WORK TO BE DONE

BRUCE WHITEMAN

WORK TO BE DONE

SELECTED ESSAYS AND REVIEWS

A JOHN METCALF BOOK

BIBLIOASIS
WINDSOR, ONTARIO

FIRST EDITION
10 9 8 7 6 5 4 3 2 1

Library and Archives Canada Cataloguing in Publication
Title: Work to be done : selected essays and reviews / Bruce Whiteman.
Names: Whiteman, Bruce, 1952– author.
Identifiers: Canadiana (print) 20230579345 | Canadiana (ebook) 2023057937X
     ISBN 9781771966092 (softcover) | ISBN 9781771966108 (EPUB)
Classification: LCC PS8595.H475 W68 2024 | DDC C814/.6—dc23

Edited by John Metcalf
Copyedited by Chandra Wohleber
Cover and text designed by Ingrid Paulson

Published with the generous assistance of the Canada Council for the Arts, which last year invested $153 million to bring the arts to Canadians throughout the country, and the financial support of the Government of Canada. Biblioasis also acknowledges the support of the Ontario Arts Council (OAC), an agency of the Government of Ontario, which last year funded 1,709 individual artists and 1,078 organizations in 204 communities across Ontario, for a total of $52.1 million, and the contribution of the Government of Ontario through the Ontario Book Publishing Tax Credit and Ontario Creates.

PRINTED AND BOUND IN CANADA

For George Fetherling (old friend)
and John Climenhage (new pal)

Poetics is the study of work to be done.

IGOR STRAVINSKY, *THE POETICS OF MUSIC*

TABLE OF CONTENTS

ONE

THE ART OF POETRY

WHAT'S POETRY?

Does one know what's poetry and what isn't?
JEAN COCTEAU, ORPHÉE

A pril is National Poetry Month, thirty days out of the year when poetry gets a nod from libraries, publishers, and other cogs in the literary machine that usually give it short shrift. If you are on Knopf's email list, you will have received a poem per day during April, a pleasant arrangement that they might consider making permanent. The University of California Press and New Directions celebrated the event more frugally, by offering discounts on their poetry list. The Academy of American Poets, which inaugurated NPM in the United States in 1996, sponsored various poetry-related events that included tweeting opportunities for poets, among other up-to-the-minute cutting-edge attempts to keep poetry at the forefront of the North American psyche. It was hopeless, of course. The average Canadian or American doesn't give a pinch of prairie dog scat for poetry. The American psyche is more interested in Civil War reenactments than in poetry. An American is a thousand times more likely to know who Jed Clampett was than Amy Clampitt. Canadian readers are no different.

Arguments about how to apportion the blame for this situation are endless and fruitless. One can point a finger at the education system, at the rise of electronic media, at the provincialism and anti-intellectualism of North American society, at the ubiquitous MFA programs, or at the poets themselves. Modernism made poetry too difficult even for the average intelligent reader to understand, goes one explanation, and the audience never recovered its interest. Poets took advantage of the vocal and formal changes introduced by Whitman, Cummings, and Williams and began passing off almost anything as poetry, further alienating readers, goes another. There is just *too much poetry* goes another still, and without a way to tell the good from the bad, the self-proclaimed from the genuinely talented, readers simply turned off the poetry channel altogether. All of these explanations have some force, but none or even all of them taken together can account for the fact that a civilized society has turned away from a literary form that is perhaps the oldest in the history of the world. Humans made pictures before they started to imagine the world in verbal form, but as soon as they did, poetry was the natural and normal recourse. Myth itself, the ancestor of all fiction, was recorded in poetic form in the ancient Near East and the classical world alike. Myths recounted in prose are so late a literary development as practically to be denominated modern.

What does it mean anymore to be a poet? Henry Miller, who as far as I know wrote very little poetry, thought that the poet's "status and condition" revealed "the true state of a people's vitality."* Whitman before him was convinced that a country was not even recognizable as such until it produced great poetry. "A barren void" exists without it, he wrote, no matter how advanced the nation's intellectual and political growth. Since his day, America has produced a lot of great poetry, of course, although its exact relationship to the country's enduring history is hard to measure. Yet poets like Hart Crane, William Carlos Williams, Dennis Lee, Anne Waldman, many Québécois poets, and others certainly worked and still work from a platform that includes a

---

* *The Time of the Assassins: A Study of Rimbaud* (New York: New Directions, 1956), p. viii.

recognition of the polity and poetry's place in defining it. In the twenty-first century, do poets attest to or reflect anything that relates to the nature of their citizenship? And if so, does the citizenry care or pay attention? The answer to the first question is certainly yes—think of the poetry written against the Iraq and Afghanistan wars, for example—but the answer to the second question is unfortunately no. Congress keeps affirming the appointment of various distinguished American poets to be poet laureate, and the poets, conservative to a man and woman largely, keep coming up with programs that try to bring poetry to the people in a meaningful way. None of these efforts seems radically effective or long-lasting, and certainly none has had any rooted effect on the nature of what it is to be an American citizen in our age. Perhaps the United States is too decadent a country for poetry to matter in a political sense anymore. That it matters in other ways to a large proportion of the country's citizens is also demonstrably not the case. Few people think poetry to be integral to their intellectual, emotional, or passional lives. The constitution of most bookstores' stock proves that contention. Is it still true, then, as Guy Davenport wrote forty years ago in a review of Stanley Burnshaw's book *The Seamless Web*, that "poetry is the voice of a poet at its birth, the voice of a people in its ultimate fulfillment as a successful and useful work of art"?*

Well, again, what does it mean to be a poet anymore? Sometimes even the poets don't know, or at any rate don't seem prone to letting on. The conservative East Coast poet Mark Strand, for one, suggests that "Not writing is the best way to write." Standing on an aesthetic plinth in a polar opposite corner, Robert Kelly, a poet in the avant-garde tradition of Ezra Pound and Charles Olson, proposes that poetry is "lucid incomprehensibility." Neither of these ideas strikes one as helpful, and indeed they seem rather puerile contentions for distinguished poets to be uttering. Perhaps we are in what Mallarmé called

---

* *The Geography of the Imagination* (New York: Pantheon, 1992), p. 214.

incubatory times, a time of deep change for poetry, a time when a thousand voices making contradictory and sometimes incomprehensible claims for poetry can be heard. Is any sort of consensus likely to emerge from this cacophony? Does it matter? Has poetry any essential *quidditas* that remains even during a period when the art seems to have no central aesthetic being and little honour among readers?

Real poets go on writing no matter what the culture of receptivity is around them. Literary history easily furnishes many examples of poets who did not become joiners or barber-surgeons or airplane pilots when their books found no readers or largely hostile ones. If today only a very few poets do not have other jobs, it is because they were brought up that way. Their sense of calling remains immutable, even if what they think their poems are good for and where they come from know no end of variety. Perhaps "calling," with its overtone of divine representation, is not the right word for what is, finally, an inborn compulsion centred on the music of language. There is a commonality among those who have thought about poetry, going all the way back to the ancients, that one is born and not made a poet. The made-up poets, and there have been thousands, the ones who assume poetry rather than follow its drive, fall pretty quickly by the wayside. They are the boring self-expressers who have little to tell us about the beautiful obliquities of language or the world, and who use poetry mainly as psychoprophylaxis or to profess things. Aristotle 2,500 years ago wanted poets to be considered separately from those who merely used poetry for specific ends (science, medicine, or philosophy). Hart Crane wrote in a letter that the real poet needed "an extraordinary capacity for surrender," and Robert Creeley, in his wonderful essay on Whitman's late work in *On Earth*, his last book, refers to poetry's "correspondences and determined intimacies of feeling—all the physical reception that being human constitutes."

In two lines from Creeley's poem "For John Weiners" an essential truth about poetry is confided:

When you are a poet as he was, you have no confusions, you write
The words you are given to, you are possessed or protected by a vision.

—

Perhaps the order of the elements is strange here, but Creeley has it exactly right: the poet has a vision (by which he means nothing especially or necessarily spiritual, but rather a cogent and penetrative view of the world and his experience in it), he or she has no confusions about *that*, whatever confusions he may suffer on other planes, and the poems are given to her, all at a go or word by word, from some startlingly unspecific and mysterious source, call it what you will. It is that receptivity that constitutes poetic brilliance. The poem is what the poet transmits. Of course she also puts things there more consciously: thematic improvisations, musical scaffolding, rhythmic finesse. He may reorder the elements, dispose of excess words or discordant sounds, orchestrate line endings or sentence continuity. She is not *just* a conduit, not *just* a platform where surrealism plays out its unconducted musical fantasies, not *just* a subject for psychoanalytic free association. His control of the poem at hand ebbs and flows, as the language comes to him and he goes with its direction, unpredictably making decisions and having decisions made for him by the words as they creep or flow into ordered life from the thousand sources and the infinite characteristics that language has.

In "By Blue Ontario's Shore," Walt Whitman called the poet "the arbiter of the diverse." He or she listens, thinks, remembers, feels. On the page the words that arise from her feelings, senses, intellection, and desire will form a kind of music that will be ill or well constructed depending on a host of factors beyond the poet's control for the most part. Prosody can be studied, but it is largely about what has happened in the past, not what is at hand or going to happen in the future. The subject of the poem brings its own prosody with it. The poem makes decisions much more than the poet does.

Whitman said that the poet "judges not as the judge judges but as the sun falling round a helpless thing." He or she illuminates a subject by giving it a chance to speak through the poetic gift. Poets will have their own recognitions afterwards and may be surprised by them. Readers too will see and hear aspects of the poem that the poet was unconscious of. Whitman again, from "A Song for Occupations": "All music is what awakes from you when you are reminded by the instruments." In "The Work of Creation," included in his *Last Poems*, D. H. Lawrence wrote:

> *Even an artist knows that his work was never in his mind,*
> *he could never have thought it before it happened.*
> *A strange ache possessed him, and he entered the struggle,*
> *and out of the struggle with his material, in the spell of the urge*
> *his work took place, it came to pass, it stood up and saluted his mind.*

What makes a poet a poet is that he has that ache; the ear is where the events of the world focus and become the poem. The Bay Area poet Jack Spicer put it in as distilled a fashion as possible: "Prose invents— poetry discloses." Poetry is the voice of the world, then, prose the voice of an author.

This view proposes to erect a very lofty bar, and it is not surprising if most poets fail to leap high enough to cross it. With no obvious or universal rules any longer about what constitutes poetic language, it has become relatively simple to self-categorize everything from the maundering and the impenetrable and the prosy to the loony and the analphabetic as poetry. "Does one know what's poetry and what isn't?" was the obvious question in Cocteau's film *Orphée* when it was shown that the car radio was the medium for transmitting poetic texts, a metaphor that appealed deeply to Jack Spicer (who thought that poets were just mediums for messages from outer space) but which has a more general suggestiveness. How *does* one know what's poetry when all the old basics of rhyme, meter, strophe, elevated language, et cetera, are either a thing of the past or at any rate not de rigueur in a text that defines itself as a poem?

The answer in the end has to do with music and rhythm. All language, including prose or everyday speech, has these qualities to varying degrees, but poetry is or should be built around them. Rhythm is inherent in words, but the poet disposes the words on the page in response to how the ear hears rhythm between and among words, not just inside them. That is why William Carlos Williams's infamous "fashionable grocery list" ("2 partridges / 2 mallard ducks / a Dungeness crab," et cetera.) could be a poem as well as a grocery list. Music by contrast is the entirety of the sonic world of a poem. The ear of a good poet instinctively retains the sound of everything that has been said in a poem from the beginning to the end, whether in a short lyric or a long narrative, and establishes multiple relationships among those sounds. The Canadian poet John Newlove put it well in a wonderful poem called "White Philharmonic Novels": "This turbulent ear hears turbulent music, / the poem made up of its parts." Largely lacking end-rhyme and meter, an excerpt from the fourth section of Basil Bunting's poem *Briggflatts* (1966) embodies a sense of music that can stand for many other examples:

> *Where rats go go I,*
> *accustomed to penury,*
> *filth, disgust, and fury;*
> *evasive to persist,*
> *reject the bait*
> *yet gnaw the best.*
> *My bony feet*
> *sully shelf and dresser,*
> *keeping a beat in the dark,*
> *rap on lath*
> *till dogs bark*

> *and sleep, shed,*
> *slides from the bed.*
> *O valiant when hunters*
> *with stick and terrier bar escape*
> *or wavy ferret leaps,*
> *encroach and cede again,*
> *rat, roommate, unreconciled.*

This is an instance of poetry's quintessential beauty and truth. The vignette is part of Bunting's autobiographical narrative, a story that could well be nothing more than bar talk or next-seat-in-the-airplane confessional chatter. ("You wouldn't believe how poor I was back then.") It is the rhythmic intercessions and the polyhymnic music of the words that make it poetry. The assonance and internal rhyme are effective and readily sensed, but equally important are the attention to vowel sounds ("rap on lath") and other rhymes—the way in which, for example, at the conclusion of the passage Bunting's ear still remembers the beginning, not just in the repetition of "rat," but also in the reappearance of the long vowel ī ("I" and "unreconciled"). This is poetic music at a high level. It's what we most want from poetry. It's what makes poetry poetry, at least of a certain kind.

"So much talk of the language—when there are no ears," said Williams in Book III of *Paterson* (1949) over sixty years ago. Perhaps readers have abandoned poetry because its essential emphasis on music rather than meaning (although meaning is not irrelevant, needless to say) makes it seem less accessible. Perhaps it appears daunting in the way that chamber music can seem daunting if you are not musically trained. Prose fiction, like a symphony, offers a more ramified converse with a reader; the reader does not necessarily have to hear the language to follow the narrative. A reader who does not hear the poem has missed its essence. The verse from Creeley's poem "For John Wieners," quoted above, concludes with these lines:

We are not going anywhere, we are somewhere, here where John is,
Where he's brought us much as he might himself this evening, to listen.

That's it: the poem invites us to listen. If we refuse or brush it off, the loss is ours. Williams thought it an incalculable loss ("It is difficult / to get the news from poems / yet men die miserably every day / for lack / of what is found there"), and he was right.

EMBRACING EVERYBODY
AND WRESTLING TREES

WALT WHITMAN TURNS 200

I wouldn't want to be around you
Embracing everybody and wrestling trees.
RALPH GUSTAFSON, "LETTER TO WALT
WHITMAN" (1981)

L ike many writers, when I visit a bookstore, I usually try to make
a discreet check of the shelf in the poetry section—in my case,
the W area—to see whether any of my books is there for sale. They
rarely are, since I publish mostly with a small house in Toronto and
with various letterpress printers whose books are seldom stocked by
retail booksellers. Almost invariably, however, the exact spot where my
books ought to be, did justice reign, is occupied with volumes by Walt
Whitman; and over the years, as much as I love the poetry of that
splendid man, I have sometimes resented him and his similar name for
always getting bookstore real estate where I get none. *Leaves of Grass*
has become a sort of nemesis, a book I feel sure will continue forever
to stand alone where *The Invisible World Is in Decline*, my own long
poem, might share space. It has not been easy to make a "pact" with

Walt, as Ezra Pound did, whose relationship to Whitman was complex. He once wrote that "Mentally I am a Walt Whitman who has learned to wear a collar and a dress shirt (although at times inimical to both)." It has been difficult to incorporate Whitman into my own aesthetics—although I have done that, I think—when he persists physically, or at least bibliographically, well over a century after his death, in so unnervingly universal a fashion, just one *e* away from me.

When I recently read Cary Fagan's novel *Valentine's Fall* (2009) I felt great sympathy for the central character's friend Felix Roth, a Canadian novelist who is trying to make a success in New York, and who has a habit of rearranging books in bookstores so that his have more prominence. "I can't help myself," he says. "There's always half a shelf of *Philip* Roth and usually none of me. You try being a Jewish writer living in New York with that last name and see where it gets you." Yes indeed.

Whitman's "Song of Myself" is at the root of vast quantities of North American poetry written over the last century or so. Most everyone who composes anecdotal and confessional verse in English can thank Walt for making the poetics of the personal poem acceptable. As D. H. Lawrence put it as long ago as the 1920s, "Lots of new little poets camping on Whitman's camping-ground now."* William Carlos Williams—another *W* poet whose books usually rest very near Whitman's in most bookstores—had something to do with this as well, especially at the level of prosody. But it was Whitman who first doffed the mantle of "poet" and donned the leather jacket of "guy." He was happy to go bathe and admire himself, as he put it in the "Song," and ever since, legions of poets have followed him into the bathroom with the big mirror over the sink where they too bathe and admire themselves and write poems about it. It is telling that the title of the "Song of Myself" was simply "Walt Whitman" through seven editions and twenty years,

---

* D. H. Lawrence, *Studies in Classic American Literature* (Harmondsworth: Penguin, 1971), p. 179.

before the poet altered it. Perhaps Lawrence most astutely took Whitman's measure in that wonderful essay he included in *Studies in Classic American Literature*, one of the great books of twentieth-century criticism. He makes much fun of Whitman's easily parodied egocentrism, his loose, tropical poetic line, and his crackpot philosophizing; but he also honours Whitman's deep sense of humanity and sympathy with all living creatures, as well as his emotional and somatic health. Lawrence's deeply personal poetry owes a lot to Whitman as well, although his approach to the poetic line is much more British than American.

All poets stand in the shadows thrown by their distinguished predecessors, and despite Harold Bloom's theory that we caper and writhe when we think about how astonishing they were and how puny we are, most of us do pretty well at acknowledging them without feeling unbearably oppressed by their achievements. I for one could not live without the poems of Sappho, Catullus, Ovid, Keats, Blake, Yeats, Stevens, Pound, Lautréamont, Rimbaud, Spicer, Pessoa, Lorca, H.D., Cavafy, Creeley, and many others. I learn from these poets, admire them, steal from them once in a while, and turn to them for succor of various kinds and at various times, as all who love and write poetry do with their favourites. Karl Shapiro once wrote that when he finished a poem, he sometimes asked himself, "What would Milton [or some other master] think of this piece?" It kept him to a high standard—his own high standard, of course, not Milton's, whose work Shapiro's does not resemble at all. Whitman is on my list too. It's just that we have this onomastic relationship that makes me sometimes uneasy and occasionally cranky.

Very few admirers of Whitman's poetry know that his first book was a novel, and a temperance one at that. He said he composed it for money, and later disclaimed the book and pretended he had been drunk on port when he wrote it. (It seems common, even accepted, for writers to want to erase all evidence of their first books. At every opportunity Williams would buy up copies of his *Poems* and destroy them.) The epigraph to chapter xix of *Franklin Evans, or The Inebriate* (1842) consists of a quotation from William Cullen Bryant (Whitman would later describe him as "the good, stainless, noble old citizen and poet" who "liked the old formulas") that now sounds very unlike Whitman's interests:

> *In vain the flattering verse may breathe*
> *Of ease from pain, and rest from strife;*
> *There is a sacred dread of death,*
> *Interwoven with the strings of life.*

In retrospect, it is a curious quatrain for Whitman to cite, for no other poet of the nineteenth century so concentrated his mind on life as lived and the objects of the senses. How many poets apart from Whitman have testified to the attractiveness of an armpit's smell? It is an "aroma finer than prayer," he naughtily said, no doubt shocking just about every living American adult reader of poetry at the time.* "Copulation is no more rank to me than death is," he wrote. That line has lost some force, no doubt—who even speaks of sex anymore as copulation?—but to a reader in 1855 or even 1905 or 1955, it must have been a bomb. (Lawrence would still have recourse to "copulation" in *Pansies* in 1929, but in his prose he had already given up the word for the simpler Anglo-Saxon equivalent.) Promiscuity, old age, "unspeakable passionate love," even his genitals ("firm masculine coulter" and "nest of guarded duplicate eggs" as he put it in his sometimes wacky jargon), he lauds them all, among many qualities and facts of life that no English-language poets before him, except perhaps for Chaucer and Blake, had dared to address so directly and so warmly. Genially if a bit

---

* Basil Bunting attested similarly, a hundred years later, in his ninth ode from Book ii: "sweet sublimes from her armpit / when the young men go past // seeking silk and elaborate / manners and strange scent." Basil Bunting, *Collected Poems* (Mount Kisco, NY: Moyer Bell, 1985), p. 139. I suspect that "sweet" is a typo, but the sentiment remains the same.

loftily, he characterized much of the poetry that preceded him as "wedded to children's tales, and to mere amorousness, upholstery and superficial rhyme," which is to say, removed from real life. This was Lawrence's recognition in his essay—Whitman's force for life—and it is a recognition that all readers of Whitman come to, whether they fall in love with it or reject it. It is infinitely more valuable than Bryant's conventional commingling of death and life, which seems cheesy and superficial by comparison.

In the "Song of Myself," Whitman wrote:

> Walt Whitman, a kosmos, of Manhattan the son,
> Turbulent, fleshy, sensual, eating, drinking and breeding,
> No sentimentalist, no stander above men and women or apart from them,
> No more modest than immodest.

These are lines with a long future in the history of poetry. Poets still live under their direction, however imperiously the commandments of Anglo-American modernism may have intervened and deflected poetry into a theatre where almost none of the poets seemed to eat, drink, or breed, much less give evidence of a determined sense of fellow-feeling. Fortunately, this was not universally true. Pound and Williams may have had an odd, contestatory relationship with Whitman (Williams called him "a romantic in a bad sense" and complained eccentrically that he "revised—or failed to revise—like a politician, not an artist"),* but Hart Crane, in *The Bridge*, called Whitman the "Saunterer on free ways still ahead," and in an essay published in the same year as his poem, he recognized similarly that Whitman's "bequest is still to be realized in all its implications." It was even less true of modernist poets writing in languages other than English, and they were quick and generous in

---

* These comments come, strangely, at the end of Williams's essay on Lorca, first published in *The Kenyon Review* in 1939 and reprinted in William Carlos Williams, *Selected Essays* (New York: New Directions, 1969), p. 230.

acknowledging Whitman. Lorca, Pessoa, and Neruda, for example, delighted in a similar physical gusto, and all wrote extraordinary odes to Whitman's extraordinary poetic presence. (Lorca's ode was perhaps most beautifully and compellingly translated by Jack Spicer in his book *After Lorca.*) Cavafy, to mention a modern poet from a rather different tradition, surely read Whitman too. Cavafy's biographer, Robert Liddell, notes that among the poet's books were copies of Poe and Longfellow. Whitman is not mentioned, but it is inconceivable that Cavafy did not know Whitman's poetry. (It is not surprising to discover that Lorca, Spicer, Hart Crane, and Cavafy were all gay. Whitman was unusually forthright in expressing homoerotic desire. Later gay American poets like Robert Duncan and Allen Ginsberg were also great admirers of Whitman.) Neruda, for his part, attested to "[walking] on the grass / on the dependable dew / of Walt Whitman." Lorca described his voice as "ancient and beautiful as the fog," and Pessoa called him "the Homer of the elusive carnal flux." What could be more Whitmanesque than these lines from Pessoa's poem "A Passagem das Horas" (The Passage of Time):

> To feel everything in every way,
> To hold all opinions,
> To be sincere contradicting yourself every minute,
> To get on your own nerves with complete impartiality,
> And to love things just like God.*

This may be a little reminiscent of Keats's concept of negative capability, but it is surely full of Whitman's spirit as well.

In 2019 we celebrate Whitman's two-hundredth birthday. (He was born on May 31, 1819, in a small town on Long Island.) If his influence

---

* Fernando Pessoa, *Forever Someone Else: Selected Poems*, trans. Richard Zenith (Lisbon: Assirio & Alvim, 2008), p. 141.

on poetics has been almost inexhaustible and global, that is not the reason we continue to read *Leaves of Grass*. His reputation for high spirits, sexual honesty, and humanity is well deserved, and we forgive him, with reservations, for some of his less savory opinions—on the Fugitive Slave Law, for example. (He was in favour of it.) But Whitman was not just a blind optimist, a kind of Dale Carnegie of poetry. The "Song of Myself" and other poems like "I Sing the Body Electric," with their celebration of "beautiful, curious, breathing, laughing flesh," give any reader renewed joy in being alive. Yet Whitman was not always so manic or so optimistic. A poem such as "As I Ebb'd with the Ocean of Life," one of his most lovely, profound, and moving pieces, a poem in which he unexpectedly expresses extreme depression and lack of confidence, testifies to his depth and complexity as a man, to his uncertainties as a poet, and to his almost radical awareness of the fact that his self was little more than a windrow (his word) of jetsam, an abstract mosaic with no central core. This less frequently sounded side of Whitman's feelings is perhaps the one which speaks to us most audibly as postmoderns. Here Whitman to every reader's certain amazement admits that "I have not once had the least idea who or what I am," that his loquacious, encomiastic, and almost unremittingly sunny poems amount to nothing, that they leave his true self "untouch'd, untold, altogether unreach'd / Withdrawn far." Here in this poem, first included in the *Leaves* in 1860, occurs an almost unbearable moment in Whitman's poetry, a moment of avowal that threatens to erase all the gloriously approbational language of "Song of Myself" and the other poems that made up *Leaves of Grass* when it first appeared in 1855. Two hundred years after Whitman's birth it is the poet who "[perceives] I have not really understood any thing, not a single object, and that no man ever can," who defines himself as nothing more than "a little wash'd-up [sea]-drift," who seems the most intimate companion for readers today. His progressiveness and his optimism and his high spirits arouse admiration, but his acknowledgement of a broken self

("Tufts of straw, sands, fragments") puts all of that in a more relatable light. Our Whitman, my Whitman in any case (no *e*), is the one who is rebuked by Nature for even thinking to make poems of the visible world:

> *I perceive I have not really understood any thing, not a single object,*
> *and that no man ever can,*
> *Nature here in sight of the sea taking advantage of me to dart upon me*
> *and sting me,*
> *Because I have dared to open my mouth to sing at all.*

In the later part of his life, Whitman developed a relationship with Canada that continued and manifestly strengthened after 1892, the year he died. Richard Maurice Bucke, the Canadian alienist (as he would have called himself, neuropsychiatrist as we would say now) had a mystical experience in 1872 that involved reading Whitman's poetry, and he eventually became a close friend and was named one of the poet's three executors. Bucke included Whitman in his book *Cosmic Consciousness* (1901) as an example of historical figures (Jesus, Buddha, and Blake among many) who represented his notion of experience beyond the veil of the real world, experience of a mystical plane that they then wrote about or bore witness to. Bucke visited Whitman in Camden, New Jersey, where he lived, and Whitman came to Canada once for an extended visit, in 1880, with Bucke as his host. (In his novel *Walt Whitman's Secret*, George Fetherling has Whitman say about that trip that "Canada was as America used to be when I was young, long before the war, as long ago as to be nearer Creation than our own time, when city and country lived in harmony and the sky was blue with promise.") Bucke's book was published in 1901, just a year before he died at sixty-five in a fall on the ice. Whitman societies developed in Canada as elsewhere, most notably the Walt Whitman Fellowship of Toronto, founded in 1916, where poets and mystics (and admittedly somewhat crazy folk—many were also involved in the Canadian Society for Psychical Research) gathered to acknowledge Whitman's genius. Members included the poet, journalist, and theosophist Albert E. S. Smythe, the dressmaker, feminist, and writer Flora MacDonald Denison (whose magazine *The Sunset of Bon Echo* existed primarily to spread Whitman's reputation), the writer and cartoonist J. W. Bengough, theatre director Roy Mitchell, and many others. "Whitmania" persisted for many years. The Group of Seven painter J. E. H. MacDonald, perhaps one of the last of the cultists, used to recite Whitman to his students at the Ontario College of Art in the 1920s. In a lecture he gave at the Toronto Reference Library entitled "An Artist's View of Whitman," he called the poet "a liberator of the soul" and acknowledged his presence in his own artistic life as "air & sunlight." Albert Ernest Stafford once claimed that Toronto booksellers' shops that carried *Leaves of Grass* were raided by the police, and that the head of the Toronto public libraries had refused to let the book be made available to borrowers. But by 1926 the book reviewer William Arthur Deacon was already complaining in an essay entitled "The Whitman Cult" that the good grey poet was "being captured by persons with the instincts of priests and schoolmasters." By then, it seems, Whitman was thoroughly part of literary history and available to all. His influence, on poets ranging from Dorothy Livesay to Louis Dudek to bpNichol, would be more taken for granted than remarkable.

SAPPHO; OR, ON LOSS

Desire is not simple.

ANNE CARSON, *EROS THE BITTERSWEET*

1

For more than a thousand years, every important writer in the West was familiar with Sappho's poems. She was a celebrity, a model, a source of inspiration, admiration, parody, imitation, and theatrical fun. Her work was quarried by other poets and quoted by grammarians, by theorists of meter, and by writers on style and many other subjects, to quite a few of whom we owe a debt for saving bits of her poems, and even an entire poem, that otherwise would have vanished. There is evidence that as late as the twelfth century CE at least a good part of Sappho's poetry was still extant in Byzantium, even though a poet and writer named John Tzetzes recorded then in a work on Pindar that "the passage of time has destroyed Sappho and her works." Only another three hundred years and she might have made it across the line represented by the invention of movable type in the middle of the fifteenth century, the technological miracle that saved so much of classical literature in a permanent way when it was still under imminent threat of erasure from the world. Catullus and some of Pindar barely survived into the Gutenberg era. Sappho did not.

"Among the mutilated poets of antiquity there is none whose fragments are so beautiful as those of Sappho," said Joseph Addison in *The
Spectator* in 1711. He wrote these words almost sixty years after the first
English translation of a poem by Sappho appeared in print, John Hall's
version of one of the few largely complete poems that have survived, the
one Pound always called the "*phainetai moi*" (its first words in Greek)
and which Hall included as part of his translation of Longinus, to whom
we owe the survival of this poem. The beauty of her poems is a constant
thread in the so-called testimonia—even Socrates is reported to have
spoken of "beautiful Sappho"—in which her work, her life, and her person were commented on and alluded to across many centuries; and
beauty is what many later poets have defined her by, from Addison to
Swinburne to Bliss Carman to many twentieth-century admirers, Pound
and H.D. and William Carlos Williams among them. "Beauty" and "the
beautiful" are words that Sappho used sparingly, at least in the surviving
corpus, and there is doubtless more than a trace of a kind of covert
misogyny detectable in the almost rote attribution of "beauty" to her
work, given her historical status as the earliest known female poet writing in the West.* The poems of her closest contemporaries are rarely
described as beautiful, and it is not irrelevant that one of the early testi-
monial writers by contrast described her person as "contemptible and
quite ugly." Like virtually all of the testimonia, this one, written hundreds
of years after Sappho's death, was almost certainly reporting hearsay, if
it was not merely inventing. It is no more reliable than base gossip.

Sappho's work began to be edited by classical scholars as early as the
sixteenth century, and by the end of the nineteenth there already existed
several scholarly editions, mostly the work of German Hellenists. But as
is well known, papyrological discoveries made beginning in the 1890s

---

* In his foreword to Mary Barnard's translation of Sappho, Dudley Fitts called for "the throwing
overboard of the whole apparatus of factitious 'beauty' that has for so long attached itself to
the name of Sappho of Lesbos." *Sappho: A New Translation*, trans. Mary Barnard, foreword by
Dudley Fitts (Berkeley and Los Angeles: University of California Press, 1958; 1986), p. x.

at Oxyrhynchus in Egypt and elsewhere and extending well into the twentieth and even the twenty-first century have added much, comparatively speaking, to what we have of Sappho's poems. Nothing, however, has been added to what we know of her life, and despite continuing reference in translations to the traditional stories—that she led a school (one early commentator, with surely unintended humour, put it that she was "president of the world's first women's club," while a more recent translator speculated that she might have been a "counter-culture *guru*"),* that she was exiled for years to Sicily, that she committed suicide by jumping into the sea from a cliff after a ferryman whom she was in love with rejected her ("Sappho's last fling," Daryl Hine irreverently called this reputed death)—we know almost nothing about her. Thomas McEvilley says quite rightly that we can be confident that the writer of Sappho's poems was a woman, and that she flourished roughly between 630 and 565 BCE on the island of Lesbos (because the Greek dialect of her poems is Aeolic†), opposite modern-day Turkey, and that is about it. Everything else falls into the category of "may have been" when it is not pure fantasy.‡ Fantastic writerly reimaginings of Sappho have been legion and include such works as Pierre Louÿs's parthenogenetic "Life of Bilitis" (1894), which he appended to his supposed translation of the work of a then unknown Greek lesbian poetess, a poet whom he invented and who, according to him, knew Sappho when she was "still beautiful." Beauty again.

---

* David M. Robinson, *Sappho and Her Influence* (Boston: Marshall Jones Company, 1924), p. 29. Professor Robinson was one of the last—and surely one of the most rhetorical—defenders of Sappho from the charge of lesbianism. "It is against the nature of things that a woman who has given herself up to unnatural and inordinate practices which defy the moral instinct and throw the soul into disorder, practices which harden and petrify the soul, should be able to write in perfect obedience to the laws of vocal harmony, imaginative portrayal, and arrangement of the details of thought. The nature of things does not admit of such an inconsistency." Ibid., p. 44. The guru suggestion belongs to Terence DuQuesne, in his *Sappho of Lesbos: The Poems* (Thame, Oxon, UK: Darengo Publications, 1989), p. 12.

† Aeolic Greek differs from Attic Greek in a way similar to the difference between Québécois French and Parisian French.

‡ Thomas McEvilley, *Sappho* (Putnam: Spring Publications) 2008), p. 17.

Most of Sappho is lost. She is essentially an early modern writer, even a modern one.* Everyone who writes about her creates a new subjectivity for Sappho. It is difficult, with so few surviving poems and so much that is tatterdemalion, not to be tempted to fill in the gaps to some extent, in exactly the way by which Sir Arthur Evans created the Palace of Knossos on Crete out of rubble. (Guy Davenport called Evans "the Stalin of archeology," and of Knossos remarked that, being there, "one despairs of knowing Minoan from Victorian architecture.")† Swinburne and Bliss Carman took the bare tunes of Sappho and Wagnerized them. Charles G. D. Roberts, in his introduction to fellow Canadian poet Carman's version of Sappho, published early in the twentieth century, wrote of the "calumnies with which the ribald jesters of that later period, the corrupt and shameless writers of Athenian comedy, strove to defile her fame," and yet Carman himself had no scruples about, if not defiling Sappho's poetry, at least transforming it into something with as little relation to Sappho as an oak tree has to a maple key. Fragment 49, numbered XXIII in Carman's book, consists of two lines of Greek:

> I loved you Atthis, once long ago.
> You seemed to me a small, graceless child.‡

Carman was not aware of the second line, which comes from a separate source, and his version, which consists of eighteen lines, begins in this way:

> I loved thee, Atthis, in the long ago,
> When the great oleanders were in flower

---

* The most recent, largely complete poem to be added to the body of her work was published in 2005.

† Guy Davenport, trans. *Sappho: Poems and Fragments*. (Ann Arbor: University of Michigan Press, 1965), p. xv.

‡ This translation is taken from the Loeb edition, *Greek Lyric*, translated by David A. Campbell (Cambridge: Harvard University Press, 1982), p: 95.

In the broad herded meadows full of sun.
And we would often at the fall of dusk
Wander together by the silver stream,
When the soft grass-heads were all wet with dew
And purple-misted in the fading light. *

He continues in this manner, making a strongly heterosexual love poem out of one line of Sappho, adopting a diction far more Victorian than anything remotely archaic, strangely more sexual than Sappho ever was ("the unutterable glad release / Within the temple of the holy night"), colonizing her, in effect, for his own poetic ends. Good Carman his *Sappho* may be; good Sappho it is not. Swinburne for his part made Sappho into a *fin de siècle* vamp straight out of Gustave Moreau:

I feel thy blood against my blood: my pain
Pains thee, and lips bruise lips, and vein stings vein.
Let fruit be crushed on fruit, let flower on flower,
Breast kindle breast, and either burn one hour.
Why wilt thou follow lesser loves? Are thine
Too weak to bear these hands and lips of mine? †

In the end, there are no right or wrong versions of Sappho, really; there are just reflections, from the scholarly or the poetic translator, onto a screen, with greater or lesser interest, greater or lesser authenticity and persuasiveness.

---

* Bliss Carman, *Sappho: One Hundred Lyrics.* Introduction by Charles G.D. Roberts (Boston: L. C. Page, 1904), p. 27.

† Algernon Charles Swinburne, "Anactoria," in *Poems and Ballads,* new ed. (London: J. C. Hotten, 1866), p. 64.

2

–

Many translators have attested to the difficulties of bringing Sappho into English, difficulties that go well beyond the normal problems that translators of poetry confront. To begin with, there is the remoteness of her sensibility, the "unbelievable otherness" recognized by Anne Carson in an interview.[*] There is the provincialism of her dialect, which no translator I am familiar with has ever attempted to find an English equivalent for.[†] There is the striking fact that she is the earliest European woman poet whose work survives at all, added to the centrality of her sexual passions that are so much at variance with archaic Greek poetry by men, or indeed *any* Greek poetry by men, from Homer forward. Although I take it as a given that those sexual obsessions included lesbianism, and do not feel it necessary to rebut any of the many, many so-called defenses of Sappho from the "degenerate" and the "prurient," culturally constructed readings which are forgivable if unfortunate, nevertheless her bisexuality, to call it that, complicates and enriches her poetry and adds to the translator's burden. Although the earliest versions in English, following the poetics script of their periods, used meter and rhyme for poems which knew nothing of the latter and employed a markedly different system for the former, several twentieth- and twenty-first-century translators have tried to dress Sappho in formal costume. Walter Petersen, in a vanity press edition of Sappho published in 1918 and Marion Mills Miller, in a translation issued in 1925 with a substantial apparatus by the archaeologist David Moore Robinson, both used rhyme and four-line stanzas. Their versions of the Aphrodite ode (the only poem of

---

[*] Will Aitken, "Anne Carson, The Art of Poetry No. 88," *The Paris Review* no. 171 (Fall 2004), http://www.theparisreview.org/interviews/5420/the-art-of-poetry-no-88-anne-carson.

[†] Guy Davenport, op. cit., does use the Aeolic form of Aphrodite's name (Aphrodita) in his version of the Aphrodite ode ("Poikilothron' athanat' Aphrodita"), but this is very much an exception to the normal practice.

Sappho's to survive in its entirety) have much in common, as can be seen from the opening stanza:

> *Ah! Golden-throned immortal Aphrodite*
> *Daughter of Zeus, through wily cunning mighty,*
> *Goddess revered, to thee I pray:*
> *My soul-subduing griefs allay. (Petersen)*

> *Throned in splendor, beauteous maid of mighty*
> *Zeus, wile-weaving, immortal Aphrodite,*
> *Smile again; thy frowning so affrays me*
> *Woe overweighs me. (Miller)*

Jeffrey Duban, a cranky anti-modernist scholar ("I will be pleased in [sic] those readers who have in the pages of this translation found refuge from the plague of modernity")* used rhyme and four-line stanzas also for his versions and sought a rather old-fashioned diction as a way of attempting, unsuccessfully I would say, to recreate Sappho's archaic language. His odd, plodding rendering of the Aphrodite ode begins in this way:

> *Appareled in flowered allure, deathless*
> *deceiver, daughter of Zeus, Aphrodite!*
> *Subdue not, nor destroy, this heart, my lady,*
> *with distress.*

And while rhyme has been a rarity in Sappho translations for over half a century, the recent Penguin version designedly reverts to its use in an attempt to recruit Sappho into the new formalism camp.

---

* Jeffrey M. Duban, *Ancient and Modern Images of Sappho* (Lanham: University Press of America, 1983), p. 17.

The translator, Aaron Poochigian, a classicist and a poet, views Sappho as a singer-songwriter and opts "to translate [the fragments] as English lyric poems," using rhyme as "an important part of this tradition."*His version of the Aphrodite ode begins thus:

> Subtly bedizened Aphrodite
> Deathless daughter of Zeus, Wile-weaver,
> I beg you, Empress, do not smite me
> With anguish and fever

The tightness of this is admirable in its way (he uses exactly as many words as Durban, only four more than the Greek), but the vocabulary choice is somewhat odd. "Bedizened" feels a bit too antiquarian; "Empress" seems just wrong and misleading; "smite me," chosen for its rhyme with Aphrodite, evokes an inappropriate Biblical overtone; and "fever," once again chosen for a rhyme, is not really accurate. Poochigian's version of Fragment 130, famous for its use of the word *lusimeles* to describe Eros (almost universally translated as "loosener of limbs") and for Sappho's invention of *glukupikron* ("bittersweet") is reminiscent of the quatrain poems composed by Eliot and Pound in the 1920s:

> That impossible predator,
> Eros the Limb-Loosener,
> Bitter-sweetly and afresh
> Savages my flesh.

"Impossible predator" and "savages my flesh" raise the intensity of the Greek by a considerable factor. Rhyme, of course, is the circus-master here, as one can see from comparing Poochigian's version with Anne

---

* Sappho, *Stung with Love: Poems and Fragments*, trans. Aaron Poochigian, preface by Carol Ann Duffy (London: Penguin, 2002), p. xlv.

Carson's: "Eros the melter of limbs (now again) stirs me— / sweetbitter unmanageable creature who steals in."*

The discovery of new texts (almost all fragmentary) by Sappho in the trash heaps of Oxyrhynchus coincided roughly with a revolutionary change in English-language poetry. As the Sapphic texts were being brought painfully back into the light of history by Bernard Pyne Grenfell and Arthur Surridge Hunt, the first of whom suffered more than one nervous breakdown from overwork and died early of a heart attack while in an asylum, imagism was being codified by a group of English and American poets as a way to make poetry less bloated and saccharine. Pound, Williams, and H.D., the three American poets primarily associated with the imagist movement, all took an interest in Sappho, though out of quite distinct aesthetic inclinations. One measure of Pound's development in his early years is the startling difference between the Sapphic meter he employed in "Apparuit," a poem published in *Ripostes* (1912), with its perfumed and gossamer diction:

> *Clothed in goldish weft, delicately perfect,*
> *gone as wind! The cloth of the magical hands!*
> *Thou a slight thing, thou in access of cunning*
> *   dar'dst to assume this?*[†]

and "Papyrus," perhaps the perfect exemplar of the imagist poem, published in *Lustra* (1916) and based on Fragment 95 of Sappho, then quite recently published:

> *Spring...*
> *Too long...*
> *Gongula...*[‡]

---

* Anne Carson, trans., *If Not, Winter: Fragments of Sappho* (New York: Knopf, 2013), p. 265.

† Ezra Pound, *Poems and Translations* (New York: Library of America, 2003), p. 232.

‡ Ibid., p. 289.

This makes brief poems such as "Alba" and "In a Station of the Metro," collected in the same book, sound almost garrulous by comparison. Williams for his part would mention the loss of Sappho's poems and their partial recovery "from / outer mummy cases of papier mâché inside / Egyptian sarcophagi" in Book III of *Paterson*, and the second section of Book V opens with his translation of Fragment 31, which begins:

> Peer of the gods is that man, who
> face to face, sits listening
> to your sweet speech and lovely
> laughter.*

This almost complete poem has been translated innumerable times, but Williams's version demonstrates just how sympathetic to Sappho's limpid language the imagist-entrusted aesthetic of Williams's long poem was. As for H.D., all of her early poetry has a Greek-inspired clarity, brevity, and precision. She did not so much translate Sappho or imitate her as ventriloquize her voice, as in the group of "Fragment" poems that were published in *Hymen* (1921), of which the opening of "Fragment 113" is typical:

> Not honey,
> not the plunder of the bee
> from meadow or sand-flower
> or mountain bush;
> from winter-flower or shoot
> born of the later heat:
> not honey, not the sweet
> stain on the lips and teeth:

---

* William Carlos Williams, *Paterson* (New York: New Directions, 1963), p. 253.

> *not honey, not the deep*
> *plunge of soft belly*
> *and the clinging of the gold-edges*
> *pollen-dusted feet[...]**

Mary Barnard's widely read translation of Sappho embodies a distinct inheritance from this modernist tradition. Barnard had been urged by Pound to translate Sappho over a period of many years, as he found in her poetry a sort of essential Greek spirit that he felt made her the ideal poet to do the work. She began in earnest as she was convalescing from a serious illness (the "fragments...were great pillow-work" she admitted in her memoirs),† and she tried to create the most straightforward versions possible by employing a diction that had the naturalness of speech. She worked from J. M. Edmonds's Loeb volume, as the standard edition by Edgar Lobel and Denys Page (*Poetarum Lesbiorum Fragmenta*) was either unfamiliar to her or published too late. She included just one hundred poems and fragments and ordered them as a sort of imagined dramatic biography, from "Now, today, I shall / sing beautifully for / my friends' pleasure" to "Prosperity that / the golden Muses / gave me was no / delusion: dead, I / won't be forgotten."‡ She gave each poem/fragment a title (the Aphrodite ode she called "Prayer to My Lady of Paphos"), and in her "Footnote," she wisely rejected most of the traditional stories associated with Sappho. Unfortunately she proposes one of her own—that Sappho was something similar to a "*kapelmeister*, or...a Renaissance painter with a studio full of talented young fellows picking up the tricks of painting altarpieces"—neither of which suggestion seems remotely sensible, while the second seems unfortunate from the point of view of gender.

---

* H.D., *Collected Poems 1912–1944*, ed. Louis L. Martz (New York: New Directions, 1983), p. 131. The fragment of Sappho out of which this poem is evoked is in fact Fragment 146.

† Mary Barnard, *Assault on Mount Helicon: A Literary Memoir* (Berkeley and Los Angeles: University of California Press, 1984), p. 283.

‡ Mary Barnard, *Sappho*, np. (Sappho's poems 1 and 100.)

She tends to use a three-line stanza especially for the longer poems, and this triune structure makes her Sappho look and sound contemporary; her emphasis on the "fresh colloquial directness of speech"* adds to this contemporaneity. Here is her version of the opening lines of the Aphrodite ode:

> *Dapple-throned Aphrodite,*
> *eternal daughter of God,*
> *snare-knitter! Don't, I beg you,*
>
> *cow my heart with grief! Come,*
> *as once when you heard my far-*
> *off cry and, listening, stepped*
>
> *from your father's house to your*
> *gold car, to yoke the pair whose*
> *beautiful thick-feathered wings*
>
> *oaring down mid-air from heaven*
> *carried you to light swiftly*
> *on dark earth . . .*

For the most part this sounds compelling, a sixth-century BCE poet speaking like a modernist poet in the 1950s. One can quibble with certain choices. "God" instead of "Zeus" brings in an inevitable Christian association that is unwanted, despite the fact that the Greek word is *Dios*, and "snare-knitter" is perhaps a bit arch (snare-setter might have been less protuberant). By contrast, "Don't, I beg you, / cow my

---

* Ibid., p. 102.

heart with grief!" has the attractiveness of common parlance, and the contrast of "light" (here a verb, not an adjective) and "dark" is sublime. Richmond Lattimore's version, published just three years before Barnard's, sounds Parnassian and much too full-throated by comparison:

> *Throned in splendor, deathless, O Aphrodite,*
> *child of Zeus, charm-fashioner, I entreat you*
> *not with griefs, and bitterness to break my*
> > *Spirit, O goddess;*

> *standing by me rather, if once before now*
> *far away you heard, when I called upon you,*
> *left your father's dwelling place and descended,*
> > *yoking the golden*

> *chariot to sparrows...* *

There have been many translations into English of Sappho's poetry since Barnard's version appeared in 1958, but only two follow in the poetic line that leads back to her and through her to Pound and Williams. Guy Davenport's rendering, first published in 1965 and later revised, grew out of his lifelong devotion to the archaic in art and literature, and his conviction that the archaic and the modern made a cultural rhyme. In the Aphrodite ode, his Sappho speaks a somewhat surprising mix of the colloquial ("Come now, of all times") and the obsolete ("wildering," "bitted"), the result being a sort of tonal macaronic that creates exactly the degree of estrangement that a 2,500-year-old poem intrinsically possesses:

---

* Richmond Lattimore, *Greek Lyrics* (Chicago: University of Chicago Press, 1955), p. 24.

God's wildering daughter deathless Aphrodita,
A whittled perplexity your bright abstruse chair,
With heartbreak, lady, and breathlessness
Tame not my heart.

But come down to me, as you came before,
For if ever I cried, and you heard and came,
Come now, of all times, leaving
Your father's golden house

In that chariot pulled by sparrows reined and bitted,
Swift in their flying, a quick blur aquiver,
Beautiful, high. They drew you across steep air
Down to the black earth; ... *

Jim Powell, a classicist and poet and at one time a member of Robert Duncan's circle, extended the Pound tradition, perhaps for the final time, with a version of Sappho published in 1993. Powell wanted, he wrote, "to re-create the feel of [Sappho's] poetry in contemporary American English,"† and the result is a style predominantly demotic ("please don't hurt me") with touches of the quaint ("these my words") which, in the Aphrodite ode at any rate, feel apposite for what is, at least in its opening invocation, a traditional hymn:

Artfully adorned Aphrodite, deathless
child of Zeus and weaver of wiles I beg you
please don't hurt me, don't overcome my spirit,

---

* Davenport, op. cit., np. (his poem §1). When reissued in a book that also included Davenport's versions of Archilochos and Alkman, the poem was revised somewhat and Davenport dropped "wildering" and substituted "stunning," a less forceful choice.

† Jim Powell, *Sappho: A Garland: The Poems and Fragments of Sappho* (New York: Farrar, Strauss, Giroux, 1993), p. 45.

goddess, with longing,

but come here, if ever at other moments
hearing these my words from afar you listened
and responded: leaving your father's house, all
golden, you came then,

hitching up your chariot . . . *

(Can any American reader hear "hitch" and not think of a cowboy context?)

The classicist Marguerite Johnson published a small book about Sappho in 2007 in which she was refreshingly blunt about her subject. "For a poet," she wrote, "whose extant work comprises few complete poems, several semi-complete poems and approximately two hundred fragments—some consisting of a single word—the fascination with Sappho is excessive."[†] The river's-length of translations issued over the last fifty years certainly bears her out. Since 1965, there have been complete or partial versions by Josephine Balmer, Willis Barnstone, Anne Carson, Cid Corman, John Daley, Page duBois, Terence DuQuesne, Suzy Q. Groden, Sam Hamill, Stanley Lombardo, Sasha Newborn, Diane J. Rayor, Paul Roche, Beram Saklatvala, and Sherri Williams. Doubtless I have missed a few. Many of these renderings are competent but unaccomplished. Anne Carson's has attracted perhaps the most attention, for she is that rare thing: a great poet (at times) and an accomplished classicist. To my ear her versions sound more like trots than fully achieved English poems. She prints every scrap that has survived, including single words, and her translations hew very closely to the Greek (which is printed *en face*) in terms of word order and syntax. This is useful for the reader lack-

---

ing Greek, but the English demonstrably needs more, well, more poetry. The version by Daley and duBois is the most recent (2011), but it was printed by the Arion Press in San Francisco in an edition of just four hundred copies, most of which, at a published price of $1,750, will be owned by collectors and libraries rather than by readers of classical poetry. Daley's English (I assume that duBois, who is a well-respected scholar, was an adviser rather than a co-translator) achieves a kind of mid-Atlantic tone somewhere between old-fashioned and more contemporary:

> *Upon your intricately wrought throne, deathless Aphrodite,*
> *child of Zeus weaving lures, I beg you*
> *don't break my heart with longing nor with grief,*
> *O queen,...* *

While "weaving lures" seems to beg a question, and while most of this English has been evoked before by translators of the ode, there is nothing especially objectionable here, nor, perhaps, anything especially striking.

The "excessive" attention paid to Sappho began with Henry Thornton Wharton (1846–95), an Oxford-trained surgeon and ornithologist whose edition of the poet (Greek texts and multiple translations, as well as an extensive apparatus) went through three editions during his rather brief lifetime, and two posthumously.† Wharton did not just introduce Sappho to English-speaking readers. He manifestly sacralized her poems. Wharton's project as a whole has a strong *fin de siècle* aesthetic underlying it. The third edition of his book was designed by Aubrey Beardsley for John Lane, and he quotes extensively from Swinburne and John Addington Symonds, a poet and classicist, who prepared translations

---

* *Poetry of Sappho*, introduction by Page duBois, trans. John Daley with Page duBois, wood engravings by Anita Cowles Rearden, prints by Julie Mehretu (San Francisco: Arion Press, 2011), np.

† Henry Thornton Wharton, ed. and trans., *Sappho: Memoir, Text, Selected Renderings, and a Literal Translation*, 3rd ed. (London: John Lane, 1895). The five editions were published in 1885, 1887, 1895, 1898, and 1907.

especially for Wharton's book.* Wharton's remained the most widely read and consulted edition of Sappho in English until the first volume of J. M. Edmonds's *Lyra Graeca* was published in the Loeb Classical Library in 1922. Edmonds did not scruple from adding his own poetry to Sappho's in order to make fragments seem more whole, a practice forgivable perhaps in poet-translators but surprising for a scholar. Yet this was a temptation other scholars gave in to,† and even now it has not entirely disappeared, though it is primarily poets rather than scholars who continue to indulge in writing-as-Sappho.‡ The three main scholarly editions of Sappho prepared in the twentieth century following Edmonds were far more scrupulous, and most of the subsequent multifarious translations into English have been based on these.§ Unless some startling new discovery brings more of Sappho to light in the future, it is unlikely that a new scholarly text will ever be edited. Translations will doubtless continue to be published, as Sappho's voice, even in the fragmentary form it takes in the surviving corpus, speaks irresistibly to readers.

3

The modernist poets were attracted by the very fragmentariness of Sappho's work. Its reification of loss undeniably evokes feelings that, while not inherent to Sappho's poems as such, are difficult to suppress. The

---

* Symonds too worshipped Sappho. He once wrote: "Of all the poets of the world, of all the illustrious artists of all literatures, Sappho is the one whose every word has a peculiar and unmistakable perfume, a seal of absolute perfection and illimitable grace." Quoted in Edwin Marion Cox, *The Poems of Sappho* (London: Williams and Norgate, 1925), p. 27.

† David Moore Robinson, for example, who prepared the Greek text of Sappho for Marion Mills Miller's translation, *The Songs of Sappho* (New York: Frank-Maurice, 1925), likened the restoration of Sappho's fragments to the work of a paleontologist who "must restore a diplodocus or dinosaur from a few scattered bones" (p. 35).

‡ Beram Saklatvala admitted that he wrote "completely new lines and verses around many of the fragments." *Sappho of Lesbos, Her Works Restored* (London: Skilton, 1968), p. 17. Aaron Poochigian, op. cit., "on occasion, translated supplements proposed by scholars" (p. xlv).

§ These are the editions of Page and Lobel (1955), Eva-Maria Voigt (1971), and David A. Campbell's revised Loeb edition (1982).

scholar Richard Jenkyns warned against indulging in the nostalgia of loss while reading Sappho, but poetry inevitably incites us to emotions that are part of its being in the world, even if they are not precisely encoded in the words.* Reading Keats, who can ignore how unbearably short his life was?

The poetry that most moves us records the movements of the heart, but also what is out there in the real world, the things that die. Robins bob their heads and bump and bash the black earth for worms. Linden trees rain their leafy detritus on the ground, their erotic stuff meant to replicate a singularity. Squirrels with golden tails run up and down trees, dedicated to food and meticulous mating. Indian grass sprouts chaotically in one particular part of the American world. Corn. Thunderstorms. Train wrecks.

Love rises and sets like the sun. It should come back, but perhaps it won't. Perhaps it will resist the cycle and rest somewhere out of sight like an animal sleeping. Perhaps it will disappear entirely, haughty and withheld. Sappho felt that the beloved was far more beautiful than caparisoned cavalry or naval ships glinting in the reflected light of the sun. Her lines record that erotic emotion for the first time in Western poetry. But what if the beloved withdraws love and turns a blank and disinterested face to the lover? What then? Sappho knew that emotion too. The anonymous compiler of a ninth-century CE Byzantine etymological work cites her as saying simply "and I long and yearn" (Fragment 36). Eros becomes a linguistic arrow (arrows) to the heart, as the poet Jack Spicer once punned. Eros, errors. Loss.

The real impinges, rabbits in the dry grass, blue jays seeming to clamour for attention, Sappho's "messenger of spring, the lovely-voiced nightingale," columbine and roses and fireweed in the garden, grey clouds and adamantine weather. There is no escaping any of it. Yet

---

* Richard Jenkyns, *Three Classical Poets: Sappho, Catullus, and Juvenal* (Cambridge: Harvard University Press,1982), pp. 82–83.

somehow the present, full as it may be, rarely makes us happy. It lacks something indefinable, like missing lines in a poem, a rhyme unarticulated, a metrical completion resisted. A tattered sixth-century CE parchment begins in the middle of a sentence with either Sappho or one of her lovers saying out of the sort of adolescent agony to which lovers are subject, "... and honestly I wish I were dead" (Fragment 94). Loss is a foreshadowing of death.

We should like to allow Sappho to remind us of the continuity through 2,500 years of emotion and the inner life of an individual person. With the other great archaic poets of Greece she was among the first to speak in poetry the way one speaks to friends or to oneself rather than to a community. Bruno Snell long ago drew an important distinction: even in Sappho, as personal as her poetry strikes us, love is not generated by the heart but is a gift from Aphrodite or Eros, i.e., from a god. What is generated by the individual heart is "the emotional discord released by unhappy love."* Fragment 168B, which is not accepted as genuine by some editors but is nevertheless one of Sappho's best-known poems, is a succinct and poignant expression of loneliness and the transitoriness of life:

> *The moon and then*
> *the Pleiades*
> *go down*

> *The night is now*
> *half-gone; youth*
> *goes; I am*

> *in bed alone*†

---

* Bruno Snell, *The Discovery of the Mind: The Greek Origins of European Thought*, trans. T. G. Rosenmeyer (New York: Harper & Row, 1960), p. 65.
† Mary Barnard's translation, her poem no. 64. A. E. Housman unsurprisingly composed two

In the third edition of his *Sappho*, Wharton reproduced in "Autotype," almost as a talisman, what he called "a tiny scrap of parchment,"* now dated to the seventh century CE, on which Fragments 3 and 4 are written. They are so ruined as to be incomprehensible, but even so the texts are haunting and haunted; even as they slip off the edge of sense their message of loss and pain is perfectly clear and emotionally commanding:

> ... *spirit... completely... (if?) I can... (as long as?) I have... to shine back... (lovely?) face... caressed...* †

Adventitious our sense of loss may be in confronting such ruins as the Sapphic text presents to us, but it is not to be gainsaid. The body is so adamant. We know where it ends. Sappho knew as well. Aristotle quotes her as saying "that death is an evil: the gods have so decided, otherwise they would die."

---

different versions of this poem.

* Wharton, 3rd ed., p. 181.

† This is David Campbell's reconstruction of Fragment 4. He notes that the final word might also be read as "stained." Campbell, op. cit., p. 61.

TWO

ANTIQUITY

THE MUSES
TAUGHT ME SONG
BEYOND DIVINE

I n earlier centuries, translators of the classics would not atypically
use their preface or introduction as a bully pulpit to sermonize
against their predecessors. Even the creator of a new version of the
ancient Greek poet Hesiod, whose translator one might have thought
happy to have had a few chums in the business—Hesiod translators
being so rare—could not resist the occasion. Hesiod, unlike Homer,
has only seldom been translated into English before recent times; yet
Charles Elton, Bart., a poet, translator, and theological disputant,
seized the moment in the preface to his translation of Hesiod (1814;
second edition, 1815) to cast aspersions in no uncertain terms on the
only published English translation of Hesiod from the eighteenth century. Thomas Cooke, the translator in question, whose version was
published in 1728, is dismissed as having a "superficial knowledge of
Greek" and of being incurably "indolent." His "blunders are inexcusably
frequent and unaccountably gross" and his style is "tame and grovel-
ling." Cooke (1703–56) had been reviled in his lifetime as well, when
he publicly claimed (setting the precedent among complaining translators?) that Alexander Pope, with his translations of the *Iliad* and the

Odyssey, demonstrated conclusively that he was a poor Hellenist. For his pains, Cooke wound up in both *The Dunciad* and *The Epistle to Dr. Arbuthnot* as a figure of esoteric fun. Cooke and Elton, like George Chapman before them—the earliest translator of Hesiod (1618) and the only other English translator before the twentieth century—translated the Hesiodic corpus into rhyming couplets, and however much Sir Charles may have been determined to elevate his own version above that of his predecessor, there is not much to choose between them poetically. Here are the opening lines of Hesiod's *Works and Days* in their respective pentameters:

> *Sing, Muses, sing, from the Pierian Grove;*
> *Begin the song, and let the theme be Jove;*
> *From him ye sprung, and him ye first should praise;*
> *From your immortal Sire deduce your lays . . . (Cooke)*

> *Come, Muses! ye, that from Pieria raise*
> *The song of glory, sing your father's praise.*
> *By Jove's high will th'unknown and known of fame*
> *Exist, the nameless and the fair of name. (Elton)*

Although praised by Ben Jonson for his ability "to refine / old Hesiod's ore," Chapman's translation is perhaps only a small cut above those of his later competitors:

> *Muses! That out of your Pierian state,*
> *All worth, in sacred numbers celebrate;*
> *Use I here your faculties so much renownd,*
> *To sing your sire; and him in hymns resound . . .*

To "use" the Muses seems particularly inelegant, though the pun on him / hymn is clever enough.

—

What we know about Hesiod is comprised only of a few tidbits that he reveals in his poetry, among them (for the first time in Western literature) the poet's name. Even that is not enough to convince all classicists, some of whom think that there was no more a person called Hesiod than that there was a person called Homer. Robert Lamberton, for example, a classics scholar who used to teach at Washington University, was certain that Hesiod was "a composite that defies analysis, a tradition and not an individual voice."* This places Hesiod directly in the oral culture of archaic Greece, the preliterate period that ended sometime in the eighth century BCE when writing was adopted by the Greeks from the Phoenicians. Archaeology is not especially helpful in bringing precision to this epochal event in cultural history. M. L. West, the most distinguished of Hesiod's modern editors, states that his poetry was well known throughout Greece within a generation or two of Hesiod's death, i.e., by sometime in the early-to-mid-seventh century BCE. West himself has no doubts that Hesiod was an actual person, and that the autobiographical details in his poems are likely to be largely true. Hesiod informs us that he lived in a village called Askra near Mount Helicon, in Boeotia, today a drive of about 150 kilometres northwest of Athens. He disliked the place intensely, calling it "*oizyre kome*," a poor excuse for a village, and characterizing it as miserably cold in winter and uncomfortably hot in summer. His father had emigrated there from Kyme in Asia Minor, a longish sail across the Aegean Sea, in search of a better life. We also learn that the poet had a brother, Perses, who apparently attempted to take more than his fair share of the paternal inheritance. Finally, we encounter for the first time in literary history a poet's acknowledgement of the Muses, and Hesiod is the first witness to their names and their parentage (Zeus and Mnemosyne). He tells us that they touched him on the shoulder (as it

---

* Robert Lamberton, *Hesiod* (New Haven and London: Yale University Press, 1988), p. 36.

were) as he was looking after a flock of sheep on Mount Helicon, and promised him a sweet voice and access to "many false things / that seem like true sayings, / but...also how to speak the truth."* We cannot read this story as a merely literary convention because Hesiod was the earliest poet to characterize his beginnings as a writer as a divine visitation, thus in fact establishing the tradition to which hundreds of later poets would hew. Even in the last century, the story that Hesiod told reverberates still in Yeats's account of spirits who brought him metaphors for poetry, for example, or Jack Spicer's claim to have his poetry from "spooks" or "Martians." Whether Hesiod invented his myth of the origins of poetry out of whole cloth or simply recounted an actual psychic experience, it remains an accounting with a durable afterlife.

Only two works, the *Theogony* and the *Works and Days*, are reliably assigned to Hesiod on ancient authority and by modern scholars. Two further pieces, *The Shield of Herakles* and the *Catalogue of Women*, became associated with his name during antiquity, but were in all likelihood not composed by him. Given that it focuses on the genealogy of the gods, the title of the *Theogony* is obvious and unexceptionable; the title of *Works and Days*, though associated with the poem from ancient times, is rather more perplexing, since the poem is about much more than work and certainly contains material beyond what we would consider relevant to an almanac ("days"). George Chapman, in the earliest English translation, for good reason preferred *The Georgicks*, and at one level it is as an extended exercise in mostly rural and agricultural advice and description that the poem operates and influenced many later poets central to the pastoral tradition, from Virgil to Spenser to Seamus Heaney. But *Works and Days* remains the standard English title for Hesiod's poem, and the convention is maintained in the most recent translation by A. E. Stallings.† (That Penguin has chosen to pub-

---

* Richmond Lattimore, trans., *Hesiod* (Ann Arbor: University of Michigan Press, 1959), p. 124. These lines are from the *Theogony*.

† Hesiod, *Works and Days*, trans. A. E. Stallings (London: Penguin Books, 2018).

lish it on its own, without the usual pairing with the *Theogony*, makes the resultant book a very slim one: just thirty pages of poetry, although with prefatory material and notes the book bulks out to slightly over one hundred pages.) Stallings is widely regarded as an accomplished poet in the formalist vein; and as a trained classicist and current resident in Greece she is uniquely well placed to take on the translation of ancient Greek poetry. In an interview she once avowed that she seemed "to have an affinity for curmudgeonly didactic male poets in dead languages." Of course Hesiod is much more than that, though his curmudgeonly side and his sometimes "quaint and stilted" style sets him apart from his coeval Homer.* No one really feels any affection for Homer as a person, but it is difficult not to feel affection for a poet who counsels his readers not to pee facing the sun nor to warm oneself at the fire after lovemaking. Why not? Who knows why not! But such intimate advice makes every new reader of Hesiod feel that the poet has become a new if slightly eccentric friend.

Like Homer, Hesiod wrote in dactylic hexameters, the standard meter of ancient epic poetry in both Greek and Latin. End-rhyme was largely unknown among the ancient poets, although standard techniques for creating poetic music, such as assonance and internal rhyme, were a part of the poet's armamentarium then as now. Dactylic hexameter has always been an awkward meter in English apart from comic situations, and translators of Homer over the last few decades have generally chosen not to imitate Chapman (who used an even longer poetic line), but to employ the iambic pentameter flexibly as a general guide to creating a line, and (again, generally) not to use end-rhyme, which (*pace* Dryden and Pope) can make an ancient epic poet begin to sound like antiquity's version of an advice columnist. Hesiod, however, at least in parts of the *Works and Days*, really *was* antiquity's

---

* "If I have sometimes made Hesiod sound a little quaint and stilted, that is not unintentional: he is." Hesiod, *Theogony and Works and Days*, trans. M. L. West (Oxford: Oxford Universirty Press, 1988), p. [xxiii].

version of an advice columnist, and perhaps for that reason Stallings has chosen (like her seventeenth-, eighteenth-, and nineteenth-century predecessors) to translate the poem into rhyming couplets. She wanted, she says in her "Note on the Translation," to create "the flavor of aphorism." She also wanted "a slightly old-fashioned feel," on the basis that Hesiod would have sounded old-fashioned to readers two centuries later during the so-called classical period.

Well, yes. But what about two and a half millenia later and in a foreign language? I have already noted that there is a strong precedent from the early modern period for the use of rhyming couplets to translate Hesiod. Yet to my ear, at least, they now have a tendency to make Hesiod sound not just quaint, but downright goofy, at least in those passages in which he is not speaking like some kind of avatar of Poor Richard and in his Almanack-ese, where the couplets have an irresistible pull on our memories of sage avuncular advice of the "a friend in need is a friend indeed" sort. ("Deposit small amounts, but do / It often, and you'll find that they accrue.") The result is exceedingly far from what is now thought to be poetry's true address—surely most readers now respond to aphorism more with cynicism than with nods of approbation—and sometimes Stallings wisely uses a great deal of enjambment to try to modify the pseudo-sagacity of Hesiod's advice, especially in the "Days" section:

> Guard well in mind the days, which come from Zeus,
> Advise your slaves in their allotted use.
> For overseeing works, the thirtieth's best,
> And for dividing rations, folk attest
> Who can distinguish truth. For these days come
> From Zeus the Counsellor. Here too are some,
> The first, the fourth, the seventh, that are hollow
> (On the Sabbath, Leto gave birth to Apollo
> Of the golden sword); the eighth and ninth. Two more

> *Days of the waxing month are perfect for*
> *Mortal toil—if sheep are to be shorn,*
> *Or you are gathering in the gladsome corn,*
> *The eleventh and twelfth are fine . . .*

If this poetry sounds old-fashioned, even Augustan, that is because it is. Compare Stallings' version with Richmond Lattimore's in which, while being faithful to Hesiod's words, the translator makes the lines more robustly modern through variation in line length and indentation, as well as by avoiding older vocabulary:

> *Observe the days that come from Zeus, all*
>   *in their right order.*
> *Explain them to your workers; that the thirtieth*
>   *of the month*
> *is best for supervising works,*
>   *and for doling provisions.*
>   *And here follow the days that come to us*
>   *from the counselor*
> *Zeus, when men who judge their true nature*
> *can observe them.*
>   *First of all, the first, fourth, and seventh*
>   *of the month are holy;*
> *it was on this last that Leto gave birth to Apollo*
> *of the golden sword. Then the eighth and ninth,*
>   *two days in each month*
> *as it waxes, are excellent for mortal labors.*
> *The eleventh day, and the twelfth too,*
>   *are both very good days*
> *either for shearing sheep or for reaping*
>   *the good harvest; . . .*

Lattimore makes no attempt to translate line for line—five lines of Hesiod essentially become ten—nor does he strive to sound conventionally apothegmatic. Like Stallings's version, the result is certainly readable, but unlike hers, it sounds more like a poem in the modernist tradition. (Pound for one quotes a short section of the *Works and Days* in a beautiful passage in canto 47, and Olson, who, with his cosmological interests, not unexpectedly was more interested in the *Theogony*, begins one of the later Maximus poems with the line "The sea was born of the earth without sweet union of love Hesiod says.")

Stallings states that, as far as language is concerned, her determination is to locate "a timeless as opposed to antique diction." It is at least an arguable question as to whether there really exists something like a "timeless" diction at all. Some words certainly astonish us by their unexpected age and perdurability. In a time of gas-guzzlers, it may come as a surprise that the earliest recorded use of "guzzle" dates to the sixteenth century, in a translation by Arthur Golding (he of Ovidian fame) of a book by John Calvin. (All the same, I am not entirely persuaded by Stallings's use of "gift-guzzlers" to translate the Greek epithet *dorophagous*, which the Loeb version gives as "gift-eaters," Lattimore as "who eat bribes," and others variously as "bribe-devouring," "bribe-swallowers," and "bribe hungry." One normally guzzles a liquid, not a solid.) "A lick of work" and "divvied up," by contrast, seem largely to be colonial colloquialisms and are not attested much before the middle of the nineteenth century, while "payback" in the common sense now current barely goes back to the 1970s and "dope" ("The dope / Who's idle and awaits an empty hope") sounds inappropriate. Stallings also uses some words that seem out of date, making them timeless up to a certain point but uncommon now, words like "bounteous," "boon," "meet" (as an adjective), "thrice myriad," "gladsome," "lad" and so on. These are all perfectly good words and expressions, though perhaps they sort rather ill with others, like "brat" and "bitch" and "Daddy" (old words to be sure, but somehow contemporary-sounding). Stallings cites Robert Frost as a model for her use of language and her adoption of a "vernacular that allows...for archaism and the odd quaint or regional turn of phrase as well as highfalutin' pronouncement." This seems fair enough.

What is the *Works and Days* about, and does it remain at all relevant to us, as Homer or the archaic lyric poets unquestionably do? In the *Guide to Kulchur*, Pound suggested that "a man might still learn from Hesiod if he had no other access to agricultural knowledge. The civilized farmer will want to compare today's knowledge to Hesiod's." Of course eighty years later, in the era of corporate agriculture and tractors with GPS devices as standard equipment, no farmer is likely to care much about an ancient Greek poet's advice on when to plant and when to harvest, nor is he or she likely to have the time to be reading Hesiod as comparative literature. (Stallings tells us that on a visit to Hesiod's area, she spoke to some local winemakers, who had followed Hesiod's advice on harvesting and pressing grapes. They got miserable results.) This is to be a bit fatheaded, needless to say, since the poetry of information or the poetry of advice in whatever sector of life ages badly, and will continue to be read by future generations of readers only if there are other blandishments—cultural, linguistic, aesthetic, psychological, et cetera. The "Days" portion of Hesiod's poem will always seem rather quaint, and Stallings's language does not shirk from its quaintness:

> Fifth days, beware—
> The fifth [of the month] is terrible, a day to loathe,
> When the Furies midwifed at the birth of Oath,
> Whom strife bore as a woe to the foresworn.
> Mid-seventh, carefully strew the holy corn
> Of Demeter on the threshing floor, smooth-worn;
> The carpenters should hew a chamber's lumber,
> Or a boat's ship-shape planks, many in number.

Rhyme here, as rhyme will often do, has forced the choice of less than perfect words. The Greeks did not grow corn as such—it came to Europe only after Columbus—and every other modern translator of Hesiod translates the Greek word *akte* here as "grain." As for "foresworn," which is slightly puzzling in this context, other translators use instead "liars" or "perjurers," or even admittedly more cumbersome expressions such as "those who break their oath" or "those who take false oath," in order to avoid invoking the more common meaning of "foreswear" as "renounce." "Corn" and "foresworn" help Stallings through the challenge of rhyme, but here unfortunately function to obscure the sense somewhat. Stallings is in general very skilled at rhyme, but occasionally elsewhere she is more or less forced into questionable word choices because of the need for it, "easy" and "breezy," for example, at lines 453–54, or "befalls" and "appalls" at lines 547–48. That the North Wind "befalls" is a stretch. Lattimore's "comes down upon you" seems more accurate.

Hesiod's poem is more than a collection of random sayings and bits of moral or practical advice. Though it is repeated from the *Theogony* to some extent, the myth of Prometheus originates with the poet, as does the story of Pandora and the evils loosed on the world by an inattentive woman. (There is a streak of misogyny in Hesiod, though it is perhaps somewhat balanced by an overall crankiness in the poet's emotional makeup.) The culturally reverberant myth of the Golden Age also originates with Hesiod's poem. *Works and Days* seems most timeless in its concerns with family squabbles (much of the earlier part of the poem is addressed to Hesiod's brother) and in the end with the role and constitution of the poet himself, his inspiration, his feelings, even his career. (We are told about a poetry contest that Hesiod won; and although likely an invention, a later tradition pits Hesiod against Homer in a contest where the former took the prize because the judge decided that lines about peace were more worthy than lines about war.) At the centre of the poem is an almost Old Testament ethos. The gods send trouble to humanity for its overweening self-regard and work is the glum result, work that Hesiod makes his subject. Men and women have been ejected from Eden and must make a living by the sweat of their brows:

> For the gods have hidden livelihood away
> From men, else you could work a single day
> And easily have enough for living clear
> Without a lick of work for the whole year,
> And soon season the rudder over the smoke,
> Retire the drudging mules, the oxen's yoke.
> But Zeus hid it away, galled in his heart
> That he'd been duped by Prometheus' wry art...

(The rudder is stored over the hearth because in a perfect world it is not needed for travel nor for trade.) Yet one of Hesiod's deepest recognitions is that the days are not simply full of hard work, disappointment, and woe. Some are propitious and some are full of gladness, especially if you honour the gods ("the deathless ones"), treat your friends well, marry intelligently, and avoid sea travel. At the end of the poem, in Stallings's lovely English, we are told that "These days are gifts to those who dwell on earth." Hesiod means the days that are suitable and well auguried for certain events like begetting and childbirth, for building ships or even opening a jar; other days produce little, are "fateless" in the word that Stalling has chosen. A person needs to know the difference. But we can make Hesiod out to be saying something more general and more deeply optimistic. The closing lines of the poem contain a reference to ornithomancy and what seems to be a proverbial witticism about stepmothers and mothers, but otherwise provide a cheering and profound conclusion to the poem:

> These days are gifts to those who dwell on earth—
> The rest, haphazard, with nonspecial worth,

Fateless. One praises one day, one, another;
Few know: a day can go from stepmother
To mother. Blessed and rich is he, who's wise
In all these things, who works, and in the eyes
Of the deathless ones is blameless, one who reads
The omens of birds, avoiding all misdeeds.

I SUPPOSE YOU TO BE NO MEAN READER, SINCE YOU INTEND TO READ HOMER

Though slow to come, the tale of this achievement / will never die.
—ILIAD, BOOK I, TRANS. BARRY POWELL

In 1581, when monoglot English speakers first got an opportunity to read some of Homer's poetry in their own language, this is what he sounded like:

> I Thee beseech, O Goddesse mild,
> > The hatefull hate to plaine,
> Whereby Achilles was so wroong,
> > And grewe in suche disdaine,
> That thousandes of the Greekish Dukes,
> > In hard and heauie plight,
> To Plutoes Courte did yeelde their soules,
> > And gaping lay vpright.*

---

* Homer, *Ten Books of Homers Iliades*, trans. Arthur Hall (London: Ralph Newberie, 1581), B1^r.

Arthur Hall (1539–1605), a well-to-do landowner and member of Parliament who would spend time in prison and may have died there, was just a teenager when he acquired his copy of Hugues Salel's French translation of Homer and began his version. Like George Chapman's much more famous later version, which it preceded by almost twenty years (part of Chapman's translation first appeared in print in 1598), Hall's uses rhyme and fourteeners (here broken over two lines) to convey Homer's dactylic hexameters, the standard meter of classical epic poetry. His English is racy if crude, like much amateur Elizabethan verse. Many of his contemporaries thought Hall something of a madman—choleric, quick to get into an argument or fisticuffs, bad at managing his money and pleasing his betters (including the Queen), and generally a bit of a failure at life. Having no Greek he made his Homer out of a French version that Ezra Pound would later praise, and so remains important in the history of English literature in this indirect way, by introducing what was then a 2,300-year-old poem into a language that had only a very limited relationship to ancient Greek. Apart from proper names, only the word "plaine" in the excerpt quoted above derives from a Greek root. Of the others, three words remember their Latin equivalents, and the remainder is all solidly anchored in Germanic etymology.

Precisely four hundred years after Arthur Hall's incomplete version of the *Iliad* appeared, the English poet Christopher Logue published the first section of a partial "account" (as he called it) of the same Homeric poem. The poetics of *War Music* bear so little relation to conventional translations (and, some would say, to Homer) as to make the Logue version seem at first startlingly disconnected from what had become by 1981 a long tradition of English Homers. But from Chapman to Pope to Lattimore and Robert Fitzgerald, with many, many other versions along the way and since by poets, politicians, and scientists, as well as classicists, there had always been varying views on what constituted good Homer in English. Pope's comment that "a translator owes so much to the taste of the age in which he lives, as not to make too great a complement to a former" perhaps surprisingly can be seen to support Logue's decision to write Homer as though he were, among other things, a playwright composing for a West End theatre. Here is the opening of Achilles's cranky speech to his mother (a goddess), from Book 1 of the *Iliad*, after Agamemnon has declared that he intends to steal Briseïs, Achilles's girlfriend-as-booty:

"Mother,
You said that you and God were friends.
Over and over when you were at home
You said it. Friends. Good friends. That was your boast.
You had had me, your child, your only child
To save Him from immortal death. In turn,
Your friend, the Lord our God, gave you His word,
Mother, His word: If I, your only child
Chose to die young, by violence, far from home,
My standing would be first; be best;
The best of bests; here; and in perpepuity.
  And so I chose. Nor have I changed. But now—
By which I mean today, this instant, now—
That Shepherd of the Clouds has seen me trashed
Surely as if He sent a hand to shoo
The army into one, and then, before its eyes,
Painted my body with fresh Trojan excrement."*

The repetitions here are certainly not in the Greek, but how emotionally right they sound in this speech. One may be less lenient with Logue for turning Zeus into a Christian god (although "Shepherd of

---

* Christopher Logue, *War Music: An Account of Books 1–4 and 16–19 of Homer's* Iliad (London: University of Chicago Press, 2001), pp. 7–8.

the Clouds" is a perfectly legitimate translation of the Homeric epithet associated with the Greek deity), but the employment of modern slang words such as "trash" and "shoo" gives a wonderful immediacy and contemporaneity to Achilles's plaint.

The twin questions of style and diction are at the heart of one particular "Homeric question," that is, how to translate these ancient poems into English convincingly; and again, the answers not surprisingly have differed over the centuries since Hall and Chapman. Matthew Arnold, in a famous essay, stated unconditionally that the "union of the translator with his original, which alone can produce a good translation...takes place when the mist which stands between them—the mist of alien modes of thinking, speaking, and feeling on the translator's part—'defecates to a pure transparency,' and disappears."* More recently, an editor of Pope's version of the *Iliad* observed that "if a translation is to live, it must be thoroughly contemporary, a literary success in the style of its time and in a distinct style of its own." He adds that "the way for a writer to ensure a long life for his translation is to be a poet of a high, if not the highest, order."† If this seems like a very high standard to uphold—how many poets of the highest order read ancient Greek anymore?—it remains unarguable. Surely we continue to read Chapman's Homer and Pope's Homer rather than the Homers of Thomas Hobbes or William Sotheby or the 14th earl of Derby precisely because Chapman and Pope were highly accomplished poets before they were translators.

Barry Powell is not a poet but a retired classics professor who has maintained a longstanding professional interest in Homeric studies. He is well known in classical circles for his contention that the Greek alphabet was quite literally invented around 800 BCE specifically to

---

* Matthew Arnold, "On Translating Homer," in *On the Classical Tradition*, ed. R. H. Super (Ann Arbor: University of Michigan Press, 1960), p. 103. The citation within Arnold's text is from Coleridge, who uses "defecates" here in its rarer sense of "clarifies."

† Reuben A. Brower, "Introduction," in *The Iliad of Homer*, trans. Alexander Pope, ed. Reuben A. Brower and W. H. Bond (New York: Macmillan, 1965), p. 10.

record the Homeric poems, perhaps even from recitations by Homer himself. While he restates this theory in the introduction to his new translation of the *Iliad*, it is by no means universally or even widely accepted by scholars.* I. J. Gelb long ago derided the notion that "an intelligent Greek" overnight adapted an existing Semitic writing system by adding vowels and extra letters peculiar to Greek (phi, chi, psi, et cetera), and Powell's charming fantasy that this particular Greek managed such a feat so that the *Iliad* and the *Odyssey* could be recorded is more than a little implausible.† But Powell's translation of the *Iliad*, to which an *Odyssey* will be added in the spring of 2014, does not stand or fall on philological theories but on poetry. The central drama of Homer's war poem, the transformation of Achilles from a shallow and petulant warrior into an emotionally complex human being, will always be a compelling one; but without equally compelling poetry, few readers in the twenty-first century will be willing to wade (heroically, one might say) through twenty-four books comprising almost 16,000 lines. Never, perhaps, has Chapman's compliment, "I suppose you to be no mean reader, since you intend to read Homer," been more relevant.

Powell's poetics are summarized in his introduction. He uses "a rough five-beat line" with an emphasis on "contemporary English" and "flexibility within accuracy." All of this seems unexceptionable, although in practice his diction can sound flat and his music dull; and at times his willingness to be "contemporary" betrays him into unfortunate word choices. For example, at the end of Book 1, a spirited conversation takes place between Zeus and Hera, and Powell's translation here sounds very inconsistent tonally. Hera addresses her husband as "my clever fellow," a vocative phrase with high-born British overtones; Pope's "artful manager of Heav'n" seems too arch, but perhaps Stephen Mitchell's "You schemer" approaches the right register most

---

* Homer, *The Iliad*, trans. Barry Powell (New York: Oxford University Press, 2014).
† I. J. Gelb, *A Study of Writing*, rev. ed. (Chicago: University of Chicago Press, 1963), p. 182.

successfully. Zeus, by contrast, descends to the B-word. "You bitch!" he says a little further on, where George Chapman had used "wretch," Samuel Butler simply "wife," Logue "First Heart" (rather beautifully), and Richmond Lattimore "Dear lady," which is in fact what one will find if one looks up the Greek word used here in Liddell and Scott's *A Greek-English Lexicon*. Zeus goes on to tell Hera to "shut up and sit down!," which is simply offensive, and other phrases such as "Hang on" and "Good grief" are equally too slangy. (I am aware that Albany says to Goneril, "Shut your mouth, dame," in the final scene of *King Lear*. "Shut up and sit down!" still sounds wrong in Homer's poem.)

At a different extreme Powell's English can sound lumpish. When, for example, Agamemnon sends two soldiers to Achilles's tent to fetch Briseïs for him, Powell translates one line in this way: "They walked in silence along the sea that grows no crops." That "sea that grows no crops" is not only awkward. It is also puzzling when it needn't be. Lattimore's version is not only better poetry, it also does not confuse the reader: "They went against their will beside the beach of the barren / salt sea." Pope's "Pensive they walk along the barren sands" is equally to the point. Powell's *Iliad* contains many other examples of lines that lie half-dead on the page. "Early in the morning / they bring to them the rough fight," for example (Book III), or Hephaistos's words of complaint about Hera, who threw him out of heaven: "I had fallen far, through the will of my bitch mother! / She wanted to hide me because of my bum leg" (Book XVIII).

Powell's verse is not without occasional felicitous touches. Early in the poem he says of Chryses, whose daughter has been Agamemnon's prize and who has been disdainfully rebuffed: "He walked in silence along the resounding / sea." This is simple and quite lovely. (That it is repeated in part in the later line discussed above is typically Homeric, for repetition is an inherent characteristic of the oral style.) And in some lines spoken by Hephaistos later in Book I—"Surely this will be a nasty turn, / scarcely to be born [sic], if the two of you quarrel like this / over men who die"—the counterpoint of "born" and "die" is most ept. Powell can manage eldritch power too, as in this well-known simile from Book XVI:

> But Achilles went through the huts and urged all
> the Myrmidons to arm. And they ran out like flesh-eating wolves
> in whose hearts is an unspeakable rage—wolves who have killed
> a horned stag in the mountains and who dine upon him,
> and their cheeks are red with blood, and in a pack they course
> to the black waters of a black spring. With their thin tongues
> they lap the surface of the water, all the while vomiting
> blood and gore, and their hearts in their breasts are unflinching,
> and their bellies are gorged—even so did the leaders
> and rulers of the Myrmidons swarm forth around Patroklos,
> the companion of the grandson of Aiakos the fast runner.

This in its way is as good as Lattimore or Robert Fitzgerald, even if "the fast runner" is somewhat bathetic. It has the limitations of plain speech, but also its power, where "unflinching," for example, sounds more effective than Lattimore's slightly prissy "untremulous" or Fitzgerald's less gripping "unshaken." That "gore" and "gorged" should occur in close proximity is also a nice touch. For the most part, Powell's English has undeniable narrative drive. Yet that drive feels largely like good descriptive prose rather than poetry, and that fact, finally, makes Powell's version a failure by his own standard. "Homer seems wrong as prose," he observes in the introduction, and he is right, however massively successful the prose version by E. V. Rieu has been over the decades since it was first published by Penguin in 1950.

Stephen Mitchell is not a professional classicist but a professional translator and a poet. His version of the *Iliad* was published in 2011, and he has now brought out an *Odyssey* to accompany it.* His introduction, like Powell's, contains some contentious scholarship, drawn primarily

---

* Homer, *The Odyssey*, trans. Stephen Mitchell (New York: Atria Books, 2013).

from the work of M. L. West, a British classicist who is convinced of
several debatable theories: that there was no poet named Homer, that the
two epic poems were written by different poets, and that they date to
roughly 650 BCE, more than a century later than the conventional dating.
Mitchell states that, if he had his way, the name "Homer" would not even
adorn his book; but of course publishing constraints forced him to go
along with the traditional assignment of authorship. West was Mitchell's
mentor for both of his Homeric translations, and his *Odyssey* is dedicated
to the scholar whose edition of the *Iliad* he used, and on whose authority
he rejected Book X as a later spurious interpolation (although West himself includes it in his edition of the Greek text) and which he did not
translate for his book. That decision drew a lot of critical fire, as did his
use of slang and his decision to drop most of the Homeric epithets (swift-
footed Achilles, et cetera). The epithets have always caused controversy
among translators, with some, citing Matthew Arnold's view, feeling that
they rapidly become boring and distracting in English (Mitchell says that
they are often "merely tedious"), while others value their authenticity,
not to mention their occasional irony (Achilles is swift-footed even when
he is sitting down). Mitchell drops parts of the *Odyssey* too, although
nothing so radical as an entire book; and perhaps as a sop to the critics
who complained of this decision in his *Iliad*, these excisions (a passage
from Book XI and the first two hundred lines of Book XXIV) are translated
and included as appended material.

Mitchell's approach to the poetry of Homer is similar to Powell's.
He has used what he denominates "a pentameter with as few iambs as
possible," a line that "usually has from twelve to fourteen syllables, and
occasionally eleven or fifteen." He avoids iambs presumably to forestall
his poetry from falling into blank verse, but the flexibility of his line,
while certainly natural ("I have tried to sound natural," he claims of
his diction) can, as Powell's also can, descend into prosiness. Here is a
passage in which Athena is chatting with Telemachus, Odysseus's son:

> *"But tell me now: Are you really*
> *his son? You must be. You certainly look like him;*
> *with your face and your handsome eyes, it is really quite*
> *an amazing resemblance. Oh, I remember him well.*
> *We spent a great deal of time together before*
> *he sailed to Troy with the rest of the Argive commanders,*
> *though since that day we have never set eyes on each other."*

Did a Greek goddess ever sound more like a nosy old friend of one's mother, interrogating some nice young man after church? Or take this passage from the conclusion of Book I, again concerning Odysseus's son:

> *He opened the bedroom door, sat down on the bed,*
> *took off his tunic, and handed it to the old woman,*
> *who folded it, smoothed it, and hung it up on a hook*
> *by the side of the bed.. Then slowly she left the room . . .*

This sort of nondescript writing, which could easily come from a second-rate Hemingway short story, surely has no place in a poem. Chapman's version has all the benefits of a richly sensual language:

> *He on his bed sat, the soft weeds he wore*
> *Put off, and to the diligent old maid*
> *Gave all, who fitly all in thick folds laid,*
> *And hung them on a beame-pin neare the bed,*
> *That round about was rich embroidered.*
> *Then made she haste forth from him . . .*

All the same, Mitchell's language does achieve greater readability than Powell's, and at times it even breaks the bounds of prose and approaches the sublimity of poetry. No translator, reaching Book XI, the so-called Nekuia or visit to Hell, can avoid thinking of Ezra Pound, whose canto 1 ("And then went down to the ship") translates part of this book and makes it into the most beautiful and compelling English ever to invoke Homer. Whether that precedent is daunting or inspiring depends, I suppose, on the translator. In Mitchell's case I think it was the latter, as some parts of his Book XI are wonderfully done. After sacrificing two sheep and allowing their "dark blood [to flow] in the fosse," as Pound puts it, the ghosts from Hell appear. Mitchell's version is deeply moving even if one does have Pound's version in one's ear:

> Immediately the ghosts came swarming around me
> up out of Érebus—brides and unmarried youths,
> old men worn out by suffering, tender young girls
> with grief still fresh in their hearts, and a host of spirits
> whose flesh had been mangled by bronze-tipped spears, men killed
> in the crush of battle, still wearing their blood-stained armor.
> From all directions they crowded around the pit
> with unearthly shrieks that made me turn pale with terror.
> And I called to my comrades and told them to flay the sheep
> quickly, to burn them as offerings, and to pray
> to the lower gods, Perséphonē and grim Hades.
> Meanwhile I crouched there, holding my drawn sword over
> the pool of blood, and I wouldn't allow the ghosts
> to approach until I had questioned Tirésius.

Other passages in Book XI are equally fine, such as the simple statement made to Odysseus in Hell by the ghost of his mother, Anticlea, that "Of that same inconsolable sorrow I died," meaning the feeling of certainty that Odysseus had been killed on the return voyage from Troy. Like other reviewers, I am not convinced that Mitchell's use of slang is always warranted, and he indulges it in Book XI by having the spirit of Agamemnon call his wife "that goddamned whore," where Lattimore had used "the sluttish woman" and Robert Fagles "my treacherous queen," both renderings admittedly a little fussy. (When Odysseus addresses a female servant in Book XVIII as "You bitch," it is admittedly less of a stretch. The Greek word means literally "dog," and Fagles and even Lattimore both translated the derisive term as "bitch.") Even Achilles's famous reply to Odysseus when the former is complimented as "a great prince among the dead," while on the whole quite wonderfully done, is marred by a bit of late-twentieth-century slang:

> And he said: "Don't try to smooth-talk me into accepting
> death, Odysseus. I would much rather be
> above ground as the most destitute serf, hired out
> to some tenant farmer with hardly enough to live on,
> than to be king over all the shadowy dead."

"Smooth-talk" here sounds tonally discordant. The Greek verb means both to urge and to encourage or to console, and both William Cowper in the eighteenth century and Lattimore in the twentieth chose the latter verb. Perhaps "browbeat" is slightly too negative, although it has at least the benefit of more ancient use than "smooth-talk," which the OED does not cite as being used before the 1950s, while "browbeat" goes back to the sixteenth century. Mitchell has also dropped the adjective "shining" which Homer uses here to characterize Odysseus, presumably out of his normal habit of excising epithets. But here it feels crucial, since Odysseus shines precisely because he is still among the living and is not a shade in Hell. One regrets its absence even if one does not always regret the absence of "swift-footed" or "rosy-fingered." It is what Bernard Knox, in his long and splendid introduction to Robert Fagles's translation of the *Odyssey*, called "a truly formulaic epithet [that] does in fact seem to be poetically functional in its context."*

---

* Bernard Knox, "Introduction" to Homer, *The Odyssey*, trans. Robert Fagles (New York: Viking, 1990), p. 18.

The identity of the *Odyssey* as basically an adventure narrative, with a fair share of magical events, shipwrecks, challenges to human endurance, erotic dalliance, and (in Penelope) erotic fidelity, is surely what has kept it at the centre (a different sort of centre from the *Iliad*) of Western literature for 2,700 years through hundreds of translations, adaptations, novelizations, films, television productions, graphic novels, cartoons, and poetry. Yet there is such rebarbative strangeness at times in the poem. Reading about Odysseus beating up Arnaeus, the local beggar on Ithaca, in Book XVIII, is unedifying and indeed unappetizing. "You are a poor excuse for a man," Odysseus tells him like some mean-hearted hard-drinking cowboy in a Hollywood western. Odysseus's flagrant and wild cock-and-bull story addressed to Athena in Book XIII is embarrassing for him and for the reader. Some of the famous epic similes are beautiful. When Odysseus and Penelope finally embrace after she realizes that he is really who he claims to be in Book XXIII, the simile of loving relief—they feel like storm-tossed bodies flung at long last onto firm and safe ground—is lovely, magical even. But an example in Book X, when Homer describes Odysseus's men frisking and gamboling around him like calves around cows when they return from the fields, is puerile, even epicene. Shortly thereafter, Odysseus is sorely tempted to decapitate one of his men, and a close relative at that, merely for disagreeing with him. And the tears! There is more weeping in the *Odyssey* by men and by women (this is true of the *Iliad* as well) than in a thousand soap operas. In the Circe episode alone, one group of men weeps at being transformed into pigs, those men left back at the ship weep when Odysseus returns, the two groups of men burst into tears when they are reunited at Circe's hut, Odysseus himself sobs when Circe tells him that before returning to Ithaca he must visit the underworld, and the crew, told of this before embarking, likewise collapse in a lachrymose fog. All of these particular weepy moments happen within seven pages of Stephen Mitchell's translation. And there is much crying elsewhere as well. Clearly, as scholars have shown, there was nothing unmanly in archaic Greece about men showing their emotions.

Yet if at times one grows slightly weary of all the wailing, it certainly humanizes that other, also wearying side of archaic Greek manhood, the pugnaciousness, even the bloodthirstiness. "*Weinende Männer sind gut*," as Goethe said: weeping men are good.* Does Gulliver cry enough? Does Captain Nemo (whose name itself is a direct steal from the Cyclops episode of the *Odyssey*) ever weep? Would they not have been richer characters if they had? Would Olson's postmodern Homeric Maximus not have been a more representative figure if he had been given greater emotional depth, instead of seeking only for the narrow-minded heroic?

> *The only interesting thing*
>
> *is if one can be*
>
> *an image*
>
> *of man, "The nobleness, and the arete."*[†]

Barry Powell discusses several key Greek words in the introduction to his *Iliad*, including "kudos" (glory), "timê" (honour), and "kleos" (fame), but he left out Olson's word here, "arete" (manly qualities, according to Liddell and Scott). Olson's image of man falls short in its overemphasis on nobility and manliness. Maximus should have cried more, like Odysseus and his kind.

---

* The Goethe poem is quoted by Sabine Föllinger in her paper "Tears and Crying in Archaic Greek Poetry (especially Homer)," in *Tears in the Graeco-Roman World*, ed. Thorsten Fögen (Berlin and New York: Walter de Gruyter, 2009), p. 19.

† Charles Olson, *The Maximus Poems*, Volume Three, ed. George Butterick (New York: Grossman, 1975), p. 101.

EPICS MANQUÉS

The Greek Anthology is unique in Western literature. Consisting of thousands of poems by many dozens of poets, written over a period of over 1,500 years in a vast geographical area extending from the Greek islands to Constantinople, it is perhaps indigestible as a whole but is endlessly fascinating in bits. Two quite distinct versions survive and together make up between them fifteen books, with an appendix constituting a sixteenth, divided by subject (Christian poems, poems about art, homosexual poems, et cetera) rather than by poet or period. Few of the poems exceed eight lines and all are defined technically as epigrams, not in our sense of short witty pieces (though many are), but in the more basic sense, from the Greek, of inscriptions. Like most of classical literature the Greek Anthology survived by the slenderest of threads. Readers who remember Benjamin Jowett's stirring speech in Tom Stoppard's play *The Invention of Love*, about how extraordinarily unlikely it is that Catullus's poems withstood the ravages of time at all, will have a vivid sense of how the Greek Anthology barely escaped the fate of much of the writing of the ancient world. We are fortunate to have it. A recension prepared by the Byzantine monk Maximus Planudes in the thirteenth century, and preserved today at the Marcian Library in Venice, was printed in Florence in 1494. Planudes bowdlerized the text considerably, but fortunately a second, more complete manuscript survived and turned up in Heidelberg in 1606, where most of it still is. (Classical manuscripts frequently formed part of war booty, and a smaller portion of the Heidelberg manuscript now belongs to the Bibliothèque Nationale in Paris because of the Napoleonic depredations.) The Heidelberg manuscript, first published in the eighteenth century, forms the basis for modern scholarly editions of the Greek Anthology, with the poems known only from the Planudean version being placed in the appendix.

With its frequent ribaldries and obscenities (although as Daryl Hine has remarked, there was little if anything in ancient Greek that qualified as obscene), the Greek Anthology is essentially a modern book, known in the Renaissance to scholars but not to the general reader until the twentieth century. A nineteenth-century edition for English schoolboys naturally censored the work, and even many later translations into English omitted the stronger stuff or dropped a veil when necessary to shield the gentle reader from the risqué bits. English-speaking poets have long been game to try their hands at individual poems, including Shelley (who translated four poems and used another as the epigraph to *Adonais*) and later Ezra Pound, Richard Aldington, and Dudley Fitts, as well as, more recently, Kenneth Rexroth, Daryl Hine, W. S. Merwin, and Guy Davenport among Americans, and Robin Skelton, Peter Whigham, Tony Harrison, Edward Lucie-Smith, and Peter Porter among English and Commonwealth poets. The concision and cleverness of the poems in Greek makes for a great deal of latitude in the English of these poets, an English which ranges from romantic to imagist and from Augustan to street slang. Daryl Hine, in a translation of Book XII of the Greek Anthology that he calls *Puerilities* (2001), makes all of the poems rhyme; while Tony Harrison, executing versions of poems by Palladas for a compilation that Peter Jay put together and published in 1973,* gives us, among other amusements

---

* Peter Jay, ed., *The Greek Anthology and Other Ancient Greek Epigrams* (London: Allen Lane, 1973).

requiring a certain degree of suspended disbelief, a fourth-century CE Greek poet speaking English with a German accent:

> Mein breast, mein corset und mein legs
> ja dedicates to Juice like all gut Greigs.

Harrison opted for a tessitura that is rigorously demotic, while other versions, like that of the Loeb Classical Library or the scholarly edition of the Anthology by A. S. F. Gow and D. L. Page, are more literal and function as trots and ponies. The Greek poems can stand up robustly to all kinds of imaginings. (When the going gets tough and erotic, the Loeb edition still substitutes Latin for English.)

David R. Slavitt, a poet and well-known translator from Greek, Latin, and other languages, has now published a garland of his own translations of some 140 poems from the Greek Anthology.* His selection draws heavily from Books v (erotic poems), vii (epitaphs), ix (rhetorical epigrams), and xi (humorous pieces), while completely ignoring the Christian poems in Books i and viii and only occasionally dipping into the remaining books. In his preface he cheerfully admits to eschewing "a systematic approach" in favour of choices based on personal appeal and linguistic challenge. Slavitt has previously brought out versions of Sophocles, Ovid, Valerius Flaccus, and Aeschylus, not to mention the Latin odes of Jean Dorat (the sixteenth-century scholar and poet who helped to bring the Pléiade together), the Minor Prophets of the Old Testament, and Dante's La Vita Nuova. Like Daryl Hine and Dudley Fitts (who was one of Slavitt's teachers at the Phillips Academy), Slavitt is both classically trained and a poet, unlike, say, Guy Davenport, who took up Greek later in life and admitted that his knowledge of the language was "functional rather than philological."

---

* David R. Slavitt, *Poems from the Greek Anthology* (Riverdale-on-Hudson: Sheep Meadow Press, 2010).

Slavitt starts then from an intimate knowledge of what the Greek really says, so that if his translations stray from euphemism into execration, or from indirection into malediction, it is a deliberate choice. Two examples will show his willingness to stretch the Greek and to try to give it a very contemporary vocabulary.

First, there is the famous misogynistic two-line epigram by the fourth- or fifth-century poet Palladas (his dates are disputed) that, in Greek and without any attempt to poeticize, says: "Every woman is a cause of anger. But she has two good times, / one in the bedroom, the other in death." The Greek gets its epigrammatic bite in part from the fact that the words for "bedroom" and "death" are very similar in sound (*thalamos* and *thanatos*). Slavitt chooses to leave out the bit about "cause of anger" (a single word in the Greek), and, like Pound, he turns the two lines into three:

> Every woman has two shining moments:
> In her bridal chamber when she gets laid,
> And on her bier, when she gets laid out.

This is certainly more slangy than the Greek, but the play on "laid" is nicely done if we allow that the slang catches the spirit rather than the linguistic content of the original. Pound, for his part, is more understated, and his tone is rather removed from anything one would characterize as demotic:

> Woman? Oh, woman is a consummate rage,
> But dead, or asleep, she pleases.
> Take her. She has two excellent seasons. *

---

* Pound's translation forms the fifth section of his "Homage to Quintus Septimius Florentis Christianus," and is most readily found in *Poems and Translations* (New York: Library of America, 2003), p. 314.

A second example goes substantially further down the byways of slang and is perhaps more questionable. Marcus Argentarius is recognized as one of the more accomplished of the poets in the Greek Anthology. He has an effective poem on the subject of how a cock crowing in an untimely moment disturbs his owner's erotic dream of Pyrrha, and how he plots revenge through sacrificing the bird to Serapis, an imported Egyptian god who, appropriately for the poem, spoke to adherents in dreams. Slavitt reduces the poem from six to five lines, excising some text in the process ("You'll crow no longer at night"), as he ratchets up the man's anger well beyond the original: "you stupid chicken / . . . I'll wring your fucking neck and offer you up / on the altar of Serapis, god of dreams." Fleur Adcock, the New Zealand poet, has translated this as ". . . holy Serapis / His altar, on which I swore, / Shall have your corpse as a sacrifice," which stays quite close to the Greek. Of course there is something eschatologically appropriate about wringing a chicken's neck, despite the fact that a chicken and a cock are not the same thing and chickens normally do not crow. (The Greek word is *ornis*, which in Attic is usually a male bird, but can more generally mean a domestic fowl of any sort, thus leaving room for Slavitt's alteration. In any case an enraged awakened dreamer might well fasten on the easier word in expostulation.) Whether the adventitious "fucking" is a good or a bad thing is debatable, I suppose. Certainly it has no equivalent in the Greek.

Slavitt is fond of this sort of jazziness, and sometimes it works well through sheer audaciousness, as in this short squib by Julian Antecessor:

> *That's some beard, bud.*
> *Way beyond razors.*
> *Even beyond scissors.*
> *What you need is a goddamn scythe.**

---

* Perhaps it is helpful to give the more literal Loeb translation here: "You have such a heavy crop on your hairy face that you ought to have it cut with scythes and not with scissors."

At other times it seems forced or even old-fashioned, as in this poem by Rufinus:

> To hell with classy dames, so full of airs,
> reeking of scent, and, if they show up, they bring
> their maids, even into your bedroom.
> Give me a slave girl every time. They smell of soap,
> never talk about Homer, and are grateful
> for a good time. What could be better than that?

The language here is assuredly more colloquial than the Greek, but "classy dames" is a colloquialism from another era, and Rufinus was not trying to sound like he was a character in a Raymond Chandler novel. (The same might be said of the vocative "bud" in the Julian poem quoted earlier.) It is in the nature of slang to become dated even more quickly, perhaps, than poetic language, and while most translation is not meant for the ages, it ought at least to be for its own age. If slang is to be introduced into poems well over a millennium old, it should be current.

Arguably more than most classical poetry, the poems in the Greek Anthology resist literalism and present themselves as raw material which the translator needs to transmute to a greater or lesser extent to make English poetry out of them. Intimate emotion, though not absent from the collection, is less common by far than word play, grim observation, religious conviction (on the one hand), and cynicism (on the other). These attributes bring the poetry closer to the tenor of our times perhaps than to other epochs. David Slavitt's translations try to deploy the language of our day (with slips of the kind noted above) in a formal context of directness and a spartan sense of music. Phrases such as "What's up with that?," "bad-ass," "surf and turf," and "gabby geezer" attest to his determination to make the Greek poets sound like our contemporaries. One might complain that he ranges a little too freely across generations for his colloquialisms, since one can imagine a thirty-something saying "What's up with that?," but hardly thinking, much less saying, "gabby" or even "geezer." Vulgarisms add to the contemporaneity of the diction, and on the whole I think Slavitt is successful in bringing the Greek into an idiom that is forceful and true. His other translations demonstrate that he has range. A recent version of three of Ovid's works (the *Amores*, the *Heroides*, and the *Remedia amoris*), for example, shows him coursing through a variety of styles that suit Ovid's urbane personality and yet can reach a higher or lower tone when called for. The elegy for Tibullus (*Amores* III, 9) is beautifully rendered and concludes with the very moving line, "I pray that the earth lie lightly on your bones."*

If there is a characteristic of many of the poems in the Greek Anthology that seems modern, or perhaps just psychologically permanent—modern in all ages—it is the theme of how short life is, and how we must take the time to enjoy sex and wine and the life of the senses before it is too late. A poem by Rufinus to which Slavitt gives the title "Toast" captures the feeling:

> *Let's drink to each other, Prodike, while we still can.*
> *Age waits in the shadows, and behind it, death.*

Slavitt has shortened this piece, effectively so, and it can stand for many similar epigrams scattered through the sixteen books of the Anthology. Blithe exhortations to seize the day are only one side of this theme. It ramifies in many ways, producing poems in which self-delusion, stupidity, miserliness, and resolute virginity are anathematized, while humour, even humour in the very teeth of death, is prized. Given that many of the epigrams are inscriptions for tombs, death

---

* Ovid, *Love Poems, Letters, and Remedies*, trans. David R. Slavitt (Cambridge, MA: Harvard University Press, 2011), p. 121.

naturally haunts the collection. Lamentations about fate are common, then ("I, Dionysius of Tarsus, lie here, / sixty years old, and never married. / I wish my father hadn't either"), but equally prevalent are poems that constitute a proud provocation of death or a recognition that, if nothing else, at least death pulls in the bad guys too. How wonderful that poems of such an ancient lineage can still make us cheer out loud.

> *This stone above a hateful head*
> *crushes the bones of a son of a bitch.*
> *Earth fills his lying mouth and little rat teeth,*
> *weighs down his bowed legs, and crowns his bald pate.*
> *The rest of him rots, but then he was rotten before.*
> *The Earth has swallowed him up. We hope it won't vomit.*
>   *(Crinagoras, "Epitaph for a Bad-ass.")*

THE PLACE OF REST
FROM ALL YOU HAVE
UNDERGONE

The English poet and translator C. H. Sisson once wrote that "To know nothing of Virgil is to miss one of the clues to our poetry." Glenn W. Most, an American classicist who teaches at the Scuola Normale in Pisa, put it much more forcefully. He felt that "the legacy of Virgil to Western Literature is Western Literature." Like all such startling claims, his is both arguably true and patently exaggerated. It might be possible to squeeze much of Greek literature under Virgil's long shadow (epic of course, but also pastoral and more generally the rural poem), yet so much has happened over the last two millennia in poetry and other genres of writing that Virgil would be hard pressed to recognize as his spawn. Dante's choice of Virgil as his *cicerone* through two-thirds of the *Divina Commedia* speaks volumes for Virgil's reputation more than a thousand years after his demise in 19 BCE, a death compellingly imagined in Hermann Broch's novel *The Death of Virgil*; but it is significant too that, if there is an ancient poet who rules over a modern epic poem like *The Cantos*, it is not Virgil but Homer. "And then went down to the ship," it begins, as Pound translates from Book 11 of *The Odyssey*. The final line, almost 120 cantos and 800 pages later, is "To be men not destroyers," surely a reference to ancient epic in general and probably to Homer in particular. Unlike most of ancient literature, Virgil's work was successfully Christianized, an evolution which gave him a prominent and essential leg-up for survival through late antiquity, into the Middle Ages, and beyond. Virgil's works were printed first in 1469 and had been printed multiple times before the *editio princeps* of Homer was published in 1488. Even allowing for the relative ease of printing Latin in the incunabular age, compared to Greek, it is clear that the Roman poet was a far more desirable text for the early printers than his Greek predecessor, which means essentially that he had economic advantages in the marketplace. Virgil was a saleable commodity.

The *Aeneid* has been translated into English countless times, in whole or in part, over the last five hundred years. The record begins with William Caxton, the first person to print books in English (and England), among whose many books was an *Aeneid* that he translated, or rather paraphrased, from a French version and published in 1490. So unlike Virgil's original is it that it is usually omitted from the list of English Virgils. Indeed the translator who is usually credited with the first translation of the *Aeneid* into an Anglic language—Gavin Douglas, whose version was completed in 1513 but not published until 1553—dismissed Caxton's text with a disdainful couplet:

> *His buk is na mare like Virgil, dar I lay,*
> *Than the nyght oule resemblis the papingay.*

Douglas's vigorous Scots translation was deeply admired by Ezra Pound, among others, and remained the most accomplished version available to unlatined English readers until Dryden's, which was published in 1697. Lesser translations preceded Dryden's and lesser ones succeeded it; but the poet laureate's thousands of rhyming couplets comprised most educated readers' access to Virgil's epic poem for 250 years, until

C. Day-Lewis's version came out in 1952. Since then there have been many translations published, each with its qualities, and each usually with a stated aspiration of obedience to Virgil's Latin. Day-Lewis, like Sarah Ruden (2009) half a century later, managed to translate line for line by using a flexible six-stress hexameter, whereas a translator like Robert Fitzgerald (1984) chose a much shorter measure by which the 756 lines of Virgil's Book 1, for example, swelled to 1,031. Versions by Allen Mandelbaum (1971), Stanley Lombardo (2005), and Robert Fagles (2006) are composed in a more or less modern voice with a flexible metrical overlay: sometimes five, sometimes six, and occasionally even seven stresses in a line. Barry Powell (2016), who has also translated Homer's two epic poems, felt emboldened to claim that his *Aeneid* "is Vergil as he is, not as we wish he were." Yet his line is as flexible as any predecessor's, and he even felt confident enough to leave out what he thought were the less interesting parts of the poem: all of Books 3 and 5 and parts of every remaining book. Like Ezra Pound, whose translation of part of Book 11 of the *Odyssey* in the *Cantos* makes us wish he had translated the entire epic poem, Seamus Heaney's "classics homework" as he called it— his version of Book 6 of the *Aeneid*, the journey to the land of the dead—provokes in every reader the bootless wish that he had done more. But he was essentially carrying out a homage to his Latin teacher, and was, in any case, dead before the book was even published in 2016.

To this distinguished group of translators we can now add David Ferry's name. Ferry is well known as a poet—he has won the Ruth Lilly Poetry Prize (2011) among other prestigious awards—and he has previously published translations of Virgil's two other works, the *Eclogues* (2000) and the *Georgics* (2005), as well as versions of the *Epic of Gilgamesh* and Horace's *Odes*. His translation of the *Aeneid* was published when he was ninety-three years old.[*] It is not a version for the squeamish

---

[*] Virgil, *The Aeneid*, trans. David Ferry (Chicago: University of Chicago Press, 2017). My title comes from a line in Book VIII, in Ferry's version.

or the reader without Classical Civilization 101. There is no glossary of the names of people or places or gods, and it bears only the shortest of short introductions. If you do not know to which muse Virgil's poem is addressed, or to what Laurentium refers, Ferry is not about to help you out. Of course Virgil himself helps his readers quite a lot, through narration (for example, the story of the fall of Troy, as Aeneas describes it to Dido's court in Book 2), and through characterization, as when he identifies a particular soldier, one Messapus, as a horsebreaker who was "Neptune's son."

There is much in the *Aeneid* that Virgil modeled on Homer: the formality and seriousness of the epic story and style, the lengthy description of a hero's shield forged by a god, the crucial interference of an angry god (Juno here), the use of the hexameter line, the elaboration of epic similes, and so on. But there are differences too, largely owing to the fact that while the *Iliad* and the *Odyssey* have their roots in oral narratives, the *Aeneid* is first and foremost a literary epic poem. Virgil's authorial manuscript was saved from the flames by Augustus Caesar himself, who overruled Virgil's testamentary order to destroy it; the earliest surviving manuscripts are centuries older than their Homeric equivalents. Virgil does not have to resort to repetition in the way that Homer does (no standard epithets like "wine-dark sea" or "fleet-footed Achilles") and his syntax tends to be more complex than Homer's. But Ferry introduces a version of repetition of his own that he uses so often as to make it characteristic of his *Aeneid*. There are examples throughout the poem, but two lines from Book 7 are typical. Virgil writes at lines 787–88, *tam magis illa fremens et tristibus effera flammis / quam magis effuso crudescunt sanguine pugnae*, or "raging the more, and the madder with baleful flames, the more blood is outpoured and the fiercer waxes the fight," as the Loeb translation by G. P. Goold rather elaborately puts it. The two lines begin with a parallelism (*tam magis / quam magis*), but otherwise there is no repetition of words in them. Ferry makes of this passage a sentence full of repeated words that become almost incantatory, while also retaining Virgil's alliterations:

> *Hotter and more fierce the hotter the fighting,*
> *And the hotter and fiercer the fighting the hotter the fire*
> *Spilled forth.*

By comparison, the versions by Fagles ("And roaring all the more, its searing flames more deadly / the more blood flows and the battle grows more fierce") and Fitzgerald (". . . raging the more / With savage heat the more blood flowed, the wilder / Grew the battle"), while perfectly good, sound less evocative of the fierceness of battle.

As many translators have pointed out, there is no use in trying to recreate what Barry Powell called Virgil "as he is." "As he is" is the Latin, and it is a basic literary law that whatever English a translator composes in has to be the English of his or her own time, not some imagined equivalent English that Virgil might speak if only he lived in Manhattan or Westminster in 2018. A very few translations have had the necromantic good fortune to survive beyond their own times, but they comprise the exceptions. David Ferry's English is very much the poetic version of American English that characterizes much of poetry these days. Sometimes it feels a bit bland, especially with the famous bits in Latin that have become proverbial. "These are the tears of things for what they were, / and what has become of them," he invents for Virgil's famous *Sunt lachrymae rerum* in Book 1, sixteen English words for three in Latin. And yet over all Ferry's chosen "instrument," as he calls it in his note on meter—a rough pentameter most of the time, and iambic by preference—is by turns subtle, flexible, and strong. Over the long haul—13,362 lines (to Virgil's 9,896) the poem has cumulative power; and if it bogs down for twenty-first-century readers, as it does to some extent in the second half, that is more Virgil's fault than Ferry's. Much of the last six books is taken up with battle scenes, which can become emptily repetitive. Even *pius Aeneas* can seem like a brainless killing-machine when he dispatches soldier after poor soldier, "inspired with rage in the landscape of [his] killing," as Ferry translates a line from Book 12. And yet war in Virgil is never simply a heroic means to a debatable end, never simply "undiscriminating carnage." What contemporary reader, coming on these lines describing the fall of Troy in Book 2, will not think of our own world—will not think, for example, of Aleppo:

> *Who is it who could tell about such carnage?*
> *Whose tears could be equal to what has happened here?*
> *The ancient city, so long the queen, has fallen.*
> *Dead bodies lying everywhere on the streets,*
> *Among the houses, on the doorsteps, on*
> *The holy portals of the gods. It isn't only*
> *Trojans who have paid the price with blood.*
> *Sometimes some of them, when they could, fought back,*
> *And there are many conqueror Greeks who fell.*
> *Dire woe is everywhere, everywhere terror,*
> *Everywhere there are images of death.*

There is no word for "terror" in Virgil's Latin in this passage, but Ferry was right to add it. It is one of his subtle ways of making the *Aeneid* a thoroughly modern poem.

Some four hundred years now stretch from George Chapman's first translation of Homer's *Odyssey* into English (1615) to the many versions that have been published over the last twenty-five years or so, five in the last five years alone. (Translations of Homer into Latin and most of the vernacular languages of Europe all preceded Chapman's, and Chapman is generally thought to have relied heavily on an exisiting Latin translation as a kind of intermediary between the Greek and his English.) Emily Wilson's new translation of the *Odyssey* marks the first time that the poem has been translated into English by a woman.* Indeed as a female translator of Homer into any vernacular language, she is preceded only by Anne Dacier (1647?–1720), who published a French version of both Homeric epics around the turn of the eighteenth century. In a poem that is getting on for 3,000 years old and which depicts a culture in which gender roles are so starkly differentiated and the actions of men (especially) often make readers gulp and shiver, the sex of the translator will indisputably make a difference. Odysseus is a fully rounded character, a human being with foibles and flaws as well as strengths. The adjective that Homer first applies to him in the opening lines of the poem and frequently thereafter, *polutropos*, could in fact be translated as "well rounded," although translators over the centuries have mostly chosen among variations on either Chapman's "wisdom" ("prudent," "sagacious," "ingenious," "resourceful") or William Cowper's "shrewdness" ("crafty," "wily," "cunning," "shifty"). Wilson, who once said puckishly in an interview that one could arguably apply the Greek adjective to a straying husband (which Odysseus was, of course), chose "complicated" for that initial occurrence. But although the epithets in Greek may be invariable, as part of the Homeric inheritance from the oral tradition, Wilson, unlike some earlier translators, does not hesitate to translate the word differently at different moments, thus providing variety in the face of a problem that can seem intractable. So Odysseus becomes a "survivor" and a "fox," in addition to the more conventional "resourceful," "clever," "adaptable," and so on.

It is clear that Wilson's attitude toward Odysseus is ambivalent. Most modern readers feel the same. He does frankly stupid things at times, like taunting Polyphemus after he and his remaining men have escaped on their ship, bringing on Poseidon's increased wrath. He also does incomprehensibly violent things, even in the context of the ear-

---

* Homer, *The Odyssey*, trans. Emily Wilson (New York: W.W. Norton, 2018).

lier and dissimilar culture that constitutes Mycenean Greece. For example, he orders all the slave girls in his house executed, after the suitors are killed, for sleeping with the enemy. Wilson takes pains sometimes to place Odysseus in an even uglier light than Homer himself does. In Book 22, he is not, as Lattimore has it, "great enduring Odysseus, son of Laertes," but "the lord of suffering." He does not order that Melanthius, one of the suitors who has slipped away to find more weapons but has been noticed by the swineherd, Eumaeus, should "suffer harsh torment" (Lattimore) or "dangle in torment there for a while" (Stephen Mitchell). He tells Telemachus: "Torture him / with hours of agony before he dies." In her long and useful introduction, Wilson calls Odysseus a "liar, pirate, colonizer, deceiver, and thief" who "directly kills so many people," and even in a situation in which Odysseus is presented as emotional and empathetic—as for example in a passage where he breaks out in tears at hearing the story of his own martial success at Troy narrated by a bard—Wilson sees a sort of special pleading by Homer for sympathy that may not be deserved. To her list, she later adds "migrant," "homeless person," "colonial invader," and other names. (None of the homeless people in my Toronto neighbourhood eat meat and drink wine every day of their lives.)

Of course it is impossible not to read ancient poems through a modern lens. (That word "colonizer" in the list of Wilson's Odyssean epithets above is a dead giveaway.) Wilson's complex reading of the poems is reified in her language. Her *Odyssey* like many others is composed in a five-beat line, although also like many others the meter is often dissipated in sentences that do not sound particularly poetic. But she nicely combines the readability necessary for an epic poem of over 12,000 lines with a sensitivity to how modern English speakers speak today, thereby achieving her stated goal of wanting her version to be "readable and fluent." Her translation of Achilles's famous reply to Odysseus when they meet in Erebus in Book 11, one of the most famous moments in the poem, is quite lovely:

> *"Odysseus, you must not comfort me*
> *for death. I would prefer to be a workman,*
> *hired by a poor man on a peasant farm,*
> *than rule as king of all the dead."*

Even allowing for the differences of epoch and ideals of diction, Chapman's take on these lines sounds overdone:

> *"Urge not my death to me, nor rub that wound,*
> *I rather wish to live in earth a swain,*
> *Or serve a swain for hire, that scarce can gain*
> *Bread to sustain him, than, that life once gone,*
> *Of all the dead sway the imperial throne."*

By contrast, Wilson's willingness to present the *Odyssey* in an easygoing sort of diction can at other times grate somewhat on one's ear. In that same Book 11, when Agamemnon asks Odysseus whether Orestes (who has taken revenge on his mother's lover, Aegisthus, for murdering the king) is still alive, Wilson has Odysseus answer with a coinage straight from the boardroom: "It is / pointless to talk of hypotheticals." There are other examples of words that seem out of place, words like "payback" or "a single shot" (of wine) or "checkers" (draughts, backgammon, and dice have been the choices of earlier translators for what is admittedly a very ancient game). Hearing Zeus exclaim "You must be joking" is somewhat jarring, and to refer to the innards of goats or sheep as "giblets" is an error. (Only fowl have giblets.) When Nestor, the wise old adviser, addresses Telemachus as "Dear boy," I for one am irresistibly put in mind of George Sanders playing Lord Henry Wotton and addressing Dorian Gray in the 1945 film. Perhaps my favourite bizarre choice occurs at the opening of Book 22, when Odysseus, who has been disguised as a beggar up to this point, tearing off his tatterdemalion clothing and revealing himself in all his naked heroic glory, announces in a Schwarzeneggerlike voice, "Playtime is over." Pope's version—"One venturous game this hand hath won today, / Another, princes! yet remains to play"—uses the word "play" also but does not make the expostulation sound like it is coming from a cop.

In Wilson's introduction she discusses at some length the treatment of women in the *Odyssey*, and how translation can contribute to how that treatment is imagined or refocused. No one among contemporary readers needs to be convinced that the summary execution of the household slaves is cruel and unwarranted. Other issues are perhaps grey rather than black and white. When Agamemnon describes his own murder to Odysseus in the Nekuia (Book 11), he complains how his own wife turned her eyes away and left him to die. The adjective he flings at her in outrage is *kunteron* in Greek, which means dog-like or by extension shameless, which Chapman translated somewhat lengthily as "the most abhorr'd / By all her sex's shame," but which more modern translators have not scrupled to make into "the sluttish woman" (Lattimore) and "that goddamned whore" (Mitchell). It is clearly tempting to use the word "bitch" here, given Agamemnon's furor and the meaning of the Greek, but Wilson argues against it as "misleading." I am not so sure. In any case, she decided to use "doglike," which avoids the sexual politics of a man using the word "bitch" no matter how appropriate in the circumstances. It is not only the women in the poem that Wilson wishes to rescue from the misuse of earlier male translators. She charmingly rehabilitates the cyclops as well, calling them not "lawless [and] outrageous" as Lattimore did, or "a violent race / without any laws" in Mitchell's version, but "highminded Cyclops, / the mavericks." Those words represent a significant moral upgrade for Polyphemus and his fellow one-eyed monsters.

Despite adopting these unusual linguistic and ideological angles, Emily Wilson has produced overall a wonderfully readable translation of Homer's poem. The characters are lively and attractive, even in their worst moments; the vocabulary, if sometimes a bit too contemporary, is certainly never stuffy; she admirably achieves her aspiration of keeping "a register that is recognizably speakable and readable, while skirting between the Charybdis of artifice and the Scylla of slang." Here is a passage from Book 23, when Odysseus and Penelope, at the very end of the story, have retired to their old marriage bed:

> *And when*
> *the couple had enjoyed their lovemaking,*
> *they shared another pleasure—telling stories.*
> *She told him how she suffered as she watched*
> *the crowd of suitors ruining the house,*
> *killing so many herds of sheep and cattle*
> *and drinking so much wine, because of her.*

Never mind that sheep do not congregate in herds, the style here is simple, unadorned, and moving to boot. After Odysseus then goes on to tell his own story, the passage as a whole concludes with the lovely line, "sweet sleep released his heart from all his cares." The book continues, with Book 24 to follow, and after a scene in hell and Odysseus's reunion with his father, Laertes, we are led back into military slaughter. But wouldn't it have been wonderful if the *Odyssey* had ended there, on that note, with the hero and heroine fading into sleep in each other's arms after twenty years of separation, grief, nostalgia, and privation?

A SERIOUS MAN
WHOSE
LOVE WILL LAST

When Ezra Pound was released in 1958 from the Washington, DC, mental hospital where he had spent twelve years as an "inmate," the press asked him what the experience had been like. "Ovid had it worse," he said, to almost universal befuddlement. Publius Ovidius Naso, the greatest Latin poet of the Augustan age, spent the last ten years of his life (8–17 CE) banished to the Roman equivalent of Siberia, a city called Tomis on the far eastern edge of the empire, almost a thousand miles from Rome. (The Latin word for his banishment was *relegatio*, or relegation; had he suffered *exilium* or exile, he would have been deprived of both his property and his citizenship.) Tomis was a small port city on the Black Sea, in modern-day Romania, and although not the farthest outpost of empire in terms of distance from Rome (northwest Africa, northern Germany, Asia Minor, and the Iberian peninsula were farther away), it was definitely what any diplomat today would call a "hardship post." It was in the province of Moesia, which had come under Roman subjugation only a half century earlier, and was still exposed to constant attack by various tribes. Recent scholarship thinks that Ovid may have exaggerated the crudeness and barrenness of Tomis as part of a continuing effort over the course of his exile to be recalled, first by Augustus and, after the former's death in 14 CE, by his successor, Tiberius. All the same, to an urbane poet who had moved in the highest Roman circles and was well educated and well off, a colonial town where Latin was the language of only a tiny minority and the food and drink, not to mention the company, were doubtless atrocious, and where there was little or no literary culture and no book trade, must have seemed depressing and impossibly difficult. Cicero's fifteen-month exile in Greece a half century earlier looks almost like a pleasure trip by comparison. Ovid knew what he was in for when he set out for Tomis. One of his love poems, published sometime during the two decades before the year 1 BCE, describes his hometown of Sulmo (now Sulmona in the Abruzzo, whose main street is the Corso Ovidio) as being like the wastes of Scythia because his lover is not with him. Tomis, while politically not part of Scythia, was just next door.

But until his still unexplained banishment, Ovid lived a charmed life. He came from a well-to-do equestrian family and was expected to enter law and politics. He chose poetry instead and became famous. The literary world of his day was as cowed by Virgil as the German-speaking music world in the middle of the nineteenth century was by Beethoven; and just as Brahms, for example, repeatedly delayed publishing his first string quartet and his first symphony because of the weight of Beethoven's achievements in those forms, so Ovid and his crowd stayed away from the epic and concentrated for the most part on elegiac poetry. What could be done after Virgil's *Aeneid* that would not pale by comparison? Ovid was not by nature at ease in the epic mode in any case, and while his only pseudo-epic work, the *Metamorphoses*, did employ the dactylic hexameters of epic poetry, it is not so much a narrative as a mosaic of what in another context he called fairy tales for grown-ups. Augustus's support being something of a *sine qua non* for a poet in imperial Rome, Ovid concluded his book of changes with the advent of his sovereign ruler, Jove's counterpart on Earth, as he calls him. Yet it feels like a mere doffing of his hat, this acknowledgement by Ovid of literature's role in nation-building, and his final words propose that it is poetry that lasts, not the work of emperors no matter how brilliant. "My work will last"—*vivam* in Latin—the final word of the concluding sentence of the *Metamorphoses*, may strike us as an egotistical contention. It also turned out to be true, however, although it is ironic that Ovid had barely finished his long poem when his exile was decreed. The work would live on in glory forever, but the poet would live the last of his life remotely and in squalor and would be buried on the periphery of the country he had celebrated, however adventitiously.

The *Metamorphoses* notwithstanding, Ovid was famous in his day as a love poet, and if it was not the love poems which kept his reputation alive through almost two millennia of Christian civilization, it is those poems which today seem most contemporary through their vivid expression of romantic love and sexual politics. The *Amores*, fifty poems arranged in three books, contain so little in the way of cultural or political reference to their time that scholars have not been able to decide when they were written and made public. They patently date to the last two decades before the beginning of the new millennium, when Ovid was in his twenties and thirties, but greater exactitude is stymied by their determined focus on the lover's covert life, his feelings as well as his erotic strategies. Ovid learned a lot from the other elegiac poets of his time, especially Propertius and Tibullus (the ninth poem in Book III is a moving elegy for Tibullus), as well as from the poems of Catullus, the great love poet from two generations earlier. But despite his appropriation of the well-worn tradition of addressing his love poems to a pseudonymous woman—he calls her Corinna, although unlike Catullus's Lesbia or Tibullus's Delia, she seems to have had no real-life counterpart—his poems are if anything even more vivid and "true" than those of his coevals and predecessors. This is entirely due to his greatness as a poet. He did not "invent" love, as Tom Stoppard said of Propertius through his character A. E. Housman in *The Invention of Love*. He just wrote about it in such a way that a tradition was established, a tradition that still seems permanently true to experience.

In the early eighteenth century, Samuel Garth, a physician to the court of George I and a poet who was instrumental in seeing through the press an English version of Ovid's *Metamorphoses* translated by a group of writers including Pope, Dryden, and Addison, wrote that a translator of Ovid ought "neither to follow the Author too close out of a Critical Timorousness, nor abandon him too wantonly through a Poetick Boldness." On that scale, David R. Slavitt's new translation of the *Amores*, together with the *Heroides* (Letters of Heroic Women) and the *Remedia Amoris* (Remedies for Love's Afflictions) definitely comes closer to poetic boldness than to critical timorousness. During a recent Australian Broadcasting Corporation interview about his book, Slavitt joked that he liked to think of his translations of Ovid as renditions, i.e., not only versions but also unwarranted kidnappings of the texts.

Slavitt, who will publish his one-hundredth book in 2012 and who is well known as a poet and novelist as well as a translator from several languages, including Latin and Greek, has attempted to contrive an *Amores* with a very contemporary tone. While respecting Ovid's verse form (elegiac poetry was written in couplets with one six-beat and one five-beat line), he has not hesitated to alter, paraphrase, extend, and update Ovid's language, using current or almost current slang at times while never completely transforming the poet into an East Coast metrosexual, as indeed one could if so moved. He has resisted too much modernizing, and essential 2,000-year-old details remain. There is, for example, the fact that Ovid anathematizes a wood-and-wax writing tablet rather than a letter on paper for bringing him disappointing news about a proposed assignation, and the para-clausithyron or address to the closed door that guards his lover that constitutes the sixth poem of Book I remains what it is despite the ability of lovers today to arrange rendezvous by email and text messages, a substitution that probably would not have borne fruit. By contrast, various words and phrases do get reimagined. *Anus*, which means an old woman, becomes "an over-the-hill playgirl," while *procax*, which means forward or bold, becomes "a brassy babe" ("dame" occurs a few lines farther on) and *senex*, an old man, becomes "an old geezer." Other bits are simply invented, as in 1.8, where the sentence "and I should make it clear that she / and I were an item, as they say" has no equivalent in Ovid's Latin (and what the Latin would be for that is hard to imagine).

Slavitt can be concise when he wants to be—the opening of II.5, for instance ("No love is worth this much. Cupid, take your quiver / and go") is as brief as the Latin ("*Nullus amor tanti est-abeas, pharetrate Cupido!*")—but in general he needs substantially more space than Ovid required. Poem 1.8 is 114 lines in the original and 155 in English, and while this is not solely attributable to Slavitt's expansions, Latin being considerably more concise than English as a rule, it is certainly in part his doing. Christopher Marlowe, whose translation of the *Amores* was probably made while he was an undergraduate but was not published until after his death in 1593, managed the same poem in exactly Ovid's 114 lines. Peter Green, whose Penguin translation is perhaps the most widely read modern version, also kept this poem to 114 lines. (To be fair, Green's line is generally long and serpentine and he does not keep to six and five beats.) Marlowe's choice for *anus*, incidentally, was "trot," perfect and concise slang from another age. Green seems to have dithered about the word without making a decision. He gives us "a certain bitch, snake, hag."

Slavitt's expansion of the Latin can be unstinting. His *Remedies* is almost 200 lines longer than the Latin (993 as against 814 lines), and an example will demonstrate the reason. Toward the end of the poem, Cupid is quoted with some specific recommendations about avoiding romantic entanglements. At one point, suggesting how Paris might have acted to avoid the whole Trojan War, he says "*Ut posses odisse tuam, Pari, funera fratrum / debueras oculis substituisse tuis*," literally "To have focused on hatred, Paris, you should have turned your eyes to your brothers' deaths," admittedly not the clearest advice if a reader does not know his or her history. Slavitt fills that history in and adds a perhaps unnecessarily dismissive characterization of Paris: "Had Paris not been such a selfish ninny, / he might have thought of his brothers and how his banal romance / would end with their bloodshed on the Trojan plain." Implication and mythic reference are thus made very specific in the English. Ovid does not call Paris names nor dismiss his love affair as "banal," but this is often Slavitt's way. He will open the language up and be expository when the Latin is not, if he thinks the modern reader requires his help, and this is reasonable in the absence of notes or any sort of apparatus. Allowing for that, one might still question the choice, if one believes that the choice is the translator's to make, of the somewhat old-fashioned insult "ninny." Among alternatives, "jerk" or "asshole" both seem somewhat *too* contemporary. Perhaps "idiot" or "fool" would have been better, though neither word is quite satisfactory metrically.

Ovid was just twelve years old when the Battle of Actium was fought, and he therefore lived most of his life at a time when the Roman world was at peace. He detested military affairs, patriotism, and war, but was nevertheless content to conceive of the relationship between the sexes as just that, a war. The first word of the *Amores* is *arma* (arms), and while this undoubtedly constitutes in part an ironic kiss of the fingers in Virgil's direction (the opening phrase of the *Aeneid* is *Arma virumque cano*, "Of arms and the man I sing"), it also establishes a vocabulary of strategy and contest, both failure and victory, that on one level will characterize the poems as a whole. "Every lover is a soldier," begins 1.9, a poem that then concludes with talk of the "campaigns of night." Once the entire sequence ends, Ovid tells us that he is withdrawing from the fray of love by once again using a military metaphor: "Cupid and you, too, Venus, take your golden standards / out of my field." Yet in the forty-eight poems that come between these two, the poet's heart is rarely as objective as the narrative of erotic strategy might suggest. He may sometimes be focused on the rhetoric of success and defeat—we learn both that he is an indefatigable fornicator (nine orgasms in a night is his record) and that he has suffered from impotence ("my prick lay there as if it were dead")—but at other times he confesses to missing Corinna when she travels, to feeling embarrassed by his loose morals, and to the old conundrum of love, that you can't live with her and you can't live without her. This last is a feeling that Ovid states in such a literal and modern way ("*sic ego nec sine te nec tecum vivere possum*") as to make it sound like the opening line in a stand-up comedian's routine.

Thirty years ago and more, the Australian novelist David Malouf published a novel entitled *An Imaginary Life* that recreated Ovid's years of banishment, and in the brief afterword he wrote: "Ovid is very much an actor, inclined to exaggerate for effect, so very little of what he tells us is reliable." Classical scholars tend to take this view as well, but I think that there is little in the love poetry to support it. That the poems written from Tomis are sometimes inclined to whining and pleading goes without saying, but who, in Ovid's position, would not have done the same? That the poet was self-conscious about the value of poetry is another matter. He was confident that poetry would guarantee his immortality, and of course he was right. As a lover, he took a more paradoxical view of his poems, offering them on the one hand as a way for Corinna also to gain immortality—that is the debonair seducer talking—while complaining, on the other, that his skill has brought his lover to the attention of rivals, who ought to know that poets are inveterate prevaricators and are not to be trusted. The tales poets tell about Tantalus and Perseus are "children's stories," he says, so why would a reader take his narratives about his love life any more seriously? This paradoxical or self-serving attitude strikes me as simply a genuine symptom of erotic engagement. It's an honest desire to have it both ways, a forgivable fault of any man deeply enmeshed in "this rumpy-pumpy business," to quote Slavitt's slangy version of a phrase from the *Remedia*.

Turning from the very modern concerns of Ovid to what one tends to think of as the more removed and Olympian world of Virgil (as least as far as the *Aeneid* is concerned—he also wrote poetic texts about farming and the Arcadian life), a higher style might be expected. But in the so-called Appendix Virgiliana, the rubric under which a group of poems traditionally ascribed to Virgil has been published since Joseph Scaliger assigned it to them in 1572, and most of which have recently been translated by David Slavitt as *The Gnat and Other Minor Poems*, we find an atypical Virgil writing humorous, obscene, parodic, and very slight poems, uncharacteristic to such an extent that scholarship has pretty definitely consigned them to the realm of forgery and misattribution. Although he probably did not write these poems, then, they remain associated with his name, and undoubtedly survived for that reason alone and not for any putative innate greatness as poetry. A. E. Housman dismissed them as "the work of poetasters," and even their Loeb Classical Library editor, whom one might have forgiven a bit of special pleading, charmingly called them "motley pinchbeck." Unlike Virgil's three main books, these minor poems have rarely been translated into English. Apart from the Loeb edition which contains Henry Rushton Fairclough's rendering, and occasional translations of individual poems (Edmund Spenser, for example, published a rather free version of "The Gnat" in 1591), only one largely complete English version seems to be recorded. This translation by Joseph J. Mooney, issued in 1916 with a second edition four years later, is an extremely rare book and thus almost unknown.* All the more welcome, then, is David Slavitt's new translation.

He has translated eight of the poems in the Appendix, plus the group of four known as "Priapea," or poems about Priapus. He makes a case for them in his introduction as "appealing, charming, and affable," and proposes that they are worth his and a reader's time if the reader has "fun." I did not find them particularly fun. "The Gnat" is technically an epyllion, i.e., a miniature epic poem, and it is rather tiresome even at its short length (414 lines in Latin). "Curses," a much shorter poem, seems rather lame as cursing poems go, and "Pesto" is just that, a recipe for making the Roman equivalent of the basil, garlic, and olive oil sauce. Three further poems now assigned to the poet Ausonius are slight (although one, "Budding Roses," has a pleasant Robert Herrick–like conclusion), and the poems for Priapus, while fetchingly full of inflated pricks as one might suspect, seem even less attractive as poetry. That leaves "The Barmaid," a brief poem summed up by its last line ("*Mors aurem vellens 'vivite' ait, 'venio'*"—literally "'Live,' says death, tugging at my ear, 'for I am on my way'"), and "Lydia," the best of the lot, a poem about the loss of love:

> *My darling is no longer by my side, and no one*
> *on earth is as clever as she or nearly as lovely.*
> *I only wonder that Jove, at home in the heights,*
> *never noticed that here on earth was a greater*
> *prize than Europa or Danaë in her tower.*

The poems are a mixed bag, then, as Slavitt himself admits, but it is always a good thing to have some more or less new bits of classical

---

* It is accessible on the web at http://virgil.org/appendix/.

poetry made available in an English translation that is lively and vivid, if not always fun.

—

Ovid, *Love Poems, Letters, and Remedies of Ovid*, trans. David R. Slavitt (Cambridge, MA and London: Harvard University Press, 2011).

Virgil, *The Gnat and Other Minor Poems of Virgil*, trans. David R. Slavitt (Berkeley and Los Angeles: University of California Press, 2011).

THREE

EUROPE

VIVET

It is his lawe to violate all lawes.
MICHAEL DRAYTON, *ENGLAND'S HEROICAL EPISTLES*
(1597), ON WILLIAM SHAKESPEARE

Jonathan Bate is one of the most distinguished living Shakespeare scholars. He has academic appointments on both sides of the Atlantic, works a lot with the BBC, is on the Board of Directors of the Royal Shakespeare Company, and has even written a play about Shakespeare—a project almost any sane person, no matter how distinguished and articulate, might shy from like the plague. Why not offer to compose Beethoven's tenth or to repair the Venus de Milo? He has edited Shakespeare and has several books on the Bard to his credit, including a biography—another project which involves a great deal of funambulism, given the extreme paucity of archival evidence. But as Bate rightly states in his most recent book on the man widely considered the greatest poet in English, "Every age reinvents Shakespeare in its own image," and ours is no different. So the age needs biographies even in the face of a literary record, apart from the plays and poems themselves, that is almost silent.

Essayists and book writers eschewed the colon in titles for centuries. Neither Plutarch nor Montaigne, neither Carlyle nor even T. S. Eliot, ever wrote an essay with a title that leans on the pandemic colon, now almost de rigueur in humanities scholarship especially. The metaphor or quotation comes first ("Cracking the Stateliest Measure"); the descriptive backup phrase comes second ("Virgil's Broken Cadence in *Aeneid* I & IV"). I am willing to wager that 90 percent of the Shakespeare criticism recorded in the footnotes to Bate's new book follows this now ubiquitous format. Yet in that book, *How the Classics Made Shakespeare*, Bate leaves out the first element, perhaps in an attempt to make his study seem less daunting to the general reader. The result is a title that feels slightly undressed but rather direct and refreshing.[*] The omnipresence of Greek and Roman history and literature in Shakespeare's work has long been recognized and inventoried. Latin was at the heart of his grammar school education, despite Ben Jonson's flip dismissal of his friend's "small Latin and lesse Greek" in his memorial poem published in the First Folio in 1623, seven years after Shakespeare's death. His education may have been truncated by twenty-first-century standards, but his Latin was probably better than that of any Latin professor alive today. Of course we are all familiar with his knowledge of Plutarch (through Thomas North), of Ovid (through Arthur Golding and Christopher Marlowe), and of Livy and Pliny (through Philemon Holland). There are other Latin texts which he will have read only in the original language as a schoolboy: Terence, Virgil, Horace, and Cicero's *Offices*. Almost a third of the plays are set in antiquity, and the language of all of them is rife through and through with references to classical myth and history. Some of that language is unremarkably conventional—invocations of the Muses, for example—and some is unusually specific, such as Antony's reference to "those hands, that grasped the heaviest club," by which he means Hercules's. Bate makes it clear in the preface to his book that *How the Classics Made Shakespeare* is not meant to be a comprehensive study. (T. W. Baldwin's

---

[*]   Jonathan Bate, *How the Classics Made Shakespeare* (Princeton: Princeton University Press, 2019).

vast compilation from 1944, *Shakspere's Small Latine and Lesse Greeke*, accomplished that task). Rather he wishes to make "an extended argument about the 'classical' nature of his imagination." The book began as a series of talks given at the Warburg Institute as the first E. H. Gombrich Lectures in the Classical Tradition, and Bate acknowledges the importance of scholars associated with the Warburg, including Ernst Robert Curtius, at the end of his first chapter.

Shakespeare in Bate's telling was in many respects a bit of a regular guy. He was "probably bored" during church services. He was "the farmer's grandson from deep in the shires" and "a provincial glover's son." At the end of the sixteenth century, he moved residences in London to escape paying taxes and his case of tax evasion was reported to the Bishop of Winchester. In retirement he "[scratched] the earth in his cabbage patch," metaphorically if not literally like Horace at his Sabine farm. But of course he was also Shakespeare, the great poet and dramatist, with "the genius of Socrates, the judgment of Nestor, and the poetic art of Virgil," to cite the inscription (as Bate does in his final chapter) on the monument in his parish church in Stratford-upon-Avon. The reference to Virgil is conventional rather than specific, since of all the great poets of classical antiquity, Virgil is the one, according to Bate, whom Shakespeare probably did not read in English, or at least was not inspired by, though he will have known the basic story of the *Aeneid* and some of the shorter poems from his schooling. The first great English translation of the *Aeneid*, that of John Dryden, would only be published long after Shakespeare's death. In the latter's lifetime, there was only a translation that was begun by Thomas Phaer and completed by Thomas Twyne, and it was rather undistinguished and "curiously archaic," in Bate's description. Bate clearly has a soft spot for another partial version of the *Aeneid* that was made by Richard Stanyhurst and published when Shakespeare was in his twenties, in which the translator attempted to reproduce classical quantitative meter in English and filled his text with neologisms. Bate half-seriously suggests that Stanyhurst may have been "the Elizabethan James Joyce," but this seems more than a little fanciful. Certainly it is possible that Shakespeare read Stanyhurst's Virgil. (It was first published on the Continent in 1582, but was reprinted in London the following year.) As Bate points out, many words which are recorded in the *Oxford English Dictionary* as being used first by Shakespeare (e.g., baggage, eyeball, posthaste) appeared earlier in Stanyhurst's translation.

In his opening chapter, Bate surveys what he calls "The Intelligence of Antiquity," gives the reader an initial sense of the importance of Latin literature to Shakespeare and his age, and initiates an argument about how the Elizabethans, while devoted to the Rome of antiquity, wanting in many ways to emulate it, also wanted to establish cultural norms that derogated the Rome of their own time, i.e., Rome as the heart of Catholic Christianity. This argument resurfaces throughout *How the Classics Made Shakespeare*, and given the then still recent conversion of England to a faith separate from the Catholic Church—a change that had taken place as recently as the generation just before Shakespeare's—it is a cogent theory. While the specifics of Shakespeare's own religious practice are unknown to us, there are certainly indications in the plays and poems of allegiance to both the Catholic and Protestant faiths. Bate seems modestly prejudiced against the Catholic side, not really wanting, for example, the ghost of Hamlet's father to be represented as a refugee from Purgatory (which the text states he clearly is) so much as to be a representation of a "major part of a national endeavor to create an English Protestant culture that opposed itself to modern Rome even as it drew inspiration from ancient Rome." Again, that may well be, although Bate at the very outset of his book states that Shakespeare was "more profoundly shaped by the humanist inheritance from ancient Rome than the modern contentions between Rome and Geneva." In other words, Shakespeare the writer was not especially interested in supporting either the Reformation or the Counter-Reformation. Hamlet's father's ghost may intone the words "Remember me"—surely an allusion to the part of the mass when Jesus asks his disciples to eat and drink in remembrance of him—but, according to Bate, the ghost also "[dramatizes] the road to modernity," because he manifests a mental state, "the coinage of the brain," in Bate's words. Shades of the post-Freudian indeed.

Subsequent chapters focus on addressing the influence on Shakespeare of various Roman writers (Ovid, Cicero, Virgil, Horace, Terence) as well as exploring other inherited Roman issues: genre, rhetoric, the complex nature of erotic desire (Ovid returns for a second appearance here), the mythic figure of Hercules, Seneca and the influence of revenge tragedy, ghosts and spectres, and finally the concept of fame, or how "the cult of Shakespeare became a secular faith." Bate's knowledge of the Shakespeare literature—and it is vast beyond kenning—appears almost exhaustive, and his mastery of the canon, from the Henry VI plays and *Titus Andronicus* to *The Two Noble Kinsmen*, is unimpeachable. He even makes bold to invent a brief speech that Shakespeare might have assigned to Brutus in *Julius Caesar*, following Plutarch, a speech that would explain why Cicero was not brought into the assassination plot. His gutsy attempt at Shakespeare is modestly convincing. ("Born a coward, his fear increased by age, / He'll quench the heat of this our enterprise, / Which requires earnest execution.") No reader, I think, will be inclined to disagree with Bate's essential point, that the classics inform Shakespeare's work profoundly; the real interest of the book lies in the details, and it is there that differences of opinion may lie. Does the entire corpus of Elizabethan drama constitute "exercises in deliberative rhetoric," as though the characters are all taking part in set debate questions, debates about which the audience must then decide? Can an unlettered (read: illiterate) theatre audience constitute a "republic of letters," as Bate suggests? Is it fair to call the London play world an "entertainment industry," a phrase that summons up a contemporary parallel that includes Disney and Netflix? (Bate defends that suggestion by citing the terms of the contract establishing the

King's Men in 1603, the acting company to which Shakespeare belonged, and which was formed for the "recreation" of the people and the "solace and pleasure" of His Majesty, goals with which any Los Angeles mogul might well agree.) Was Shakespeare really "the Cicero of his age," even if he did not, as Bate admits, read that much Cicero? (Bate cites Cicero's *De re publica* as an influential text in Elizabethan England, but this is surely a mistake, as the bulk of what survives of this text was not discovered until the nineteenth century.) Was Shakespeare a devoted Epicurean, as Bate says he was? Beyond these debatable questions are other minor details that seem puzzling. Was Elizabeth Jane Weston, who wrote in Latin, not English, really "the early seventeenth century's most famous English poet in Europe"? Why is Giordano Bruno referred to as the humanist philosopher Marsilio Ficino's "English disciple," when he was Italian and lived in England for less than three years? What is the "working script" Bate refers to with respect to *Antony and Cleopatra*? Bate's use of slang is rather charming. The speakers of Ovid's *Heroides* are "heroines who have been dumped by their lovers," and "top and tail" as well as "name-check" are reverted to. He has also invented a verb which we can fervently hope will not come into widespread use: "Shakespeare is at his most Shakespearean when he bigs up imagination." All I can say to that, to quote Lord Foppington, is "Stab me vitals!"

By contrast there are many contentions that are rich and stimulating. That Shakespeare "had a bisexual imagination" will surprise no reader of the sonnets, nor will the observation that the tragedies contain much that is comedic (to the long-time horror of the French) "because he wanted them to hold up a mirror to 'actual life' in which there is no such thing as pure tragedy." More interesting is Bate's remark that those writers of Shakespeare's own time who thought about the generic roots of the sonnet form traced it to ancient epigram. Furthermore, that "the poet's art of feigning is a recurrent *topos* in Shakespeare" is a statement that could form the subject of an entire book, as is another assertion, that "the idea of erotic love as a kind of madness is everywhere in Shake-speare." (Perhaps *Timon of Athens* is an unpopular Shakespearean tragedy precisely because it wholly lacks any erotic manifestations.) Bate is also honest when he admits, more than once, that "we will never be able to recover [Shakespeare's] overt intentions" on many matters, not least on his view of posthumous reputation. Ben Jonson carefully plotted his literary afterlife. Shakespeare? Probably not. It's a good thing he had devoted friends who rescued his plays for the First Folio. He himself had not even bothered to publish half of them. The Shakespeare corpus would be substantially less voluminous without those friends, and less profound as literature and drama.

One subject that Bate addresses only piecemeal, but often, is the question of the London audience who bought tickets to and attended Shakespeare's plays. By no means was everyone in those audiences educated, and even those who were had rarely advanced beyond gram-mar school, or what we call eighth grade. When Lady Macbeth spoke about "[plucking her] nipple" away and "[dashing] the brains out" of babies, would most people in the audience really have thought of Medea, as Bate suggests, or would they simply have been horrified, as both Euripides and Shakespeare intended them to be? Or take Horace, who was known for such still famous moral maxims as "seize the day" and "never despair," as well as aesthetic shorthand remarks like "poetry is like painting" and "art should be both sweet and useful." Perhaps audiences really did recognize "consciously or unconsciously" Shake-spearean versions of Horatian bons mots, which Bate thinks were "familiar even to those who have never read the poems." No one really knows. Bate is convinced that Shakespeare's audience was full of clas-sically educated ticket-holders, people who could reliably summon up Hercules and Omphale while hearing a speech in *Antony and Cleopatra* in which they are not directly mentioned, or who would certainly think of Seneca's *Hercules Furens* during a separate speech by Antony in which Deianira and the shirt of Nessus are mentioned. And how many people in the audience would "hear an echo of a famous line in the final book of the *Aeneid*" when Aeneas, in *Troilus and Cressida*, speaks to Odysseus about a "second hope"? The more educated members of the audience, Bate thinks. But who is to know? And what percentage of that audience was sufficiently educated to appreciate the references? Did most or even many of the people who saw *The Comedy of Errors* recognize its model, Plautus's play *Menaechmi*, when it was performed in 1594? The well-educated German Paul Hentzner, who visited London at the end of the sixteenth century, and who in 1612 published "the most evocative tourist's account of Shakespeare's London" that we have, alas did not attend any plays. He was well placed to recognize Shakespeare's classical influences, but perhaps the aristocratic pupil with whom he travelled did not feel that the theatre was a place where a prince ought to be seen.

Bate is infinitely far from the class of unimaginative influence-hunters who have long occupied the lower rungs of literary criticism, going back perhaps to the earliest commentators on *The Waste Land* and other modernist poems that irresistibly cried out for footnoting. On the subject of genre, for example—think of Polonius's exhaustive list in act 2, scene 2 of *Hamlet*, the one that culminates with "tragical-comical-historical-pastoral"—and particularly that of the pastoral, Bate demonstrates how complex Shakespeare's approach to and assumption of the characteristics of the ancient categories were. The obvious forebears in the pastoral tradition, then as now, were Theocritus and Virgil. One of the stranger recognitions of the Christian writers who followed in the wake of classical antiquity, and whose efforts had such a strong effect (good and bad) on the survival rate of Greek and Latin writers, was that Virgil's fourth eclogue could be read without skewing the text at all as a pagan prophecy of the coming of Christ. The pastoral poem was never merely Arcadian—simple, peaceful, devoted to love games and herding—and in Virgil's case it ranged from erotic one-upmanship to political allegory. As Bate demonstrates, the schoolboys of Shakespeare's generation unquestionably read pastoral poetry, but instead of the *Eclogues* they were given, from a young age, the then more or less modern bucolic poems of Mantuanus (1447–1516), a neo-Latin poet who transformed Virgil's inheritance all the way into a Christian form. Bate points out that the "opening lines of Mantuan's first eclogue were among Shakespeare's very first encounters with poetry" as a schoolboy. As a playwright, this familiarity is embodied in the entirety of the canon, from *Love's Labour's Lost*, one of his earliest comedies, to the late romance plays, which all contain elements of the pastoral. Bate notes that in *Love's Labour's Lost*, the schoolmaster Holofernes is moved to quote (or misquote) the opening lines of Mantuan's first eclogue, a poke in the ribs of pedagogy as well as perhaps a sly giggle at the sanitized and Christianized version of the Mantuan pastoral which avoided not just homoerotic desire (e.g., Corydon and Alexis in Virgil's second eclogue) but desire in any way, shape, or form. "The force of sexual desire," in Bate's opinion, was one of Shakespeare's essential themes. His poking fun at a genre which had evolved toward something more prayerful than erotically playful is hardly surprising. His very first book, after all, published in the year 1593, was a poem about Venus, and in *Venus and Adonis* the goddess clearly is, to use a contemporary slang term, a cougar. There are no cougars in Arcadia.

As mentioned above, Bate admits that we do not know from any textual evidence exactly what Shakespeare thought about his literary afterlife. Did he think about "fame," a word that Bate correctly traces back through Latin to a Greek word, *pheme*, which means rumour or gossip, and that ultimately derives from a verb meaning simply "to talk"? (This is the sense of fame intended by Chaucer in titling his poem "The House of Fame," a poem Shakespeare knew from the 1598 edition of Chaucer's poetry.) The Greeks had a separate word for fame in the sense of immortal military glory. Fame is what the future talks about when it thinks about you, if indeed it does at all. The contrast between the classical and Christian attitudes toward fame is important here, for one last time arguably demonstrating the influence of classical literature on Shakespeare. Ovid ended the *Metamorphoses* with the supremely self-confident verb *vivam*: I will live, i.e., I will endure through my literary works. He was right, of course, although his texts had to suffer almost 1,500 years of touch-and-go transmission before the printing press saved them for good and the ghost of Ovid could rest assured of an undisputed reputation. Horace also crowed that his poetry would ensure his fame, more reliably than any monument however durable. Bate reads the Shakespeare sonnets as arguing that his poetry too will work to achieve immortality, though largely that effect will benefit the lover rather than the poet ("So long as men can breathe and eyes can see, / So long lives this and this gives life to thee"). Shakespeare's own immortality, so obvious to us now, came about largely through not just the First Folio (Beaumont and Fletcher achieved "folio immortality" too, but their reputation is not even within striking distance of the Bard's), but through a series of acts of scholarship (Nicholas Rowe's edition of 1709) and what was once called bardolatry. The actor David Garrick collected Shakespeare and produced an extravaganza to celebrate Shakespeare's bicentenary that, in Bate's amusing observation, "not only turned Stratford-upon-Avon into a tourist attraction: it inaugurated the very idea of a summer arts festival." From the mid-eighteenth century to our own day, Shakespeare has never really had a serious rival for the title of English's greatest poet, much less fallen completely out of favour. Yet perhaps it is to stretch the truth to maintain, as Bate does in his closing pages, that "the cult of Shakespeare was indeed becoming a secular faith." It's an intriguing but finally inapt analogy. Where I live, there are school boards that are replacing what in my day was the inevitable series of Shakespeare plays in the high school curriculum (*Julius Caesar, Romeo and Juliet, Macbeth, Othello*) with texts by Canadian Indigenous writers. The cult has apostates, then, as well as celebrants.

I WHO WAS ONCE THE
FAVOURITE OF THE GODS

The German writer Johann Gottfried Herder once proposed that "[a] poet is the creator of the nation around him, he gives them a world to see and has their souls in his hand to lead them to that world." Has there ever been a time when such an idea seemed further from the truth, or from the facts of life as lived, than it does in 2018? Almost 250 years ago, when Goethe was fast approaching his majority (he was born on August 28, 1749), a statement such as Herder's, far from raising eyebrows, would have been widely admired and honoured as an ineffable truth. These days poets mill around like ants, gamely trying to address issues of politics, or religion, or ecology, or human history; but for the most part no one pays the least bit of attention. So little is poetry respected in 2018 that it requires a deeply learned historical imagination to understand and acknowledge how famous Goethe the poet became at the age of twenty-four for a play—a play!— that now seems much too ill constructed and fly-blown for performance in any form save perhaps in the cinema or on television, where medievalism currently flourishes. Goethe's play *Götz von Berlichungen*, anonymously published in 1773, made him the darling of Germany, was staged in several cities despite its unwieldiness, and created a degree of adulation that bordered on fanaticism. (A few years later it provided Mozart with an obscene insult around which he built a six-voice canon, K.231.) Rüdiger Safranski, Goethe's latest biographer, claims that in the wake of *Götz*, when "Goethe set off from Frankfurt on one of his hikes, he sometimes had a train of young girls and children following him."[*] Only perhaps in a culture and at such a time when poetry, as Safranski amusingly puts it, was "prophecy in homeopathic doses," could such a thing be conceivable. Like Virgil, whose works became a source for a kind of fortune-telling (the so-called *sortes Virgilianae*), Goethe too became something other than just a writer. As Safranski notes, with him "the cult of the star author began," a cult that still bedevils us. The publication of *The Sorrows of Young Werther*, a year after *Götz*, cemented Goethe's European reputation— Safranski claims that virtually every literate person in Germany read the novel—although, like later writers with early success, Goethe would eventually resent *Werther* and the hold it came to have on the literate public of Europe.

Although he by no means lacked the faculty of self-criticism, no one was more convinced of Goethe's greatness than Goethe himself. The very first sentence in Safranski's biography tells us how Goethe, in *Poetry and Truth*, would claim how fortunate Frankfurt was in having him as a native son. Safranski rather blandly admits at one point that "Modesty was clearly not Goethe's strong suit," while providing many instances in both behaviour and print of what, equally clearly, was in fact Goethe's lifelong egoism, naming it at one point a "sometimes somnambulistic self-assurance." That creative people need to be egocentric is obvious and hardly worth arguing about, except that in Goethe's case the wreckage from his personal behaviour—friendships that foundered on his actions, relationships with women that were determinately one-sided, and the gerrymandering of personal contacts to benefit himself

---

[*] Rüdiger Safranski, *Goethe: Life as a Work of Art*, trans. David Dollenmayer (New York: Liveright Publishing, 2017).

(as when he more or less forced his son to marry a woman the son did not love because he, Goethe, was attracted to her)—can be found all throughout his long life. Safranski describes the young Goethe as "cocky and insouciant," which seems unexceptionable in a talented writer who had yet to prove himself. After his permanent removal to Weimar at the age of twenty-six, when he was dismissed in a private letter by Count Johann Görtz, the Duke's former tutor, as "a boy in need of daily improvement with the rod," Goethe became the intellectual- and writer-in-residence in a small, provincial duchy, where he was lionized and which he helped substantially to transform into a signifi-cant centre first of *Sturm und Drang* culture and later of what came to be called Weimar Classicism. Duke Karl August, who was the grand-nephew of Frederick the Great of Prussia, was eight years younger than Goethe and an aspirant to cultured and enlightened despotism. Goethe found "cheerful mediocrity" in Weimar when he arrived there in 1775. Half a century and more ago, Walter Bruford sketched the Weimar of that time: a town of barely 6,000 inhabitants ruled over by a duke who had to convince Goethe eventually to permit his elevation to the nobil-ity (von Goethe, he became) so that he could even be allowed at court. The palace had burned down the year before Goethe arrived and was still a ruin. It would not be rebuilt until 1803. The streets were narrow, industry "negligible," and the main east–west highway that ran from Frankfurt to Leipzig was miles away. The place smelled bad, as admit-tedly most eighteenth-century European towns did, and was largely unlit at night because of the expense. There were just four doctors in town and, measured by income, the middle class hardly existed.* And to this minor place, Goethe, whose reputation was already in the ascen-dant, and who came from a moneyed family and was not compelled to get a "job," despite his professional training in the law, confined himself

---

* W. H. Bruford, *Culture and Society in Classical Weimar, 1775–1806* (Cambridge, UK: Cambridge University Press, 1962), pp. 53 et seq.

for most of his adult life, "this narrow little world," as he called it in a poem entitled "To Fate." Weimar, it seems, was his fate.

Is there any legitimacy in the view that Goethe simply wasted years of his life in a cultural backwater, in what José Ortega y Gasset called "a ridiculous Lilliputian court," living out his great long life as what Heinrich Heine derisively labelled "a servant of princes"? As one of the duke's three privy councillors, in the first ten years of his Weimar period Goethe was involved in consideration of some 23,000 agenda items on every subject imaginable, from foreign policy to the construction of new butchers' stalls in the town, and he surely must have felt at times as though his genius was being buried beneath a mountain of official paper. His gifts for the sorts of special responsibilities that the duke eventually gave him—improving roads, for example, and ameliorating the working conditions in the mines at Ilmenau, fifty kilometres southwest of Weimar—admittedly were not remarkable. His early attempts at road construction went vastly over budget and had to be halted for lack of funds; and the Ilmenau mines in the end were what Safranski calls "an economic disaster, consuming enormous amounts of money and producing no results." Yet he had better success managing the duke's militia, where his remit was to reduce expenses rather than to add to them. (He helped to restore the duchy's financial health by cutting the army from 500 to a mere 136 men.) Many if not most poets would find this sort of day job soul-destroying, but Goethe seems to have had a deep longing to take part in the active world of men, if that is the right way to put it. His Christianity was too eccentric for him to take holy orders, and he had no interest in taking up arms as a professional soldier; his role as a bureaucrat, by contrast, helped to spur his scientific passions and gave him the reassurance of contributing to the common good, an instinctual need not felt by all poets then or now, but strongly experienced by Goethe throughout his life.

At least outside of Germany, Goethe is perhaps more admired than read. He is one of those monuments of culture whom everyone salutes from afar while, in the real world, they secretly ignore him and go back to reading Dante or Rousseau or Tolstoy or Proust or even, heaven help us, Jane Austen. *Faust*, which Goethe laboured at over a lifetime and which always figures on lists of the masterpieces of world literature, along with *Moby Dick* and *The Divine Comedy* and *Don Quixote*, is rarely performed (Goethe's talent, according to Safranski, was "more narrative than dramatic"), even if its characters (Faust, Gretchen, Mephistopheles) are universally recognized and the final line, "*das ewige Weibliche / Zieht uns hinan*" (the Eternal Feminine leads us ever onwards) is perhaps Goethe's most famous. The opera *Faust*, by Gounod, is performed a thousand times for every production of its source play. Music, in fact, has been extraordinarily kind to Goethe. Schubert, Beethoven, Schumann, Wolf, and other composers found his lyric poetry deeply adaptable to music and set it famously again and again, while the poetry itself—again, outside Germany—is far less well known than, say, the poems of Blake or Wordsworth or Keats, roughly contemporary poets writing in English, not to mention Victor Hugo, a poet from a later generation, obviously, and a writer whose novels Goethe reviled. (He thought *The Hunchback of Notre Dame* "the most abominable book ever written."[*]) Goethe has also been fortunate in his translators. Poets like Shelley in the nineteenth century and C. Day-Lewis in the twentieth took on *Faust*, Sir Walter Scott translated *Götz von Berlichungen*, and Thomas Carlyle made an English version of *Wilhelm Meister's Travels*. The great poet Gérard de Nerval translated *Faust* into French and his version remains in print to this day. Michael Hamburger, perhaps the best translator of Goethe's poetry in the modern era, thought that Goethe's most accomplished poems were "hardly translatable into English,"[†] an opinion which, if valid, must go a long

---

[*] Gerhart Hoffmesier, "Reception in Germany and Abroad," in *The Cambridge Companion to Goethe*, ed. Lesley Sharpe (Cambridge, UK: Cambridge University Press, 2002), p. 239.

[†] Johann Wolfgang von Goethe, *Roman Elegies and Other Poems and Epigrams*, trans. Michael Hamburger (London: Anvil Press Poetry, 2006), p. 11.

way toward explaining why Goethe is more honoured than read, when even highly effective translators of apparently consummate work are stymied by some aspect of the language that cannot convincingly be recreated in another language.

If in his working life Goethe was often pulled between the conflicting demands of poetry and statecraft, in the life of his imagination and his intellectual concerns, the conflict was that between poetry and science. Mainly self-taught as a scientist, with interests especially in plants, minerals, anatomy, and the theory of colour, Goethe was anything but representative of the scientist of his age. Famously anti-Newtonian in particular but in general carrying on a lifelong dispute with the tenets of experimental research (which he termed a "pathology") as it came to dominate science during and after the seventeenth century, Goethe mostly experienced nature rather than experimenting with it. If we remember that he would eventually call his autobiography *Dichtung und Wahrheit* (Poetry and Truth), it becomes less peculiar that, as a scientist, Goethe largely resisted theory and felt that phenomena were themselves the theory, that truth lay before our eyes, not secreted in things we cannot see. He felt that many specialists depended too much on precedent and received wisdom and not sufficiently on direct observation. "Let no one search behind the phenomena; they are themselves the science," Safranski quotes Goethe as writing. This goes so profoundly against the grain in scientific research, now and even during Goethe's lifetime, that it is easy to dismiss Goethe as an amateur, if not a crank. As a theorist of colour, that is exactly the reception his *Zur Farbenlehre* (On the Theory of Colours) met when it was published in 1810. A few artists found it congenial and even compelling, but the scientific community was dismissive, with a later academic relegating it to the ash heap of history as the "stillborn bagatelle of a dilettantish autodidact," according to Safranski.

Goethe's other famous "discovery" concerned what is called the intermaxillary bone, a bone that is detectable in the embryo at an early stage but that is invisible in adults except in pathological situations. Its existence mattered for Goethe, because it supposedly helped to differentiate humans from apes and to confirm that what he called the archetype of vertebrates—a kind of architectural drawing made by nature—was followed uniformly throughout vertebrate species. Other contemporary scientists like Johann Friedrich Blumenbach disagreed, and the intermaxillary bone is now a rejected bit of anatomical description. Goethe's scientific work was extensive and not carried out entirely in vain, but Erich Heller's description of Goethe's mind as a kind of well-equipped halfway house in which "you cannot be quite sure whether it looks like the Academy of ancient Greece or the Cavendish Laboratory at Cambridge"[*] goes a long way toward explaining his mixed reputation as a scientific observer and writer.

Nicholas Boyle, whose *Goethe: The Poet and the Age* (1991–2000) remains the most substantial biography of the writer in English, began his study by noting how extensively well-documented Goethe's life is at the level of texts and primary documents. Some 12,000 letters from Goethe are extant, and 20,000 to him can be traced in archives across Europe. His correspondence with Schiller alone filled six volumes when it was first published in 1828–29. The Weimar edition of Goethe's works, printed between 1887 and 1919, consists of 143 volumes, leading one scholar to refer dispiritedly to "the unmanageable quantity of things that Goethe has said";[†] and the literature on Goethe, biographical and critical, is so large and multilingual as to deter any reader from even considering mastering it all. Faced with such a mountain of material, Goethe's biographers have tended to carve a tunnel through it rather than ascending it and writing in triumph from the summit. Rüdiger Safranski's strategy is similar to that adopted by Albert Bielschowsky in his *Goethe, Sein Leben und Sein Werken* (1895),

---

[*] Erich Heller, *The Disinherited Mind: Essays in Modern German Literature and Thought* (London: Bowes & Bowes, 1975). p. 15.

[†] Ibid., p. 18.

in which the works figure far more importantly than the times and Goethe's life is examined as a carefully constructed text or work of art. Goethe's letters and writings, as well as Johann Peter Eckermann's *Conversations with Goethe* and other primary documents, are a constant source of quotation for Safranski, but rather than rewording them and footnoting them, they occur in the text in italics and are identified in the apparatus. In this way Goethe's voice is constantly and naturally invoked and adds intimacy to a biography that might otherwise have grown too distant from its subject. These citations can be startling, even when they are little more than *disjecta membra*. "The person who acts is always unscrupulous," said Goethe. "No one has a conscience except the contemplative person." At other times, a quotation helps us to see an ordinary man lurking inside the genius on a plinth. He wonders whether one could "apply a searing iron to one's pubic hair and curl them with a curling iron." The Germans, he wrote elsewhere, would benefit from lightening up. "They make life more difficult than is proper by looking for deep thoughts and ideas everywhere and putting them into everything." In the age of Kant and Hegel, this seems a perspicacious observation.

Nicholas Boyle was convinced that Goethe's life did not follow the usual trajectory of the long-lived writer from youthful liberalism (Goethe himself liked the Pietist word *Offenherzigheit*, openheartedness) to aged conservatism. But the Goethe of Safranski's portrait does not seem quite so obvious an exception to the rule. To some extent Goethe always possessed characteristics of both extremes, given his ideal in which the artist creates as nature created—not slavishly following models but effusing, as it were—and yet following the precepts and examples set by the Ancients. This bilateral literary fidelity seems characteristic of German romanticism, with writers like Winckelmann, Hölderlin, and Friedrich Schlegel striking lifelong Janus-like poses with one look in a backward direction to the Ancients and one in the opposite direction toward the future and their contemporary muse, the human heart. However much Goethe came to regret his more unbuttoned early works such as *Werther*, even later works like the poetry of the *West-Eastern Divan* are dominated by what Safranski calls "his inexhaustibly recurring themes": love, song, drink. Goethe in old age famously told Eckermann that classical art was "sound" or "healthy," while Romantic art was "sick," in an odd premonitory observation that would later animate Max Nordau's book *Degeneration*. As for his more strictly political views, Goethe showed himself as a traditionalist for most of his life. His admiration for Napoleon, whom he met at the end of September 1806, and whose approbation, he said, constituted a moment when "nothing higher and more gratifying could happen to me in my whole life," was unbounded. When Metternich in 1819 used as a pretext the assassination of the writer August von Kotzebue to pass the so-called Carlsbad Decrees, which limited freedom of the press among other repressive actions, Goethe was "completely in agreement with the decrees." So much for Boyle's contention that Goethe never suffered from "reactionary nostalgia."

There are several successful and pleasing elements in Safranski's fine biography, not least that David Dollenmayer has translated it from German with panache and fluency. His translations of Goethe's poetry are especially noteworthy, as he usually manages to keep the rhyme and other formal characteristics alive without wrenching his English too forcefully. The book would have benefitted from illustrations—it has not a one save the frontispiece and the dust-jacket portrait—but, by contrast, Safranski's genial habit of using cultural allusions in his prose is charming (he incorporates references to such things as "an obscure object of desire" and "in the shadow of young girls in flower" subtly and without footnoting them), and his regular use of what he calls "reflections"—short chapters in which he attempts to sum up the life so far and to reflect on it—is very welcome. These reflections are like natural resting-points for the reader, moments in which to take stock before plunging into yet another thicket of events, writings, and turmoil. Even in a book of well over five hundred pages, Safranski sometimes leaves information out that one would have been happy to learn. Why, for example, did Goethe's early literary works not bring in much money, despite their almost unprecedented popularity? Was Goethe's first infatuation, with Anna Katharina Schönkopf, sexual in nature? (Safranski is in general somewhat hesitant when it comes to Goethe's sex life, apart from the obvious affair he had in Italy, which he wrote a superb suite of poems about, the *Roman Elegies*.) While it is undeniably true that *Werther* had a profound influence on literature and even on the way that Europeans began "to talk about whatever was on their mind," from the vantage of literary history, suggesting that this frame of mind is new seems slightly purblind, given the revolution in consciousness represented by the lyric poetry of Greece composed 3,500 years before Goethe's novel. In terms of individual sentiment, private feeling, and personal *angst* there is little in *Werther* that cannot be found in Sappho and Alcaeus. It is also at the very least debatable that psychoanalysis belongs in the same category as physiognomy, the psychological assessment tool promoted heavily by Goethe's quondam friend Johann Kaspar Lavater. Safranski rejects both as "a mixture of serious scientific inquiry and parlor game." And I for one cannot believe that "the world consists almost completely of the images the media offer us." "Primary reality" is probably "shot through with the imaginary" far less now than it was in Goethe's era, much less in the Renaissance or earlier.

These are minor cavils, however, and do not much detract from a magisterial biography. Almost like Goethe himself, who was profoundly fearful of death and its ceremonies and never attended funerals, even of those closest to him, Safranski leaves us at the very instant of the writer's death when, as he puts it, the author of *Werther* and *Faust* "nestled comfortably into the left-hand corner of his chair," without, as far as Safranski has been able to discover, saying anything at all about "More light!"

A GENIUS AND A GOD

Perhaps the only sign of my genius is the fact
that my affairs are seldom in order.
LUDWIG VAN BEETHOVEN, IN A LETTER
TO FRANZ ANTON HOFFMEISTER, APRIL 22, 1801

O ne of Beethoven's forebears—his great-great-great-great grand-
mother, if I counted correctly, one Josyne van Beethoven—was
burned at the stake as a witch in the late sixteenth century, a time
when so-called witchcraft was widely feared and reviled throughout
Europe and punished severely. Beethoven's two grandmothers both
ended their days in asylums for the insane; and when the composer's
father, Jean (or Johann), died in 1792—Beethoven had turned twenty-
two just two days earlier—word went around that the authorities had
taken note of his passing and rued the fact that now the city's alcohol
taxes would suffer a permanent reduction. Jean's own father, Beethoven's grandfather Louis, was a somewhat distinguished musician, but
had had a side business as a wine merchant which helped to establish
a family history of alcoholism that the composer was not able to avoid.
Although Beethoven was not a drunkard and probably did not drink
more than the average middle-class Viennese citizen in the early nineteenth century, the autopsy performed on him after his death in the

spring of 1827 showed beyond doubt that his liver was severely dam-
aged, undoubtedly due to a lifetime's consumption of beer and wine.
Given all the slaps to his mortality that Beethoven suffered over the
course of fifty-six years—everything from deafness and eye problems
to smallpox, pancreatitis, erysipelas, gout, lower back pain, gastric
problems, typhus, possibly inflammatory bowel disease, ascites, and
many other minor ailments—no one can claim that he died of alcoholism as such. Drinking however was certainly a contributing factor to
his early death.

Beethoven was a lifelong learner. Trained at first by his father, who
seems to have been a rather unsympathetic figure though not the
tyrant depicted in many early biographies, his only modestly famous
teacher as a child was an organist and composer named Christian Got-
tlob Neefe, who crucially taught Beethoven the entirety of Bach's
Well-Tempered Clavier. In his early twenties, Beethoven moved from
Bonn (his birthplace) to Vienna. The distance was a little under nine
hundred kilometres, but it took a week to get there via various coaches.
He went specifically to study with Haydn, his elder by almost forty
years and then the most famous composer in Europe. Beethoven was
already an accomplished pianist, but he felt the need of further studies
in composition. Haydn taught by both textbook and personal example.
He made Beethoven work through Johann Joseph Fux's counterpoint
text (*Gradus ad Parnassum*), no doubt then as now a tiresome but valuable experience. But according to Jan Caeyers's newly translated
biography, Haydn allowed Beethoven to look on as he worked at various important compositions, including the Symphony no. 99 and the
string quartets that would eventually be published as op. 71 and op. 74.*
Haydn, incidentally, also taught Beethoven to play chess. After about
eighteen months, Haydn was off to London and recommended Beetho-

---

* Jan Caeyers, *Beethoven: A Life*, trans. Brent Annable (Oakland: University of California Press,
2020). Reviewers in Vienna called Beethoven a "genius" and a "god" as early as 1796.

ven to yet another teacher, Johann Albrechtsberger, who for a further eighteen months continued to extend Beethoven's knowledge of counterpoint. But if Albrechtsberger was Beethoven's last composition teacher, he nevertheless continued on his own to study the scores of past masters. Even as he lay dying, he was working through a number of volumes of a complete edition of Handel's works, sent to him as a gift by one Johann Andreas Stumpff, a German piano and harp manufacturer who lived in London. It would be decades before Beethoven's three years of counterpoint studies with those two masters would bear fruit. When it finally did, in the late piano sonatas and string quartets and elsewhere, it would revolutionize European art music. It is ironic that such a revolution in musical composition would be due so largely to techniques that the rococo and classical masters had almost entirely rejected as old-fashioned.

Beethoven's lifelong study included literature as well. He was not well educated, as he left school before the *Gymnasium*, though at the age of ten he did receive some private tutoring in Latin, French, and Italian. His skills at arithmetic and mathematics were poor all his life, and his handwriting was execrable. As an adult, he was able to correspond in somewhat fractured French but not in English, and of course he had a composer's basic knowledge of Italian (which he supplemented in 1813 by taking private lessons) and was able to set Latin liturgical texts. Beethoven did not count numerous poets among his friends as Schubert later did, but he read Shakespeare and Schiller especially for pleasure and inspiration. The librettist of Beethoven's only opera, *Fidelio*, was improbably the composer's lawyer, who based it on a French story originally written for another composer. The texts for Beethoven's song cycle, *An die ferne Geliebte* (*To the Distant Beloved*, op. 98), were in a similarly odd fashion commissioned from a medical student and never published separately as poetry. Beethoven met Goethe—the two titans of the German artistic world did not become friends, perhaps predictably—and there are settings of Goethe's poems scattered throughout the composer's catalogue, though not nearly in such profusion as would be true of later German composers. Beethoven's reading, according to Caeyers, became more dedicated after he composed his song cycle, which was something of a farewell to the last woman he had pursued seriously. Recognizing in 1816 that he would probably be alone for the remainder of his life, the composer took solace in literature and, to a lesser degree, in philosophy and theology as well. He read or reread some of the ancients (Plutarch was a favourite), sampled Kant, and "felt an affinity" for the Deist theologian Christoph Christian Sturm. A heavily annotated copy of Sturm's *Betrachtungen über die Werke Gottes im Reiche der Natur* (Reflections on the Works of God in Nature) was found in Beethoven's library after his death.

For the past forty years, and through at least two revisions, the authoritative biography of Beethoven in English has been Maynard Solomon's *Beethoven*. Solomon was a record producer before he became a musicologist. (He famously was the first to sign the Weavers, Joan Baez, and Country Joe and the Fish, among others.) His life of Beethoven is richly detailed and deeply researched. But it has been almost twenty years since its last revision, and with research on Beethoven's career and music ongoing, and given that 2020 is the 250th anniversary year of the composer's birth in 1770, it is an appropriate moment for the appearance of Caeyers's biography, which was originally published in Dutch in 2009. Jan Caeyers is a musicologist, but also a practising musician, mainly a conductor. His book is demonstrably a "life" and not so much a "life and works," as Solomon's is. There are relatively few musical examples, and where the works are concerned, Caeyers restricts himself mainly to description rather than analysis. I suppose this means that readers unable to follow a score or unfamiliar with musical language will feel more at home; but it is difficult to engage with Beethoven's importance and radical extensions of form and harmony without analyzing the work to some extent. The translation by Brent Annable is mostly excellent and fluent, despite the occasional euphuism ("The claims of [Archduke Rudolph's] pianism must of course be first denuded of their panegyric mantle") and the occasional grammatical lapse—using "between" rather than "among" in describing a feature common to the late string quartets, for example, or a singular verb where a plural is correct. ("The time, place, and circumstances of Beethoven and Schubert's first meeting remains a mystery.") The writer and the translator both might perhaps have thought twice about telling us that advice given to Beethoven by friends about child rearing "generally fell on deaf ears." Well, yes, it did. And yes, Beethoven "turned a deaf ear" later to certain requests from his nephew, such as visiting his father's grave one year after he had died.

Beethoven never travelled outside of the areas we now think of as Germany, Austria, and the Netherlands. As fine a pianist as he was, he did not tour in the way the following generation of pianists such as Thalberg, Liszt, Moscheles, and others did. Haydn and Mozart, his two greatest immediate predecessors, saw much more of the world than he did. His deafness was mostly to blame for this, although Caeyers makes clear that he loathed travel in any case. Once Beethoven had moved from Bonn to Vienna in 1792, he pretty much stayed there, apart from time spent in the surrounding countryside on holiday or on doctor's orders. So his life in the world is not full of incident. His emotional life is another and quite different story, and Caeyers is very good at narrating the significant upheavals that Beethoven suffered in his inner life: the early deaths of his parents, his fruitless search for a woman to marry, the increasing deafness that led him to draft the famous Heiligenstadt Testament of 1802 in which he took stock of his life, and the endless troubles he took on (and in part caused) when he intervened in the life of his young nephew Karl, among others. The tatterdemalion genius is also well documented, the Beethoven who could not keep house and worked amid a dusty whirlwind of papers, abandoned and rotting food, empty wine bottles, and general filth. His financial life is also ably evoked. Beethoven was born into a world in which composers depended on the largesse of the aristocracy. He died in one from which that sense of noblesse oblige had vanished in the aftermath of 1815. Beethoven was able to support himself as a pianist when he was young, but deafness put a stop to that source of income, and for much of his life he was constantly on the lookout for rent money. This he found in a variety of ways, not least by rather shrewdly milking the music-publishing world in a way one might not have expected from an innumerate genius. Caeyers sometimes gives us almost too much information—about the financial history of the *Missa Solemnis*, op. 123, for example—but in general his well-documented explorations of the composer's ragged fiscal existence are a welcome tonic.

Although, as already pointed out, this biography is more focused on the life than the work, the work was obviously at the centre of Beethoven's everyday existence, and Caeyers addresses it throughout the book. We get accounts of some of the central compositions, including the *Eroica* Symphony, *Fidelio*, *An die ferne Geliebte*, the Ninth Symphony, *Missa Solemnis*, and others. While we learn perhaps more than we need to know about *Wellington's Victory*, a piece of bombast that most listeners will never hear and don't need to, oddly there is little or nothing in the book about other, much more significant works, such as the *Sonate Pathétique*, op. 13 (Beethoven's earliest, truly romantic composition) or the *Archduke Trio*, op. 97, perhaps the last of Beethoven's "Heroic" or middle-period pieces and much performed still today. The late piano sonatas and string quartets are discussed somewhat unevenly in terms of coverage, and confusion exists between the two sonatas, op. 101 and op. 110, for which a musical example is misidentified. The "cyclopean" and "diabolical" *Hammerklavier Sonata*, op. 106 (other extreme adjectives, as Caeyers points out, have been used as well), gets its due, as do the great *Diabelli Variations*, op. 120, which according to Caeyers reach "new, almost philosophical heights."

(The "almost" could certainly have been dropped.) The late string quartets, from op. 127 to op. 135, which today almost everyone places among the great masterpieces of classical music, are discussed at some length, and Caeyers addresses the fact that, in Beethoven's day, they were largely considered wild and even unplayable; their ascent to the peak of recognized greatness took many decades. Yet Caeyers is somewhat dismissive of the C-sharp Minor Quartet, op. 131, which, he says, "comes across as a forty-minute-long improvisation" and can be seen as "a concatenated stream of fragments" with episodes that are both "deliberate and desultory." His description of the first three movements of the Ninth Symphony is equally underwhelming: "nearly forty minutes of seemingly innocent entertainment in the form of three perfectly ordinary symphonic movements." Anyone who can hear "innocent entertainment" in the opening movement of Beethoven's Ninth is hearing something I've certainly never registered. Personally I agree with Debussy: "The Ninth Symphony...was a demonstration of genius, a sublime desire to augment and to liberate the usual forms by giving them the harmonious proportions of a fresco."* This is poetic and personal, of course, not musicological and analytical. But Debussy, who in general had little use for the symphony as a form, recognized the achievement that the Ninth represented at the levels of both form and feeling.

Caeyers gets to tell some wonderful stories. There is the meeting of Beethoven and Rossini, for example. Caeyers calls it, deliciously, "a communicative shambles." The year was 1822, and Beethoven was of course profoundly deaf by this time. Rossini was already staggeringly famous and excessively wealthy, and Vienna at that time was experiencing a sort of jungle fever for the composer of *The Barber of Seville*. He admired the *Eroica*, and that admiration led to the meeting. Rossini

---

* Claude Debussy, *Monsieur Croche: The Dilettante Hater*, trans. B. N. Langdon Davies (New York: Lear Publishers, 1948), p. 35. In this essay, Debussy said the oddest thing: "A symphony is usually built up on a chant heard by the composer as a child." Ibid., p. 37.

lived like royalty, so he was startled to see the conditions in which Beethoven lived. "Dirty and disorderly" were his words. Beethoven said all the wrong things about Rossini's operas in a conversation made challenging not only because of the composer's deafness, but because Rossini did not speak German. Caeyers quotes Schumann on the nature of that unlikely and ill-fated encounter: "A butterfly has crossed the path of an eagle, and the eagle swerved away to avoid crushing the butterfly with the strength of its wings." The meeting with Carl Maria von Weber a year later went much better. Beethoven's sense of humour is not usually noticed by biographers, but the composer of the fate motif from the Symphony no. 5 and the man who reportedly shook his fist at the heavens as he died undeniably had a good one. There is, for example, a long series of brief and little-known canons that Beethoven composed that are meant to inspire laughter. One, dedicated to his sometime friend Johann Nepomuk Mälzel, the inventor of a widely used metronome, employs the already amusing and metronome-like main theme from the second movement of the composer's Symphony no. 8 as the theme for a four-voice canon. Caeyers records but does not make anything of a rather hilarious coincidence in Beethoven's life. Toward the end, his doctor's name was Dr Wagner and his lawyer's name was Mr Bach. One wonders if his dentist's name was . . . Herr Brahms?

Beethoven lived at a supremely critical time in the history of European art music. His earliest published works—the three piano trios of op. 1 or the three piano sonatas of op. 2, among much else—largely belong to the eighteenth century and reflect the compositional values of Haydn, Mozart, and his own teachers. His last works, though obviously still reflecting the basic techniques and harmonic usages of the common practice period, reflect a totally changed world, both inner and outer. Sonata form and traditional counterpoint, including fugue, remain predominant (the latter entering Beethoven's compositions almost for the first time), but Beethoven reaches extremes of emotional expression by pushing and pulling out of shape all of the technical resources he inherited from his forebears. Between these two periods came what musicologists call his "Heroic" or middle period, beginning arguably with the violin sonatas of op. 30 and the piano sonatas of op. 31 and extending all the way to the works with opus numbers in the nineties, including transitional pieces like the strange but compelling E-Minor piano sonata, op. 90, of which Caeyers writes, "Rarely had Beethoven's music ever sounded so natural, and Schubert's spirit feels very close by." This is the period of the works still most widely performed—the *Eroica* and the Symphonies no. 5, 6, and 7, the *Emperor* Piano Concerto, the Violin Concerto, and many others— but it is arguably the period of least relevance to us today as listeners. Of course the works I have just mentioned remain as landmarks in the history of music (especially the *Eroica*), but their boisterous self-confidence and ebullient high spirits now feel vaguely empty, not unconvincing so much as off the mark emotionally. Perhaps the fourth Piano Concerto, op. 58, the *Appassionata* Sonata, op. 57, and *Fidelio*, op. 72, are the great exceptions. Beethoven's deep belief in transformative politics and his then still enduring expectations for human love combined to produce an opera of spiritual certitude and beauty. The love duet between Fidelio/Leonore and her husband, Florestan ("Oh Nameless Joy"), and the final scene that follows take the music into an ethereal realm unknown to the conventional rescue opera or indeed to many operas of any type, including much that was to come in both Germany and Italy. "Heroic" gestures may have been counterintuitive and therefore valuable as counterweights in the Biedermeier period, but their cultural value has diminished greatly since then.

By contrast Beethoven's late works feel as relevant and emotionally convincing as ever, perhaps more so. The change truly begins with the A Major Piano Sonata, op. 101, composed in 1816 and the first of the works that Caeyers accounts for in the last section of his book, entitled "The Lonely Way." It is Caeyers's contention that in that year Beethoven abandoned the search for love, a decision embodied in the song cycle

To the Distant Beloved and crucial to the development of his late style. The A Major Sonata has all the characteristics formally of late Beethoven. It is in this piece, for example, that Beethoven finally abandons the old convention of the Alberti bass. Its opening movement, while in sonata form, is extraordinarily compact (only 102 bars) and is marked to be played at a very leisurely tempo. So much for the sonata-allegro of old, as it were. The second movement is in a fairly remote key (F major) and is, of all things, a march. The slow movement is, again, extremely brief at only twenty bars, though within those twenty bars Beethoven achieves a great deal of concentrated pathos, an almost self-indulgent depressive affect that the finale—which starts with a reminiscence of the main theme of the opening movement, an idea that Beethoven will use again in the finale of the Ninth Symphony, where all three of the proceeding movements are briefly recapitulated—completely wipes away. Importantly, the development section of the final movement is a fugue, the textural technique that Beethoven used so extensively in his last works. What is extraordinary about the sonata, and a significant developmental change from his twenty-seven earlier piano sonatas, is the concatenation of the lyrical and the tragic, the concentrated and the expansive, and the range of emotions embodied in the music. It begins tentatively, yearningly, but ends with a short dramatic flourish that, rhythmically, is reflected in the opening of the sonata that follows, the "cyclopean" *Hammerklavier* of 1817, a piece that Beethoven himself predicted would need half a century before it could be understood. Even in the twentieth century, many serious pianists did not record it. Horowitz never did, nor did Rubenstein. Even now the Liszt Piano Sonata, which owes so much formally to the *Hammerklavier*, is recorded ten times for every recording of op. 106.

But it is the last string quartets that remain Beethoven's quintessential achievement, a body of music of bottomless grace, redemption, joy, despair, spirituality, and technical wonder. Caeyers's chapter devoted to these works is fittingly entitled "The Discovery of Heaven."

Heavenly they are, and it is no matter that in Beethoven's time they were dismissed as hard to play and hard to understand. They contain moments of powerful psychic pressure, such as the lead-up to the return of the main theme in the finale of op. 131, and moments of pure unalloyed ecstasy, such as the climax of the slow movement of op. 132. Fate—Beethoven's fate, and our fate almost two hundred years later—is embodied in this music, and not just in its obvious verbal manifestation in the motto inscribed over the last movement of the last of the quartets, the op. 135 in F major: "Must it be? It must be!," a bit of extra-musical *ludus gravis* that Kundera adopted as central to his great novel *The Unbearable Lightness of Being*. There is childlike music in these final quartets, and there is music of great sorrow, predictive of death to come. Music has rarely been so expressive of what it is to be human.

A VIKING ON THE LOOSE
FROM HIS LONGBOAT

A few years ago when I was in Paris and wandering around the Sorbonne, I stumbled on a small museum devoted to medical history. I rang at the front door, as instructed, and the middle-aged man who answered told me that the cost of admission was eight euros, or twelve euros if I wished to take photographs. He also explained that he did not make change. When I replied that I did not have the exact change, he went on to say that there was a café behind the museum, and that perhaps I could buy a coffee there in order to get the right change. He then led me through the museum to the café, and when I saw the contents of the place *en passant* I decided immediately that photographs were a must. There were hundreds of medical specimens in ancient glass jars, most of them with labels written by hand, as well as a small library that seemed to consist primarily of sixteenth- and seventeenth-century books on shelves that ran up the wall almost to the ceiling. I bought a coffee, got the right change, walked back around to the front door, and rang a second time. This time, with the correct change, I was admitted and left to wander. It was an extraordinary place. Among other things, there were brains in jars that had been anatomized by Paul Broca, the neuroanatomist whose name gives us Broca's area, the part of the brain where language is processed. Broca was also one of the teachers of Isidore Ducasse, the great poet better known as the Comte de Lautréamont, author of the *Chants de Maldoror*, the extraordinary proto-surrealist work that would influence a later generation of French poets including André Breton. The bits in bottles ultimately became too overwhelmingly creepy and sent me hurrying from the museum, after I'd taken many photographs of parts of those who, while long gone, in this odd and eerily touching way, were not forgotten.

This was the Musée Dupuytren, named for Guillaume Dupuytren (1777–1835), who is best remembered for lending his name to Dupuytren's contracture, a hand disease in which one or more fingers will not lie flat and curl toward the palm, and for the surgery to correct the condition that he invented. I did not know then that he was also the mentor of Gustave Flaubert's father, Achille-Cléophas Flaubert, whose appointment to the Hotel-Dieu, the main hospital in Rouen, he arranged, and where Flaubert *père* established himself as a renowned surgeon and professor. Flaubert *fils* would later have to consult another Dupuytren student, Philippe Ricord, a Paris-based specialist in venereal diseases, after Flaubert contracted syphilis during his long journey in the Middle East with his great friend Maxime Du Camp. The writer Flaubert inherited his physician father's eye for physical detail, and it is no surprise to learn from the Goncourt brothers' *Journal* that Flaubert had a bronze bust of Hippocrates on the fireplace mantel in his study. (A similar bust can be spotted in Dr Bovary's home in Sophie Barthes's 2014 film version of *Madame Bovary*.) Flaubert the anatomist of French bourgeois life under Louis-Philippe maintained throughout his career that science—not religion, not utopian theories, and certainly not bourgeois ideals of comfort and achievement—ought to rule as a force of government and as the basis for civic life. Never a success as a student—he was expelled from high school and flunked out of law school—Flaubert nonetheless turned himself into not just the greatest French writer of his century, but also a major critic of French society. Overt criticism is largely confined to his voluminous correspondence;

in his fiction it is up to the reader to interpret character and story and to gauge the criticism implicit in the details. It was the details, and the right words to capture them, of which Flaubert was a master.

Despite his hatred for middle-class life and middle-class people, with their bland chatter and their uninspiring aspirations, their philo-progenitive focus on family and their obeisance to the altar, Flaubert was middle class himself in almost every way that mattered. He lived for most of his life on family money, and although he rarely had to struggle to keep himself in modest style (house in the provinces, apartment in Paris, weekly "at homes" when he was in the city, and so on), money was always a dominant concern, even as he refused to deal with it directly. He treated his publishers almost like tradesmen, refusing to negotiate contracts with them and assigning others to do this on his behalf. He travelled and ate well and was already showing signs of bourgeois over-indulgence by the time he was thirty: venereal disease, incipient obesity, extensive medical problems, bad teeth, et cetera. In January of 1851, still only twenty-nine, Flaubert wrote disconsolately to a friend from Naples, as he was making his way back to France, of his "fattened face," his "double chin and jowls." He encouraged his niece to marry a man whom she clearly did not love, mainly because he was financially stable and socially acceptable. Of course in other, essential ways, Flaubert held back from bourgeois life, refusing to marry and dedicating himself to writing with an almost sacerdotal devotion. His mother chided his work ethic, and its resultant inhuman coldness, in a famous and stinging insult, when she told him that his "passion for sentences had dried up his heart" ("*Ta rage des phrases t'a déséché le coeur*"). That was not really true, as Flaubert's letters amply demonstrate. He was a faithful friend, an honest and valued critic of others' literary work, and a boon companion and salon attendee. His relationships with women were hardly above reproach, but bourgeois they were certainly not. His long and deep friendship with George Sand proves how capable he was at maintaining a relationship with a woman that was not in the least sexual.

Flaubert's life has been written many times before now, from early biographical studies such as Émile Faguet's *Flaubert* (1899) and John Charles Tarver's *Gustave Flaubert As Seen in His Works and Correspondence* (1895), to recent biographies in English by Herbert R. Lottman (1989), Geoffrey Wall (2002), and Frederick Brown (2006). The new English translation of Michel Winock's *Flaubert* is most easily distinguished from other studies by the fact Winock is not a literary critic but a historian.[*] Winock, who has also written biographies of Clemenceau and Madame de Staël among other books, is an emeritus professor at Sciences-Po in Paris. His book was published originally in French in 2013 to excellent reviews. The English version by Nicholas Elliott is extraordinarily well done: fluent, stylistically accurate, creative, and always as lively as Winock's French. Here, for example, is Winock's brief description of the character Jacques Arnoux from *Sentimental Education*:

> Dans sa boutique de Montmartre, Arnoux reçoit des peintres, qu'il exploite sans vergogne; vend trè cher des toiles sans valeur aux gogos, pour lesquelles il exhibe des factures fausses; fais exécuter des pastiches de grands maîtres pour les "amateurs éclaireés."[†]

Elliott's version is spirited and convincing:

> In his store on Boulevard Montmartre, Arnoux shamelessly exploits painters; sells suckers his worthless paintings at blue-chip prices, conning them with fake bills of sale; and turns out pastiches of old masters for "ignorant art-collectors."

---

[*] Michel Winock, *Flaubert*, trans. Nicholas Elliott (Cambridge, MA: Belknap Press, 2016). I take my title from one of the many critical characterizations of Flaubert recorded by the Goncourt brothers in their *Journal*.

[†] Michel Winock, *Flaubert* (Paris: Gallimard, 2013), pp. 298–299.

"Blue-chip prices" is particularly nice. Of course it is the translator's job to convince the reader that he or she is reading a text originally written in the target language. Elliott does that superbly well with *Flaubert*. It is a bit scandalous that the publisher, Belknap Press, did not accord him a brief biographical note on the dust jacket. He richly deserved it.

Flaubert once wrote in a letter to his lover, Louise Colet, of his disdain for "la patrie":

> I am no more modern than I am ancient, no more French than Chinese; and the idea of *la patrie*, the fatherland—that is, the obligation to live on a bit of earth colored red or blue on a map, and to detest the other bits colored green or black—has always seemed to me narrow, restricted and ferociously stupid.

"Stupid" was a key word for Flaubert. He detested what he denominated stupidity above all, and it was the main theme in *Bouvard and Pecuchet,* his final novel, even as it had been a less conspicuous but important theme in both *Madame Bovary* and *Sentimental Education*. Stupid or not, the influence of France and, in particular, the France of the July Monarchy, the 1848 Revolution, the Second Republic and the coup of 1851, and the Second Empire, on Flaubert as a person and a writer, is indisputable, however much he may have tried to avoid recognition of the impact of his "homeland" or taken fictional refuge in ancient history. (Two of the three stories in *Three Tales* as well as *Salammbô* and *The Temptation of Saint Anthony* are set in antiquity or medieval Europe.) It is precisely the historical background of Flaubert's times, both its conscious and its invisible impingments on the writer's sensibility, on which Winock is especially revelatory. While never ignoring the opposing force in Flaubert's development that was the search for style, objectivity, truth, and beauty (words of almost equal frequency in Flaubert's letters along with "stupid" and "stupidity"), Winock takes great pains to draw the context carefully. French political history during the middle third of the nineteenth century is complicated, to say the least, with the structure of government changing radically at several points and the role of the legislative assembly, as well as the role of the king/president/emperor, shifting often under varying pressures both internal and external to France. Winock is a master of all of this, and with contemporary French history at the heart of his interest, it is clear that, unlike many readers, his favourite Flaubert novel is not *Madame Bovary* but *Sentimental Education*. Frédéric Moreau's sentimental education is of course focused on what Charcot would later famously call *la chose génitale*, and money—getting it and spending it—is a strong undercurrent in the novel as well. But it is in a world dominated by political events that Frédéric and his acquaintances and friends act out their lives. The hero even decides at one point to run for public office, but quits in despair before voting day.

This does not mean that Winock is any less interesting on *Madame Bovary*, despite its intense focus on character and relationships and its relative lack of political context. The politics of Flaubert's fictional town of Yonville are primarily local. The apothecary Homais is a town booster—he writes a weekly column about local events for a Rouen newspaper, the *Fanal de Rouen*—and it is his boosterism that leads to the bungled surgery that Dr Bovary performs on the unfortunate Hippolyte, just one of the many ways in which Bovary haplessly contrives to lose Emma's faith and affection, as well as his own reputation. At the agricultural fair described in part 2 of the novel, the visiting counsellor, one Lieuvain, invokes Louis-Philippe, "that Monarch, that Sovereign, that dearly beloved King, to whom nothing that touches the public well-being or private prosperity of his people is ever a matter of indifference,"* but his invocation is rote and part of a long speech that is notable for its fustiness and tiresome clichés. He and the other dignitaries present are described as all dressing exactly alike, as all looking exactly alike, and as

---

* Gustave Flaubert, *Madame Bovary*, trans. Gerard Hopkins (Oxford: Oxford University Press, 1981), p. 134.

all acting exactly alike. His dreary speech is intercalated with the scene of Emma and Rodolphe sitting in the unoccupied council chambers of the town hall, watching the proceedings, and its emptiness is clearly meant to cast a dismissive light on the growing intimacy of the two soon-to-be lovers. This is about as far as national politics impinge on the world of *Madame Bovary*. Dr Bovary "has no political ideas for the simple reason that he has no ideas at all," as Winock points out. The local priest "is a simpleton without the slightest sense of human psychology," much less any informed sense of the wider world. Even Homais, whose opinions are presented in some depth, becomes a symbol of what Flaubert despised about French society: an adorer of the lowbrow verses of Pierre-Jean de Bérenger (the Rod McKuen of his time and place), and, ultimately, a recipient of the Legion of Honour. The recognition from the state comprises the novel's concluding line, and respect is the very last thing we are meant as readers to feel toward Homais. "Honors dishonor, titles degrade, employment makes stupid," as Flaubert later said.

Not surprisingly, given his bent to historical accounting, Winock is very thorough in tracing the critical and popular response to Flaubert's books. He quotes extensively from the newspapers of the time, which reviewed new books at length in a way that by our standards today is almost inconceivable. But the reviews in fact began even before the novelist submitted his manuscripts to his publishers (first Michel Lévy and later Georges Charpentier), for Flaubert would both send portions of his unpublished drafts to friends, and read them aloud in his house at Croisset and elsewhere. Winock cites Maxine Du Camp's testimony that he spent three weeks with Flaubert listening to and reading the manuscript of *Sentimental Education*, arguing about grammar and style; he also affirmed that the novelist often preferred what sounded well to what was grammatically correct. (This from the greatest stylist of his century!) With publication of the novel in November of 1869, comments from friends who had received inscribed copies constituted the second wave of reader reaction. (Victor Hugo told him he had insight and style, unlike Balzac, who only had insight.) Compliments from friends were clearly welcome, since the press was almost uniformly hostile to the novel. George Sand published a rave review in *La Liberté*, but she wrote the piece as a friend in response to Flaubert's plea for a positive critique. Most critics complained vociferously about the characters (irredeemably motivated by selfishness), their actions (immoral and unworthy), and the supposed artlessness and "plotlessness" of the writing. The novelist Jules Barbey d'Aurevilly, who had also denigrated *Madame Bovary* twelve years earlier, went so far as to call Flaubert "just a bric-a-brac maker," surely one of the greater purblind critical appraisals in French literature. Zola, whose review was not precipitated by a request from Flaubert, knew better. Flaubert was "a poet transformed into a naturalist, Homer turned into Cuvier."

In that same review, Zola went on to comment on the music of Flaubert's prose. For his part, Winock several times comments on Flaubert's deliberate avoidance of poetic/musical techniques like assonance and alliteration in his writing. It is of course a staple of the Flaubert story that he was exceedingly self-critical, often supposedly spending hours on a single sentence, or days on a single page, frequently discarding pages of writing because of his Olympian standards. If assonance and consonance, not to mention alliteration, were a bugbear, however, what are we make of the opening paragraph of *Madame Bovary*?

> Nous étions à l'étude, quand le Proviseur entra, suivi d'un *nouveau* habillé en bourgeois et d'un garçon de classe qui portait un grand pupitre. Ceux qui dormaient se réveillèrent, et chacun se leva comme surpris dans son travail.[*]

---

[*] Gustave Flaubert, *Madame Bovary*, in *Œuvres I*, ed. A. Thibaudet and R. Dumesnil (Paris: Gallimard, 1951), p. 293. Gerard Hopkins translates the passage in this way: "We were in the preparation room when the head came in, followed by a new boy in ordinary day clothes, and by a school servant carrying a large desk. Those of us who were asleep woke up, and we all rose to our feet doing our best to give the impression that we had been interrupted in the midst of our labours." Op. cit., p. 1.

Read aloud, consonance and alliteration above all are remarkably audible here: three *e* words in the first two phrases, ten *s* sounds if you elide the first two words, and a general mellifluousness that, admittedly, is not atypical of even the least literary French prose, given the nature of French vowels. This passage sounds to my ear at least like prose from which the writer has definitely not attempted to exclude the music of language. In summing up the route by which it came to be recognized as a masterpiece and a provocative early example of the anti-hero novel, Winock describes *Sentimental Education* as "atonal" ("this—shall we say—atonal novel that follows the mediocre lives of ordinary humanity"). It is a strange word to choose. Certainly the book has a sort of picaresque plot, a story somewhat without a centre, as atonal music also does; but in terms of the linguistic music of Flaubert's novel, "atonal," with its specific musical reference to routine dissonance and formal unpredictability, seems inappropriate. George Sand recognized that her great friend was a troubadour, or so she often addressed him in her letters, a poet whose poems were meant to be sung. Proust and Kundera would both later state that, with Flaubert, the novel became the equal of the poem. Poetic techniques were an essential aspect of the evolution.

The latter part of Flaubert's life was dominated by death—the death of his mother (he was fifty when she died) and the deaths of friends. Winock tells us that the writer coined a word to describe his increasing certainty through the 1870s that life was becoming unbearable: *insupportation*, from *insupportable*, the French word for intolerable. Louis Bouilhet, a close friend from Flaubert's earliest days, died in 1869, Théophile Gautier in 1872, and George Sand in 1876. There were others. Flaubert's last decade was also roiled by financial disaster. He had allowed his niece's husband, Ernest Commanville, to look after much of his money, and Commanville lost it, coming close to bankruptcy. (A report in a newspaper informed readers that Flaubert "lost nearly his entire fortune in a commercial enterprise he had entered into purely out of kindness for a relative." The papers were critical of his books, but they could be charitable to him as a person.) There were compensations in friends still living: Zola, Turgenev, the surviving Goncourt brother, Edmond, the young Guy de Maupassant who was a disciple as well as a companion. But the writer who had always borne a streak of cynicism and loathing for life on earth, grew even more melancholy as the end neared. His desperate cri-de-cœur in a late letter—"Where is there anyone who relishes a good sentence?"—is funny but also pitiable.

Michel Winock has written a compelling and stylish biography, and Nicholas Elliott has brought it into English with flare and skill. Almost without blemish—Albert de Broglie unaccountably becomes Alfred on page 385, and there are a handful of typographical errors in the text—the English translation is a pleasure to read. Some quotations lack references, and a few persons named in the text are not identified. (Who, for example, was Paul Collardez, one of the "three great minds in my life" referred to in his journal by Edmond de Goncourt, along with artist Paul Gavarni and chemist Marcellin Berthelot?) The illustrations, taken wholly from the French edition but not reproduced in colour as some of the latter were, contain only one photograph of Flaubert. Winock states that "photographs and portraits of Flaubert are rare," but surely one or two others could have been included. Finally, the artist who painted the scene from an opera based on *Salammbô*—whose composer, Ernest Reyer, is not credited—is not identified in the cut-line beneath the photograph, but only in the illustration acknowledgements at the end of the book. (He was Giuseppe De Nittis, an Italian painter who showed at the very first impressionist exhibition in Paris.) These are very minor cavils about a book that, in French, can stand on the shelf with others by Flaubert scholars such as Jean Bruneau and René Dumesnil, and in English, with books by Francis Steegmuller and Geoffrey Wall—all very good company for a book about "the most meticulous craftsman of prose fiction the world had ever seen,"* who once said, "One must divide one's existence into two parts: to live as a bourgeois and to think as a demigod."

---

* Hugh Kenner, "Gustave Flaubert: Comedian of the Enlightenment," in *Gustave Flaubert*, ed. Harold Bloom (New York and Philadelphia: Chelsea House Publishers, 1989), p. 12.

HAVE FAITH AND
HAVE NO FEAR

I n 1928, Freud published a short essay on Dostoevsky ("Dostoevsky and Parricide") that has fallen into disrepute on several quite reasonable grounds. His view of the writer's epilepsy as psychogenic ("the neurotic in himself") is considered dubious in modern medical practice, and his opinion that "The future of human civilization will have little to thank him for" now seems positively eccentric. (Admittedly Freud was speaking here more of Dostoevsky as a moralist than as a novelist. *The Brothers Karamazov*, in Freud's view, is "the most magnificent novel ever written.") But it is easy to see why Freud could not resist psychoanalyzing Dostoevsky posthumously. The Russian writer lost his mother to tuberculosis when he was fifteen; he lost his father three years later, probably murdered by his own servants; and he suffered almost lifelong medical and behavioural complaints that at one time were easily psychologized: a gambling addiction, hemorrhoids, and epilepsy. He also came within moments of being executed by firing squad in his late twenties, an experience that would leave most people permanently traumatized. ("Who can say that human nature can bear a thing like that without going mad," Prince Myshkin asks early in *The Idiot*. Dostoevsky's almost-execution may have been staged, but the effect was still horrendous.) And that is not even to mention his four years in a Siberian *katorga*, a prison camp where he was sent after the Tsar commuted his death sentence and where he endured hard labour and appalling living conditions. He then spent several years in the Russian army before being released back into the west of the country where he was able to pick up his literary career once again. Far from being merely one of what therapists like to call the "wounded well," Dostoevsky really was profoundly wounded. Writing only a few years after Freud's article, S. S. Smith and A. Isotoff were certain that Dostoevsky suffered from what we would now call bipolar disorder: "A modern Manichean victim, like most of his characters, of the eternal warfare between Darkness and Light, he lived in a state either of ecstatic hyperesthesia, or of depression so profound that only the dark night of the soul, described by St. John of the Cross, can compare with it."*

The wounds that plagued Dostoevsky for much of his life are most obviously on display in his novel *The Idiot* (1868), in which the central character, Prince Myshkin, is an epileptic. The title, which is phonologically identical in Russian, was already an established psychiatric term by the middle of the nineteenth century, when it referred to a patient who was "congenitally deficient in reasoning powers" (*Oxford English Dictionary*); a lunatic, by contrast, was someone who lost his powers of reason later in life. (The colloquial meaning of "idiot," as a normally reasonable person who does something stupid, was also common in Dostoevsky's time. The OED cites *Barnaby Rudge* [1841]: "You idiot, do you know what peril you stand in?") Prince Myshkin is treated for his disease in the way that many *demi-fous*—"neurotics, hysterics, anorexics and sufferers from a newly fashionable disorder, 'neurasthenia,' or weakness of the nerves"—were at the time, if they came from an affluent family: he was shipped off to a clinic in Switzerland.† Many characters describe the prince as an idiot, even in his

---

* S. S. Smith and A. Isotoff, "The Abnormal from Within: Dostoevsky," *The Psychoanalytic Review* 22 (January 1, 1935), p. 364.

† Andrew Scull, *Madness in Civilization: A Cultural History of Insanity* (Princeton and Oxford: Princeton University Press, 2015), p. 273.

hearing; it would be disgraceful if Dostoevsky did not tell us early on that even Prince Myshkin used the word in self-description: "The frequent bouts of his illness had made almost a complete idiot of him (the prince's own word)."* While inexperience undeniably makes the prince act in sometimes naive ways, as a character he is idiotic in neither the psychiatric nor the colloquial meaning of the word. Assuredly he lacks the sense of humour that comes with sophistication; but as we are reminded by the minor character Fernischenko, "only unwitty people speak the truth."† He knows that love matters, that fellow-feeling matters, that forgiveness matters, that "compassion is the most important, perhaps the sole law of human existence."‡ Those apperceptions are inspissate in the Christological model that Dostoevsky adopted for his main character.

"Paradise is a difficult business," remarks another prince in *The Idiot*, Prince S, one of just three people in the novel who lack family names and who seem more to be embodied voices than fully fleshed-out characters. The observation is made to Prince Myshkin who, in Prince S's view, wishes "to establish paradise on earth." In the end, of course, nothing goes well for Prince Myshkin. Of the two women whom he pursues alternately, one rejects him and the other is murdered. He fails in his first and only attempt to integrate into high society, talking too much, accidentally smashing a precious Chinese vase, and ultimately collapsing in an epileptic seizure. His descriptions of the two most identifiably Dostoevskian experiences—the seizure (and the aura that precedes it) and the execution commuted at the last possible moment—constitute high points of the novel and are embodied in extraordinary writing. Sometimes, however, the narrative bogs down in almost pointless chit-chat and stories of only vague relevance

---

* Fyodor Dostoevsky, *The Idiot*, trans. Alan Meyers (Oxford: Oxford University Press, 1992), p. 28. Prince Myshkin is still being described as an idiot in the final paragraph of the novel.
† Ibid., p. 146.
‡ Ibid., p. 242.

to the plot or to character development. In this way the novel only too readily betrays its lack of formal planning, something that the author himself admitted and which has long puzzled and irritated readers. The critic Mikhail Bakhtin famously saw in this seeming extemporization qualities he denominated "polyphonic" and "carnivalesque." Readers might be more inclined to agree with various of the novel's characters who variously complain "How long is this to go on?," and "Too much talk," and even "How tedious this is!"

Joseph Frank (1918–2013), who devoted decades of his life to writing the multivolume life of Dostoevsky that remains the standard biography in any language (five volumes, 1976–2002), admitted this unevenness too. In his recent book, *Lectures on Dostoevsky*, he explores the composition history of *The Idiot*, remarking on how different it is from all the other major novels, and suggesting that the somewhat ad-libbed plot accounts for "a plethora of incidents that are only loosely (if at all) connected with the main plot lines of the novel."[*] But the lack of formal cogency in *The Idiot* does not ultimately prevent it from being a great novel, in Frank's view. It is "the most autobiographical of his novels," as it is also "one of the greatest works in which an attempt is made to project a contemporary Christ figure," and it "contains the most original [scenes] that Dostoevsky ever wrote."

Joseph Frank spent most of his teaching career at Princeton; but after he retired, Stanford invited him annually to give a ten-week lecture course on Dostoevsky. Those lectures form the bulk of *Lectures on Dostoevsky*, to which have been added a biographical foreword by Robin Feuer Miller, a brief preface by the translator Marina Brodskaya (who audited Frank's Stanford course and was a friend), and a review of Frank's biography of Dostoevsky by David Foster Wallace that appeared originally in *The Village Voice* and that apparently pleased

---

[*] Joseph Frank, *Lectures on Dostoevsky*, ed. Marina Brodskaya and Marguerite Frank (Princeton: Princeton University Press, 2019).

Frank very much. An appendix lists a selection of adaptations made of Dostoevsky's works for film and television. (I took the title of this essay from a line in a film not on that list but demonstrably influenced by *The Idiot*, Visconti's *Rocco and His Brothers*.) The lectures are clearly directed at an undergraduate or non-specialist audience and cover seven of Dostoevsky's books: six novels and the semi-fictional memoir, *The House of the Dead*. Frank makes it clear from the opening sentence that he will focus on both the books and the "main literary and ideological elements" in Dostoevsky's writing. In other words, the lectures fall into the welcome category of literary and cultural criticism, with no evidence anywhere of the influence of critical theory. It is not until halfway through the book, in the second of his two lectures on *Crime and Punishment*, that Frank asks the question that his emphasis on context provokes, namely whether reading books that require us "[to search] out ideas and ideological quarrels that have long been forgotten" is worth the time and effort. His answer is straightforward and rather refreshing. While too much ideological or social or religious context can become a critical end in itself and deflect the aim of commentary away from rather than directly at the books themselves and their "higher or more general level," too little leads readers to see the books only "in terms of the most general psychological and philosophical categories," an equal if opposite critical defect. Frank tries to balance the two frameworks in his book and succeeds extremely well.

Vladimir Nabokov's well-known *Lectures on Russian Literature* (1981) are unmistakably the work of a practising writer, with all the insights and the personal likes and dislikes of one artist accounting for the greatness or lack of it in his predecessors clearly on display; Frank's book is just as obviously the work of a scholar and academic. Frank had personal opinions, needless to say. Who, having spent the better part of his life and career investigating the work of a single writer, would not? Nabokov, for example, thought that the scene in *Crime and Punishment* in which Raskolnikov and Sonya, the whore with a heart of gold, read the New

Testament together, was "nonsense" and "a shoddy literary trick," and that it contained a "sentence that for sheer stupidity has hardly the equal in world-famous literature."* Frank, by contrast, while recognizing that Sonya "can be considered a hackneyed character," thinks that Dostoevsky endowed her with "a level of intensity and purity that is unrivaled." Nabokov's dislike of Dostoevsky as a writer, despite his renown as one of the world's greatest novelists, might make a reader question his objectivity, for all that his venomous reputation-bashing can be amusing. (He was delighted to quote Turgenev as having said that Dostoevsky was "a new pimple on the face of Russian literature.") Unlike Nabokov, Frank did not speak Russian (though he read it well), but he tries to be more even-handed in appraising individual works and the writerly aspects of individual novels: plot, character, et cetera. He does not, where philosophical ideals are concerned, dismiss Dostoevsky's evolution from a Westernizer into a Slavophile out of hand, as Nabokov does; he merely notes it and points out that the writer did not unquestioningly accept all the doctrines of Slavophilia, such as its support for serfdom. (His czarist sympathies were firmly cemented in the spring of 1861 when Alexander II emancipated the serfs.) As a further example of Frank's balanced views, we can note that, while he does mention Freud's article, twice in fact, he merely notes in the first instance that it is "famous," and in the second instance points out that Dostoevsky's published journals tend to disprove the notion that the writer was merely recreating his own negative character traits in his fictional characters (one of Freud's contentions), and that he was by contrast a "highly self-conscious writer."

Unlike Nabokov, then, Frank sees it as his responsibility to accept Dostoevsky's ideological and emotional choices—his kenotic Christianity, his belief in certain aspects of utopian socialism, his resistance to

---

* Vladimir Nabokov, *Lectures on Russian Literature*, ed. Fredson Bowers (New York: Harcourt, 1981), p. 110.

Western European standards and mores—rather than to criticize them for being retrograde or provincial or sentimental. Where the first is at issue, for example—Dostoevsky's adherence to Christian principles— Nabokov mocks this as constituting "the truly irritating side of Dostoevsky as 'philosopher,'" whereas Frank uses the published notebooks to explore Dostoevsky's personal beliefs (citing some journal entries he made as he endured a vigil beside the dead body of his first wife, among other sources) and the facts of his life experience as parallels to events in the novels. Dostoevsky turned to Christ in the moment before his supposed execution—*Nous serons avec le Christ*, he said to the man beside him just as the bullet was expected—and depended on the New Testament to help him through the travails of his imprisonment. (His copy of the New Testament, now in the Russian State Library, is one of only a handful of his personal books that have survived.) The later novels are full of Christian themes, symbols, and attributes, famously in the epilogue to *Crime and Punishment*, in the figure of Father Zosima in *The Brothers Karamazov* (and indeed throughout that novel), and in the central character of *The Idiot*. Frank is a sensitive and informed explorer of those aspects of the fiction. Take the example of the Holbein painting in a crucial passage of *The Idiot*. (Two different Holbein paintings are in fact used in the novel. In the earlier and less significant case, Holbein's painting known as *The Madonna of the Burgomeister Meyer* or the *Darmstadt Madonna* is briefly alluded to by Prince Myshkin when he is trying to characterize the face of Alexandra Ivanovna Yepanchin.) A copy of Holbein's *Christ in the Tomb*, which Dostoevsky saw in Dresden during his European travels, hangs in the house of the wealthy merchant Rogozhin, and it occasions responses from Rogozhin himself (who sees it as evidence that Christ was merely a man, whose body was subject to corruption), the Prince, and the young consumptive, Ippolit Terentyev, whose reaction is to see the triumph of nature over faith in the brutally realistic depiction of Christ's entombment. Prince Myshkin finds Holbein's representation of the dead Christ difficult to incorporate into his understanding of the nature of the Son of Man and the divinity in all men. Frank sees two key themes in the Prince's response to the Holbein painting: first, that the "human...need for faith transcends both the plane of rational reflection and that of empirical evidence," and secondly, a parallel to Kierkegaard's idea of the "teleological suspension of the ethical" (which he cites). "Myshkin's practical failure [that is, in everyday life] ought not to weaken the values of Christian love and religious faith that he embodies." These observations get right to the heart of the novel and its central character.

Frank is equally astute about that most famous story within a story of Dostoevsky's, the "Legend of the Grand Inquisitor" that comes in the fifth chapter of *The Brothers Karamazov*. Frank terms it with forgivable exaggeration "one of the most beautifully subtle creations in all of literature." The "Legend" is told by Ivan Karamazov to his brother Alyosha (a novice in the Orthodox Church), and concerns the return of Jesus to earth in Seville during the heyday of the Spanish Inquisition. He is arrested by an aged cardinal, the Grand Inquisitor, who places him in a cell and informs him that he is to be burned at the stake the following day. The Inquisitor visits Jesus in his cell and tells him that his coming is unfortunate and unneeded, because the Roman Catholic Church has essentially replaced him as the mediator between people and God. He tells Jesus: "We have taken the sword of Caesar, and in taking it, of course, have rejected Thee and followed him." Frank is at pains to remind us that the narrator of the Legend is not Dostoevsky himself, but a character, and that his (Ivan's) motivation is complex. He has an "irrational love of life," Frank observes, but is also disillusioned by the suffering he sees all around him. Ivan, in the figure of the Grand Inquisitor, insists that the very things rejected by Christ during his forty days in the desert, when he was tempted by the Devil three times, are what the Church can offer to its adherents. Christ, by contrast, in Frank's words, "did not want to base his authority over man on material proofs of his power of one sort or another but solely on the free gift of man's love based on faith." This view, according to Frank, provides an analogical embodiment of "all the major plot lines [in the novel]...the same conflict between the material, the sensual, and faith, love, trust." The Grand Inquisitor "[denies] people the very essence of Christian faith, as Dostoevsky saw it," which is to say freedom of will or moral autonomy. And that, of course, is a central theme that runs through all of the writer's mature fiction.

Dostoevsky's espousal of Christianity is anything but a simple topic, and Frank addresses how it evolved over his lifetime in several chapters of his book. Despite the novelist's connections in his twenties with members of more than one intellectual circle that embraced atheism and non-Christian utopian socialism, Frank is convinced that even at that time Dostoevsky was a faithful communicant. In his chapter on *The House of the Dead*, he singles out Dostoevsky's "last words" before his commuted execution as evidence that in 1849 he was a Christian. (The fellow prisoner to whom he made the remark, one Nikolay Speshnev, clearly not a co-religionist, rejoined simply "*Un peu de poussière.*") With the experience of prison that followed, Dostoevsky gained what Frank calls "an eschatological perspective" that was largely inimical to the standards of the realist novel in which the "aim was to dramatize the more mundane and quotidian aspects of human life." (All the same, Dostoevsky admired writers like Dickens and Balzac. His first published book was a translation of *Eugénie Grandet.*) Frank seldom finds fault with Dostoevsky as a writer, but he understands this perspective, this "world of eschatological apprehension," as the source of the writer's inability to portray "the personal and the social" in a convincing way. (People rarely dine or do laundry or go on outings in Dostoevsky's novels. No one plays the piano or attends a play at the Mikhailovsky Theatre. The one major social scene in *The Idiot* first turns into a farce and then into a stage set for tragedy and failure. The funeral banquet scene in *Crime and Punishment* turns into a rancorous

food fight.) Life is always viewed "in relation to the supernatural prospect of eternity" and is underpinned by "the human necessity of
religion." Dostoevsky's life experience played against the fashionable
interests of the Belinsky circle (where he toyed with avant-garde literary and philosophical ideas) and of the Petrachevsky Circle (where he
toyed with avant-garde social and nationalist ideas, and was arrested
as a result), just as he rejected the nihilist adoption of atheism, rooted
in the influence of Feuerbach's *Essence of Christianity.* (Feuerbach was
very much in the air during Dostoevsky's young manhood, but Frank
does not specify whether the writer read that much discussed book.)
Frank is adamant that, despite Feuerbach's rationalistic view that man
had created God, and not the other way around, Dostoevsky saw the
essence of Christianity as the foundation of "the Russian national
character," and that this deeply held viewpoint "[furnished] the themes
of his major works."

In his introduction to the Pevear and Volokhonsky translation of *The
Brothers Karamazov,* Malcolm v. Jones estimates that there may exist
"thousands [of books] and hundreds of thousands [of articles] about Dostoevsky."* Even in such an ocean of commentary, and thinking for the
moment only of books and articles in English, Joseph Frank's *Lectures on
Dostoevsky* will have an important place. His knowledge of the novels
and the life are peerless and his prose is lucid and accessible, as "interesting and exciting—and as readable" as the writer of a propaedeutic
should be. He *likes* his subject, even after decades of in-depth reading
and research, and is able to communicate that affection even as he delves
into complex intellectual history and philosophical quarrels that are long
gone from the cultural scene. (The text and notes contain a few repetitions that are inherent in written lectures, but that is a minor flaw.)
Frank does not set out to emphasize Dostoevsky's continuing relevance

---

* Fyodor Dostoevsky, *The Brothers Karamazov,* trans. Richard Pevear and Larissa Volokhonsky
(New York: Knopf, 1992), p. ix.

almost a century and a half after his death, though perhaps that explains the inclusion of the list of film and television adaptations, which includes works from as recent as 2019. Andrei Tarkovsky's film *Andrei Rublev* is not on that list, nor should it be. But in the wonderful scene between Rublev and Theophanes the Greek, it is impossible not to hear Dostoevsky in the older painter's way of counselling his friend and student in light of the latter's admission that he has killed a man. "Live between divine forgiveness and your own torment." That could have been an epigraph to Joseph Frank's wonderful book.

I BITE ROOKS

When I was growing up in mid-century middle-class Toronto, in a house with a grand piano but no swimming pool in a neighbourhood of engineers and doctors and sales managers (my father), the polished wooden shelves in the den were largely filled with middlebrow books, novels like *Tortilla Flat* and *The Ugly American* and *The Good Earth*, biographies (I remember Ernest Newman's life of Richard Wagner), and sets. My parents' shelves contained no Hemingway, no Fitzgerald, no Joyce, no classical literature, and no poetry. Perhaps *A Child's Garden of Verses* was there. The only highbrow work I can recall was a two-volume edition in quarter-cloth and bluish-grey boards of Scott Moncrieff's translation of Proust, an English version of *À la recherche du temps perdu* under the Shakespearean title *Remembrance of Things Past* that every North American antiquarian bookseller over fifty knows well and has seen a hundred times. So common was it at one period that I assume it must have been a Book of the Month Club selection in the 1950s, when surely most copies went largely unread in households, like my parents', where Book of the Month Club selections penetrated but literary books were a rarity.

The legend that Proust kills translators no doubt has its roots in the fact that the author himself died before his *roman-fleuve* was completed and that the same fate attended its first translator, C. K. Scott

Moncrieff, who died at forty in 1930, leaving the final volume of À la recherche, Le Temps retrouvé, to be englished by his friend Sydney Schiff, under the pen name Stephen Hudson. Proust complained a little about his English translator, in particular about Scott Moncrieff's choice of title; but in truth he was blessed to have someone dedicated to bringing his immense and complicated book into English, someone who had all the necessary linguistic skills as well as a similar, or rather parallel, social background, someone who, like Proust, aspired to mix with his social betters. Scott Moncrieff's own homosexuality also gave him a unique insight into Proust's world, even if he had to adjust Proust's text somewhat for the more puritanical British reading public, choosing, for example, to call the fourth volume of Proust's work Cities of the Plain when his publisher balked at the more blatant "Sodom and Gomorrah." Mildly bloodied but unbowed, he took to referring to that book as "Cissies [sic] of the Plain" in private conversation and correspondence.

We know this bit of persiflage because it is mentioned in Jean Findlay's recent life of Scott Moncrieff, to whom she is related.* (He was her mother's great-uncle.) Findlay had access to a wonderful trove of family documents, letters, and diaries; the use of these, together with material in public repositories—especially an eleventh-hour discovery of Scott Moncrieff's long and intimate letters to Vyvyan Holland, now at the Humanities Research Center at Texas—has produced a richly detailed biography of a fascinating literary figure. Findlay has called her book Chasing Lost Time, and of course that is a direct translation of the title of Proust's novel, the book which in a sense made Scott Moncrieff famous, or as famous as translators ever become. Findlay is able to gather testimony to suggest that not only is the Scott Moncrieff translation good, it is even, in the eyes of some (notably Joseph Conrad, who spoke French fluently, but also John Middleton Murry), better

---

* Jean Findlay, Chasing Lost Time: The Life of C .K. Scott Moncrieff: Soldier, Spy, and Translator (New York: Farrar, Straus and Giroux, 2015).

than the original. This is a minority opinion, but it does testify to Scott Moncrieff's achievement of a flexible, at times profound, and always beautiful prose style that perfectly embodies Proust's French. If it is sometimes criticized as flowery or even euphuistic, and too obviously of its time, one might counter that those words apply equally to the original; and while the recent translation rendered by not one but seven different translators (Lydia Davis and others) has been touted as more accurate and easier to follow, readers faced with a choice will be choosing not necessarily between good and better versions but versions that aspire to different "Englishes."

Charles Kenneth Scott Moncrieff (CKSM or Charlie) was born into a well-to-do middle-class Scottish family in 1889. His father, George, was a sheriff and his mother, Meg, a writer, diarist, and later a spiritualist of such conviction that some of her diaries were destroyed by her grandchildren as registering a sensibility that they feared bordered on the psychotic. Charlie was the Benjamin in the family, the youngest of three boys, and with the age gap between him and his two older brothers (born in 1879 and 1881), both of whom were sent to boarding school, he spent much of his childhood as an only child and grew up "blithely," as Findlay puts it. He read and wrote poetry from an early age, and from the age of six would recite Milton's "Ode on the Morning of Christ's Nativity"—a poem of 244 lines—every Christmas morning, "even," says Findlay, "when he was alone." He was fortunate in his schooling, starting at eight with a German schoolmaster who believed equally in the three Rs and the pedagogical value of poetry, music, and the natural world. At fourteen he was admitted to Winchester College as a scholar, where on the whole he was quite happy and where he discovered his homosexuality. On a visit to London to see his brother, CKSM met Robert Ross, Oscar Wilde's first male lover and his literary executor, and he began to spend time at Ross's home and salon, where "the literary homosexual coterie" met and talked. Among the men in Ross's circle whom CKSM took to was Christopher Millard, a Wilde collector and antiquarian bookseller who was jailed twice for gross indecency and probably played a role in the development of CKSM's intimate life. Millard was also a convert to Catholicism, and CKSM would follow in his footsteps in that area as well some years later, in July 1915.

CKSM failed to get into either of the Oxbridge universities, so he attended the University of Edinburgh and graduated with degrees in both law and English literature. During his university years he was a member of the army cadet force, and was once chosen to accompany a group of cadets on a trip to Canada, where they visited Montreal, Toronto, and parts farther west that Findlay does not specify. When war broke out, then, he had clearly been prepared by his upbringing and experience to go. Findlay is excellent on the unconscious training that CKSM had undergone in the years leading up to 1914:

> The urge to glory was too simple a sentiment to describe the impulse that thrust Charles to war, but it was certainly part. The public school ethos glamorized warfare: studying the classics meant engaging in poetry and prose about Greek and Roman warriors, and the team spirit nurtured by sport on the playing fields enhanced partisan feeling. War was the ultimate team game, with the highest stakes.

CKSM spent some time early in the war guarding the south coast of England against an invasion—an invasion that of course never came—but by late October 1914, he was at the front. He would be there off and on for almost three years. He lost teeth, suffered from trench foot and trench fever, and finally, in April 1917, at a battle site called Monchy-le-Preux, was badly wounded in the leg by a British shell that missed its mark and blew up near him, leaving him with a permanent limp. He won several medals and experienced the deaths of many friends, not least Wilfred Owen, with whom he was in love; but his belief in the glory of war never really wavered. After his recovery, he spent the

remainder of the war in military intelligence, working under a Major
Dansey who, by coincidence, was thought to have been "corrupted" by
Robert Ross at one point in his life. Wilfred Owen's death in the very
last month of the war hurt CKSM deeply, but he would nevertheless
write, in a dedication, of wishing "to live…honorably and to die gal-
lantly." Whether such a high ideal, seemingly unannealed by CKSM's
actual experience of the ghastliness of war, can be applied to him, is a
moot question. Certainly Owen's friends did not think CKSM honour-
able: literary friends like Robert Graves took to snubbing him because
of the rumour that he had seduced Owen. The evidence is not incon-
trovertible, and Findlay does not take a stand on the truth or falseness
of the story.

It is not surprising in retrospect that CKSM's earliest translation
projects should have been the *Chanson de Roland*, a poem about the
glory and tragedy of a long-ago war in France, and *Beowulf*, another
epic poem from roughly the same period and also about warfare and
honour. CKSM was already in the first postwar years making important
friends, as he gradually settled into the life of a reviewer and translator,
having realized early on that he was not at heart a poet. The *Chanson
de Roland*, published in 1919, was graced with an introduction by G. K.
Chesterton and a poetics note by George Saintsbury, whom CKSM had
come to know at university; and the *Beowulf* of 1921 sported an introduction by Viscount Northcliffe, the newspaper baron and for a brief
period CKSM's boss. J. C. Squire, Compton Mackenzie, and Edmund
Gosse took an interest in CKSM's career as well, and Noël Coward
became a friend. As far back as the war years CKSM had been an avid
reviewer, and his forthrightness in condemning what he considered
second-rate work made him some enemies, not least among them the
Sitwells, whose poetry (Osbert's and Edith's) he thought respectively
"facile" and "largely devoid of meaning," to cite Findlay. (CKSM would
find himself satirized in Osbert Sitwell's 1924 book *Triple Fugue* as
"Clubfoot the Avenger." He was in good company, given that Sitwell

also based insalubrious characters on Edmund Gosse, Lady Ottoline Morrell, and the anthologist and arts patron Edward Marsh.)

CKSM had only a dozen years after the war in which to carry out the work that is his legacy, before an early death in 1930 from esophageal cancer, a disease which Findlay intimates was caused by his sex life.* In 1923 he was recruited by British intelligence and moved to Italy, where he worked as a low-level spy, apparently sending reports on troop maneuvers and the like from Pisa, Rome, and elsewhere. (The records about his work as an intelligence agent were destroyed in 1932, so Findlay is unable to discuss this part of his life in anything but the most general manner.) He was paid a small salary for this work, but he also depended on his reviewing and translation for a significant part of his income; and although he lived very modestly, he contributed to his nieces' and nephews' upkeep generously after the death of his brother John in 1920 from a gunshot wound that was officially deemed an accident but may have been either suicide or murder. CKSM first proposed translating Proust to Constable & Co. in 1919, when he began to work on *Du Côté de chez Swann* without a contract, but the London firm rejected his idea. (I wonder whether it may have been the novelist and bibliophile Michael Sadleir who made that questionable decision. Both he and CKSM were present at the Paris Peace Conference after the war ended and may have met. Sadleir had been working at Constable since 1912 and would become a director in 1920.) CKSM then went on to propose Proust to Chatto & Windus, who in 1921 agreed to publish an English translation and paid him a generous advance for the first volume. Henry Holt would be the American publisher and, as it later turned out, a solid ally. Proust himself would see only this first installment. He wrote to CKSM just five weeks before his death in 1922, admitting that he had not read the entire book ("my English is

---

* There is some evidence that oral sex with multiple partners may be linked to cancers of the throat. Lacking medical records from the time, Findlay's contention is a theory rather than a proven fact.

so appalling") and complimenting the publishers while complaining about the English title both of the overall work and of *Swann's Way* ("If you had added the word 'to' you would have saved everything").

Proust would occupy CKSM for the remainder of his life, but he was not the only author to attract his attention. He translated several books by Stendhal, including *The Charterhouse of Parma* and *The Red and the Black*, as well as the letters of Heloise and Abelard. He also became devoted to Pirandello whom, unlike his other authors, he was able to meet and befriend. At one point he seriously considered translating Pirandello's entire output, a massive oeuvre that included even then (he did not die until 1936) hundreds of short stories, many novels and plays, and several volumes of poetry. In the end CKSM translated just three of Pirandello's books, and copyright issues made even that limited work complicated and something of an endurance test. Those books did not sell well, leading CKSM to mutter to his publisher that "the trouble is that English people won't read a book that requires the slightest effort." All of this work did pay off in one sense, establishing him as a well-known *littérateur* and supporting his modest but not pinched lifestyle. When asked at a luncheon once what he did, he replied, "I *bite rooks*—I mean, I translate books." But in the late 1920s, as he approached forty, he began to feel ill and was already, in Findlay's possibly exaggerated view, "old in spirit" and "cantankerous." The day before his fortieth birthday he described himself as "creeping gradually into my grave," and shortly thereafter an X-ray found a growth in his neck that was eventually diagnosed as terminal cancer. Famous friends, including Chesterton, Richard Aldington, and Evelyn Waugh (who had at one time aspired to be CKSM's secretary), visited him at his deathbed in a Roman hospital. He died on February 28, 1930.

While one might on principle be distrustful of a biography written by a descendant of the subject, Jean Findlay avoids any sort of historical favouritism, even, at one summing-up point, seemingly complimenting CKSM as at once a great military leader and "a great pansy," a word that may well have been in use in her subject's prime and (by her testimony) used with affection by a great friend of his, but which now has surely acquired too much of a derogatory luster to be useful any longer. And what, one wonders, is a great pansy anyway? She makes a good case for CKSM's minority view of World War I as a war of honour, even in this centenary-year-plus-one when the vast majority of new histories and reprinted memoirs look back on that war as little more than a vast and savage waste of human life and a con on the common soldier, with doubtful if not tragic outcomes in Germany and the Middle East. While one often wonders with biographies just how the writer knows a certain detail of observation or setting or speech, Findlay has had such a detailed and extensive archive to work with that one is never in doubt about whether she is imagining the details that make a life come alive. When, for example, her subject met Sinclair Lewis and his wife and young son on a train in Italy in 1923 and spent the day with them, we learn that they stopped at Padua to see the frescoes at the chapel of the Madonna dell'Arena, and that CKSM read from his translation of Proust's description of the art as they walked around, before taking dinner at a café that CKSM described amusingly in a letter as "open all night like Paul Morand." Such detail makes *Chasing Lost Time* an absorbing account of CKSM's life and a pleasure to read.

Findlay gets a few things wrong, and is guilty of a more significant offence. She underwhelmingly describes Ada Leverson as someone who corresponded with Oscar Wilde and was "known for her connections... with [him]," when in fact Leverson was not just a good friend, but the friend who took Wilde in when most of his friends abandoned him in the wake of the 1895 arrest. She refers at one point to D. H. Lawrence's "autobiography," although as far as I know, Lawrence never wrote or published such a work. She gets the title of the second volume of CKSM's Proust wrong once, calling it *In a Budding Grove*, rather than *Within a Budding Grove*, and I rather wish she had explained what "s.a.w." was, beyond telling us in a note that it was the code used by CKSM and

Vyvyan Holland for fellatio. More seriously, Findlay has reproduced word for word three sentences from Wikipedia in summarizing the history of Winchester College.* Wikipedia is an irresistible source of general information for writers needing background on a subject germane to but not at the centre of their work, and few can stop themselves from at least consulting it. The link between consultation and unacknowledged quotation is an easy one to comprehend, even when it constitutes an unconscious act, but for all that not really forgivable.

Despite having learned French as a child from a nanny, CKSM claimed insouciantly to have little grammar and less vocabulary, and friends testified to his sometimes rather louche work habits. Giuseppi Orioli, the publisher of the first edition of *Lady Chatterley's Lover* (a book which CKSM thought vile and dirty-minded) bore witness to "Charles's translation method [as] a casual part of daily life":

> He carried in his left hand the French volume he was translating, read a few lines of it, interrupted his reading in order to talk to me, and then took a notebook out of his pocket and wrote in English the few lines he had just read, leaning against a pine tree.

It seems unlikely that anyone could manage to get through well over a million words of Proust in this charmingly unfocused manner, and CKSM must also have spent a good deal of time in the more formal pose of a translator at work, huddled over a desk with the *Grand Robert* and other dictionaries and reference works at hand. It has often been pointed out that he made errors, introduced alternative wordings, expanded here and trimmed there, and sometimes made Proust's sentences more serpentine and anfractuous than they are in French. But

---

* The passage in Findlay's book is this: "... Winchester College was founded in 1382 by William of Wykeham, Bishop of Winchester and Chancellor to both Edward III and Richard II.... The first 70 'poor scholars' entered the school in 1394. It was founded in conjunction with New College, Oxford, for which it was designed to act as a feeder."

it is by his *Remembrance of Things Past* that CKSM will be, well, remembered; for the beauty of its prose and its almost unerring evocation of Proust's worlds, both inner and outer, make it one of the greatest of all English translations. Here are a few sentences from the opening paragraph of Part Two of *Cities of the Plain*:

> The moon was now in the sky like a section of an orange delicately peeled though slightly bruised. But a few hours later it was to be fashioned of the most enduring gold. Nestling alone behind it, a poor little star was to serve as sole companion to the lonely moon, while the latter, keeping its friend protected but striding ahead more boldly, would brandish like an irresistible weapon, like an oriental symbol, its broad, magnificent golden crescent.

John Sturrock, who translated *Sodom and Gomorrah* for the new Penguin version, does well with this passage too, but his "delicately peeled but with a small bite out of it" seems to me to break the magic of the description, and his "made of the most resistant gold" has less evocativeness than CKSM's slightly more formal use of "fashioned" and "enduring." The argument as to the respective merits of CKSM's Proust and Penguin's Proust will never be settled, but certainly there is much to be said for the entire work, or most of the entire work, coming into English through the typewriter and pen of a single translator rather than a group of seven translators. Like William Adlington's version of *The Golden Ass* or Chapman's Homer, CKSM's Proust will always be read because it is Proust and because it is CKSM, a supple, at times demanding, and always brilliant work of English literature.

THE UNIVERSE IS
SO VERY MARVELLOUS;
OR, WHAT YOU HAVE
DONE, ODYSSEUS

D avid Moody's recently completed biography of Ezra Pound is so much more than the "portrait" of his title; or if it is a portrait, Pound's face or person is set on a canvas that is both vast and finely detailed. At over 1,700 pages, divided into three volumes, the work makes even its bespoke blurbs seem atrociously modest. Leon Edel's biography of Henry James may be longer, and Robert Crawford's in-progress study of T. S. Eliot's life may come close when finished, in scope and detail, to the magisterial quality of Moody. But *Ezra Pound: Poet* will surely stand for a long time as one of the great literary biographies; it is inconceivable to imagine that any other life of its subject will be necessary into the far future.

Even now, over forty years after his death, Pound remains a writer who provokes strong opinions both pro and contra. In an essay reprinted in his recent collection *Poetry Notebook*, Clive James, for example, dismisses *The Cantos* as "a nut-job blog before the fact."* Moody is very

---

* Clive James, *Poetry Notebook: Reflections on the Intensity of Language* (New York: Picador, 2015), p. 30.

clearly on Pound's side—to write so extensive a book about someone with whom one is essentially out of sympathy would make no sense except as extreme penance—without ever attempting to whitewash the poet's faults as a human being and a writer. The work is fair-handed, then. Moody carefully documents the various Pound cruces—his fascism, his anti-Semitism, his mental state at various times, his relationships with women—and his opinions always rest on precise and extensive research in the archives. (The notes section in the concluding volume extends to just over 100 pages.) He is critical, even deeply critical, when criticism is warranted; but on balance, he would unhesitatingly vote for Pound as a major poet—finally one of the central questions in a biography of any poet. He is also convinced that Pound was neither a fascist nor a traitor, and that the legal shapeshifting that got him sent to St. Elizabeths Hospital was "a travesty of psychiatry and justice." These views are stated baldly on the first page of the final volume; in the welter of detail that will follow, we always know where Moody stands on the key issues.

The third and last volume of Moody's work covers the years from 1939 until Pound's death in 1972.* Moody's subtitle (*The Tragic Years*) is entirely apt, for as every reader of poetry knows, Pound's wartime activities in Italy led to his arrest in 1945 and a charge of treason against the United States, a capital crime at the time (and still).† Pound was ultimately not forced to stand trial and was instead warehoused (to use the contemporary slang expression) in a mental hospital in Washington, D.C., where, among the criminally insane and the incurably ill, he made a life and went on with his work until 1958, when the charges were finally dropped and he was allowed to return to Italy. In

---

* A. David Moody, *Ezra Pound: Poet: A Portrait of the Man and His Work. Vol. 3: The Tragic Years, 1939–1972* (Oxford: Oxford University Press, 2015).

† An earlier biography of Pound had used the same subtitle for a much larger slice of Pound's life. See J. J. Wilhelm, *Ezra Pound: The Tragic Years, 1925–1972* (University Park: Pennsylvania State University Press, 1994).

Italy he gradually lapsed into ill health and depression and stopped writing altogether, his final years perhaps best captured by the well-known anecdote concerning his comment during a performance he was present at of Beckett's *Fin de partie:* "Ç'est moi dans la poubelle." That's me in the trash can. By that time (1967), the *Cantos* were long over, more abandoned than completed; some eight years earlier Pound had described himself as "a blown husk that is finished." It was an immensely sad coda to an astonshing life.

"The tragic years" began in 1939 with the outbreak of the European war that coincided with Pound's maturing obsessions about money and economics generally. His convictions that usury was the root cause of war, or at any rate would be the root cause of this war, and that the United States should stay out of it, eventuated in his becoming what Moody calls "a dutifully dissident exile," with radio talks from Rome directed at America beginning in 1941 that often contained anti-Semitic remarks but never openly counselled American troops to revolt. At one point he was being paid 11,000 lire per month for his broadcasts, although he was careful to maintain that this was not a salary but a kind of honorarium. As he had in *Guide to Kulchur* (1938), at this time Pound was still pushing the value of the Greek and Roman classics, unlikely as that obsession now seems in those circumstances. To the head of the Fascist Ministry of Popular Culture, Fernando Mezzasoma, Pound wrote in late 1944, that all Italian scholars should read the classics "so as to find therein the reason the enemy wants to suppress or diminish the studies of the sources of our culture and our political wisdom." His use of the word "enemy" was both correct and worrisome, of course. Pound sent Mezzasoma some Italian translations of various of the *Cantos*, probably made by his daughter, Mary, which he thought might be "useful." These activities—going to bat for Aristotle and Virgil and sending a Fascist minister his own poetry—seem more innocent, even simple-minded now, than traitorous. They are the actions not of a crackpot but of a naïf. No less so is the interview that Pound had in

1933 with Mussolini, a phrase of which he recorded in canto 41: "'Ma questo,' / said the Boss, 'è divertente.' / catching the point before the aesthetes had got there." Not really. Pound made far too much of that word "divertente" (funny, amusing); and although in retrospect one may be disgusted at the thought of a major American poet consorting with Mussolini, the naiveté is in truth not so much revolting as merely saddening. It took Pound a lifetime to learn that "nothing matters but the quality / of the affection— / in the end—that has carved the trace in the mind" (canto 76).

When Pound was transferred from FBI custody to the infamous DTC (Disciplinary Training Center) of the *Pisan Cantos* on May 24, 1945, his shoelaces, belt, and tie were removed to ensure that he did not try to commit suicide, something that would surely never have occurred to him. Moody tells us that the DTC at that time housed 3,500 "insubordinates, deserters, gangsters, murderers, rapists, thieves," and one famous poet. Pound was confined there until mid-November, when he was flown to Washington to face treason charges. His lawyer, Julien Cornell, who was brought into the Pound case by James Laughlin, Pound's publisher, would later claim that the poet "lost his memory" in the Pisan cage and that he experienced a three-month period of "violent insanity" there. Moody is no fan of Mr. Cornell, his plan to have Pound declared mentally unfit to stand trial, and the book he later wrote about the case, *The Trial of Ezra Pound* (1967). With a modicum of overkill he labels Cornell's view that Pound was crazy as "this deliberately false fiction," although he does allow for the fact that Cornell would not have been able to read *The Pisan Cantos* (not published until 1948) and that Pound himself did not fight against his lawyer's chosen line of defence. Had Cornell read the poems written in the DTC he could not possibly have thought that Pound's memory was affected by his incarceration in the cage. Memory, as has been pointed out by many critics and noticed by every reader of *The Pisan Cantos*, is what saved him from mental collapse; and if his manumission from the cage left him with any lingering psychiatric problem it was nothing worse than claustrophobia, as a newspaper report of his hearing on November 27, 1945, pointed out. The poems themselves, whatever else they are, constitute an extraordinary archive of Pound's personal recollections and his reading over a period of fifty years, all evoked without benefit of records or books to consult. Pound touchingly describes himself there as "a man on whom the sun has gone down" and applies to himself Odysseus's pointedly deceptive self-description as Οὖτις, "No One." "Yet hath his mind entire," he might have added, to cite his own translation of the phrase from the *Odyssey* describing Tiresias in Hades with which canto 47 opens.

While he waited for his insanity hearing, Pound was sent to St. Elizabeths, an institution then housing almost 7,000 patients, where he was at first confined to Howard Hall, "the maximum security ward for the most dangerous and violent of the criminally insane," in Moody's words. He was put under the care of a young psychiatrist, Dr Jerome Kavka, who, among other things, had Pound take the Rorschach inkblot test. It revealed little that was surprising—"marked pedantry" makes one smile and "marked aggression in interpersonal relations" could have been borne witness to by any number of Pound's friends, never mind his enemies. "Oligophrenic responses" probably meant little more than disinterest on Pound's part in the whole process. Moody quotes extensively from archival transcripts in narrating the insanity hearing, at which the basic argument for Pound was that a trial "would be rather dangerous to his welfare," as one psychiatrist phrased it. The jury required just three minutes to come to the unanimous opinion that Pound was of "unsound mind." Pound's friends present at the hearing— Laughlin and Charles Olson among them—were happy with the outcome. Moody by contrast quotes Thomas Szasz's opinion that the Pound hearing "placed a blot on the pages of contemporary American history." His own view is that Pound's incarceration at a mental hospital represented nothing less than a "lasting miscarriage of justice."

So began Pound's twelve years of life "in jug," as he put it to Wyndham Lewis. (He also called his new home "the bughouse.") After a year in Howard Hall ("the hell hole"), Pound was moved to a different ward, where he had a larger room and had to contend less with seriously mentally ill fellow patients. He also began to have guests and visitors, and many famous and aspiring writers, poets, academics, and groupies of all kinds joined Dorothy Pound on the lawn during the afternoons when Pound was receiving. (Some time slots he reserved for special visitors.) And he worked—at his translation of the Confucian Odes and of two Greek plays, and at *Rock-Drill* and *Thrones*, the two sections of *The Cantos* that come after *The Pisan Cantos*. Moody points out how odd it is that what he calls the "twenty-five St. Elizabeths cantos" contain so little of Pound's actual life at the hospital:

> Their world is made up out of books, and so immersed is the poet in his reading and in his making that his actual world is indeed blotted out. The reader can easily forget where Pound was as he wrote them. *

Perhaps this was a necessary psychological strategy for the poet. In any case it represented a major shift from the cantos written in the DTC, which combine Pound's usual wide body of quotation and allusion with resolutely personal confession and emotional outcries. That potent combination is part of the reason that *The Pisan Cantos* won the Bollingen Prize, to considerable scandal and outcry. ("All hell did break loose" is Moody's summation of the public response to Pound's winning the prize.) Neither of the two succeeding sections of Pound's long poem was likely ever to win a prize. They were written, as Moody says, "for the few, and the non-specialists are in effect bidden to occupy themselves meanwhile with the tea and cake."† Of course moments of naked speech do

---

* Moody, op. cit., p. 346.
† Ibid., p. 350.

flash through the extensive citations in Chinese and Greek, as when Pound, in canto 95, speaks of "Love, gone as lightning, / enduring 5000 years" and acknowledges that "there is something decent in the universe / if I can feel all this, *dicto millesimo* / At the age of whatever." (That "whatever" sounds peculiarly contemporary.) But overall, the sign over the portal to the St. Elizabeths cantos reads "Lasciate ogni speranza" if you have not read the right books, and obscure ones they often are at that. Carroll F. Terrell's annotations to canto 89 include fourteen major sources in addition to works by Dante and Sophocles, not to mention a further extensive list of "background" reading. His explicatory entry on this canto runs to twenty-six pages.*

Almost from the start of Pound's exile at St. Elizabeths, efforts began to be made to have him released. Old literary friends like William Carlos Williams, Archibald MacLeish, Ernest Hemingway, T. S. Eliot (from a distance), and others often conspired to have the US government drop the charges so that Pound could resume a normal life. They wrote letters and they published attestations. In the end it was Robert Frost, who had reservations about Pound as a person and as a poet, but who had good connections in the Eisenhower administration (he apparently called himself "a Grover Cleveland Democrat") and was friendly with Attorney General William P. Rogers, who helped to spring the lock. A motion was filed in April 1958 to have the indictment against Pound dismissed, and so it was. Pound remained without legal status and the psychiatric evaluation that labelled him insane was not changed; but he was free to leave the asylum and to return to Italy. The latter was something of a surprise, as even his most faithful and industrious supporters had always doubted that he would ever get his passport back. As Moody writes, Pound "was now a medical case requiring a compassionate judgment."† On June 30, 1958, Pound together

---

* Carroll F. Terrell, *A Companion to the Cantos of Ezra Pound* (Berkeley: University of California Press, 1984), pp. 513–539.
† Moody, op. cit., p. 428.

with his wife and his young admirer Marcella Spann sailed for Italy. The coda to his life had begun.

Moody spends a brief seventy pages on the last fourteen years of Pound's life. *The Cantos* came to an end in mere fragments only a year after Pound settled back in Italy, and he gradually sank into what Dorothy called "self-abasement," long stretches of silence, depression, and ill health. Old friends died (Hemingway, Eliot, Dag Hammarskjöld, H.D.), further contributing to his bleak view of things. Amidst so much that he felt to be grim he could still tell a journalist "The universe is so very marvellous," but on the whole these years were, as Moody bluntly calls them, an afterlife. He underwent a prostatectomy and in the mid-1960s was prescribed amitryptyline, an antidepressant that had been approved by the USDA only in 1961. Olga Rudge thought that the drug made Pound worse. His last years were spent living with Olga in Venice, and when they attended Stravinsky's funeral there in the spring of 1971, it must have felt like a dress rehearsal. Like Stravinsky and Diaghilev, Pound would be buried in the "Stranieri" section of the cemetery on San Michele, the Venetian isle of the dead. A simple stone plaque marks his grave.

David Moody, while clearly devoted as a biographer to defending Pound's honour, especially where the crucial stains on the poet's reputation are concerned, has above all made his book a work of the most profound scholarship. All events and opinions are solidly documented, and Moody never blushes at the expression of hard truths. Dorothy Pound is shown to have been manipulative and self-centred, and there is no doubt that she did everything she could to make sure that Pound's estate benefited Omar Pound (her son, but not Pound's) rather than Mary de Rachewiltz (Pound's daughter, but not hers). She is quoted as saying brutally that Pound's incarceration at St. Elizabeths gave her some relief: "At least I know where he's sleeping tonight." (This remark, or one very similar to it, is often attributed to Queen Alexandra, when informed that her husband, Edward VII, had died; one should not put too much faith in its accuracy.) James Laughlin and Julien Cornell, heroes in some tellings of the Pound saga, are portrayed less as staunch friends and protectors than as ultimately responsible for Pound's twelve-year stay "in jug," almost certainly a longer term than would have been the case had Pound been found guilty of treason and put in jail. (Iva Toguri D'Aquino, "Tokyo Rose," whose case was very similar to Pound's, was sentenced to a ten-year prison term, but was released after just six years. The treason statute demanded "not less than five years;" and while execution was also a possible sentence, it is highly unlikely that Pound would have been shot.) Moody leaves out little. We learn, to our despair, that during World War II Pound read and recommended to friends both *Mein Kampf* and *The Protocols of the Elders of Zion*. But to our amusement and pleasure, we also learn that, during that same war, with a shortage of both butter and oil plaguing Italy, Pound was pressing peanut butter and the growing of peanuts on his Italian friends. By contrast, Moody does occasionally have to plead ignorance. There is, for example, the case of Sheri Martinelli, a young bohemian artist with whom Pound fell in love in the 1950s after she began visiting him at the hospital. Were they lovers? Moody's admission is a simple and refreshing "God knows."

Moody's critical skills as a reader of Pound's poetry, while exercised at relatively short length, are always keen and on the mark. Each of the four sections of *The Cantos* that date to "the tragic years"—*The Pisan Cantos*, *Rock-Drill*, *Thrones*, and *Drafts and Fragments*—receives a short reading, and all benefit from Moody's critical attention. During an interview that Pound gave to Pier Paolo Pasolini in 1968, he was at pains to dispel the common view that the quotations found in *The Cantos* were chosen more or less at random. No, Pound said, it was "music. Musical themes that find each other out."* Moody no doubt has that remark in mind when he finds evidence of musical organization in *The*

---

* Quoted in Moody, op. cit., p. 505.

Pisan Cantos, for he employs a good deal of musical vocabulary in his analysis: overture, scherzo, counterpoint, counter-subject, verbal music, et cetera. About the daunting difficulties of *Rock-Drill* and *Thrones*, Moody is realistic: a reader must either become fluent in Pound's sources or "move on to the cantos that are accessible to the non-expert."* *Drafts and Fragments* is viewed as a return to the personal cast that had made *The Pisan Cantos* so admirable and moving. While it is painful to see Pound stagger and fall, as the *Drafts and Fragments* too obviously record, the passages of simple beauty predominate and remain in the mind:

> *No dog, no horse, and no goat,*
> *The long flank, the firm breast*
> > *and to know beauty and death and despair*
> *and to think that what has been shall be*
> > *flowing, ever unstill. (canto 113)*

Moody characterizes the final cantos as embodying "a radical reorientation" in their emphasis on "immediate personal experience."† Even as Pound's work came to an end, he made sure to leave the traces of his heart: "Give light against falling poison!"

In the preface to the concluding volume of his biography, David Moody asks a question that every reader of Pound's work must perforce confront: Can a man who at times said vile things and held abominable opinions also write lasting poetry? His answer, not surprisingly, is a determined yes, although he phrases it rather oddly. Pound's poetry, he says, "is of enduring utility."‡ Utility? That hardly seems the right word, except perhaps for other poets, even if Pound himself, like Olson and Creeley in his wake, was never shy of speaking about "use." Enduring beauty is more like it. Pound uttered and enacted

---

* Ibid., p. 353.
† Ibid., p. 449.
‡ Ibid., p. xiv.

despicable notions, he experienced pain and harsh life conditions and emotional trauma—"more knowledge of his fate than any man should have" were Robert Lowell's sympathetic words—and he composed some of the greatest poetry of his time. Moody's accomplished and compellingly fascinating portrait demonstrates these paradoxical truths beyond any reasonable doubt.

DREAM OF FAIR
TO MIDDLING POETRY

s it ridiculous, in the year 2015, to give Samuel Beckett as poet a mixed, even a negative review? While it would be no more seemingly ill conceived, from our later vantage point, than the reviews his poetry received in the early years of his career—they were mostly uncomprehending or dismissive—nevertheless he did later win universal fame and the Nobel Prize, primarily as a novelist and playwright, admittedly. Beckett himself was unsure at various times of the value of his poetry. The year before George Reavey published his first collection of poems, *Echo's Bones and Other Precipitates* (Europa Press, 1935), Beckett wrote to his friend A. J. Leventhal and admitted ashamedly, "My poems are worthless." Of course a poet experiencing a *crise de confidence* is hardly unusual; and Beckett, almost thirty and with only the slimmest of slim pamphlets yet to his credit (*Whoroscope*, 1930), can be forgiven for doubting himself beneath the cloak of privacy of a personal letter. In an earlier letter to Thomas MacGreevy, Beckett dismissed much of his poetry with a more nuanced view, saying that it was mostly what he called in French *facultatif*, by which he meant it was the product of his will rather than of emotional necessity. "I would have been no worse off for not having written it. Is that a very hairless way of thinking of poetry?" he asked in the letter.* He then goes on to characterize poetry that is optional or unnecessary (i.e., *facultatif*) as Jesuitical, and cites Mallarmé's work as an example.

Poetry is not the genre Beckett is best remembered or most often read for—the editors of a new edition of his *Collected Poems* call poetry "this most neglected part of Beckett's oeuvre"—and in the end it would not bulk large in his output. This new edition contains just 250 pages of poetry, and a good deal of that consists of translations from French and Spanish.† Yet his final composition was a poem, and poetry's concisions and excisions clearly had a determining influence on his evolving minimalist theatrical aesthetic. As long ago as 1970, the critic Lawrence E. Harvey saw in Beckett's poetry "the manifesto of the prose and drama to come,"‡ by which he meant everything after *Watt* (1953). In conversations with Harvey in 1962, Beckett had allowed himself to praise poems of his own such as "Moly"; even earlier, before those first poems had accrued the rosy hue bestowed by time, he could say of "Serena I," one of the poems in his first collection, that it was "*très émouvant*."§ A woman called Nuala Costello, whom Beckett met in Paris through James Joyce's children, Lucia and Giorgio, was sent a rather strange and somewhat repellent poem in a letter in February 1934. This poem, entitled "Seats of Honour," was only published for the first time in the initial volume of the Beckett *Letters* in 2009 and has not formed part of his poetic corpus until this new version of his *Collected Poems*. After confessing that the poem has not been well received generally, he says at first, "I don't care much for it myself." "But," he goes on, "that it is a poem and not verse, that it is a prayer

---

* Letter of October 18, 1932, in *The Letters of Samuel Beckett, Vol. 1: 1929–1940*, eds. Martha Dow Fehsenfeld and Lois More Overbeck (Cambridge, UK: Cambridge University Press, 2009), p. 133.

† Samuel Beckett, *The Collected Poems*, ed. Seán Lawlor and John Pilling (New York: Grove Press, 2012). The cited words are from the preface, p. xvii.

‡ Lawrence E. Harvey, *Samuel Beckett: Poet and Critic* (Princeton: Princeton University Press, 1970), p. x.

§ Both comments are noted in the "Commentary" to *The Collected Poems*, pp. 283, 301.

and not a collect, I have not the slightest doubt, not the slightest."* Lawlor and Pilling denominate this as Beckett's earliest statement allying poetry and prayer. Prayer seems an almost freakish alliance for Beckett to invoke, given the intensely bleak and godless world that was to become his regular territory. Is prayer or even God what Beckett the poet stammers at in "what is the word," his last poem, where whatever it is that is glimpsed (barely, it seems) remains unspoken? The poem's longest line—"folly for to need to seem to glimpse afaint far away over there what—"—never quite lets us know for certain.

Beckett's poetry evolved significantly. His deep involvement in the Joyce circle when he was still in his early twenties and just starting to write poetry, and when Joyce himself was working on *Finnegans Wake*, left an imprint on the early poems that is unmistakable and not especially happy. "Whoroscope," which infamously was written in an evening in order to meet a contest deadline, is the product of a recently post-adolescent mind stuffed with learning and jocularity and determined to mime the techniques of "Work in Progress," as Joyce's final novel was then known:

> *Fallor, ergo sum!*
> *The coy lecher!*
> *He tolle'd and legge'd*
> *and he buttoned across a redemptorist cardigan.*
> *Very well, then:*
> *I'm a bold boy, I know,*
> *so I'm not my son*
> *(even supposing I were a concierge)*
> *nor Joachim my father's*
> *but the chip of a perfect block that is neither old nor new,*
> *the lonely petal of a high bright rose.*

---

* *The Letters of Samuel Beckett*, op. cit., p. 188.

The combination of philosophy (Descartes, the poem's subject), religion (St. Augustine), the everyday and the spiritual (that Redemptorist sweater), the obscene (Beckett liked the word "concierge," since he heard in it the two French slang words for the male and female sex organs), together with what feels like a line from a Celtic Revival poem ("the lonely petal of a high bright rose") is commonplace in Joyce and is here recreated in Beckett's syncretic fantasy. Fifteen years later Beckett wrote "Saint-Lô," a brief poem about a bombed-out town that is highly thought of: four different critics have called it his "masterpiece." It is a minor piece, really, three lines of trochaic tetrameter with a shortened final line, but the language, at least, is far more authentic and forceful than the learned sillinesses of "Whoroscope:"

> *Vire will wind in other shadows*
> *unborn through the bright ways tremble*
> *and the old mind ghost-forsaken*
> *sink into its havoc*

And then there is the poetry of Beckett's last phase, minimalist, austere, mostly unpunctuated and uncapitalized, seemingly spoken in the teeth of a deep unwillingness to speak at all. Theatre can be wordless and still have power (witness the two plays called *Act Without Words*), but poetry cannot attain that seeming endpoint. Beckett almost gets there, as his final poem (quoted briefly above) stutters into that space where there is nothing left to say. "what is the word" begins in this way:

> *folly -*
> *folly for to -*
> *for to -*
> *what is the word -*
> *folly from this -*
> *all this -*

> *folly from all this -*
> *given -*
> *folly given all this -*
> *seeing -*
> *folly seeing all this -*

The poem continues for another forty-two lines, consistently in this aphasic style, ending inconclusively in two restatements of the title phrase. There is no poetry that can follow. This is poetry's *consummatum est.*

Canonization tends to bring hierophants and scholiasts in its wake, and as a younger member of that generation we think of as the great modernists, Beckett, like Joyce, Pound, Eliot, and others, has had and continues to attract his fair share. The Beckett industry, more bluntly put, thrives. The 250 pages of poetry in the new *Collected Poems* are matched almost page for page by an extensive exegetical text by the editors, and on the whole it is a vastly learned and enormously helpful commentary. Like Servius on Virgil or Cristoforo Landino on Dante, Lawlor and Pilling have compiled thousands of detailed notes on Beckett's poetic corpus. They explain Irishisms (e.g., "skinnymalinks"), scholarly and literary allusions (to a bewildering array of writers, philosophers, et al.), rare words (e.g. "litibule," "supplejack"), and phrases and words from foreign languages (e.g., "*algor*," "*Hochzeit*," "*kakoethes*"). It is pleasant to learn that, like Keats, Beckett absorbed some of his classical mythology from Lemprière's *Dictionary*. The editors are assiduous about comparative material (Beckett's use of X will remind them of Y and Z and sometimes A through D as well), and extraordinarily thorough about the manuscript and publication histories of each poem. Alternative and variant readings are given exhaustively. The notes mostly do not stray into the evaluative territory of the literary critic, although occasionally Lawlor and Pilling cannot help themselves. "Spring Song," for example, a hermetic effusion from 1932 that has not appeared in print until its inclusion here, is characterized as "SB at his most obscure" and as a poem which "it is difficult to believe...gave Beckett much satisfaction."* This is slightly dangerous ground, given that poets often mistake the worth of their work, thinking good poems bad and bad poems good. Constant reference to the first two volumes of the Beckett *Letters* is made, as well as to a long list of studies, bibliographies, biographies, and other incarnations of Beckett scholarship.

There are a few errors, but this is no surprise given the length and detailed nature of the commentary. (A poem entitled "Malacoda," for example, has almost three pages of commentary and annotation, including references to Dante's *De monarchia*, Beethoven's final string quartet, *The Book of Common Prayer*, a painting by Jan van Huysum at the National Gallery in London, and much else besides.) The mistakes that caught my attention are minor: a botched citation of the Latin tag *de mortuis nil nisi bonum*, a reference to 1 Corinthians 16:42 when chapter 15 is meant (p. 295), a reference to a "famous group of melodies by Debussy" (they mean songs, *mélodies* being the French equivalent of *Lieder* or art songs, p. 330), the misdating of the Lisbon earthquake to 1756 (p. 383), and the misreading of "pia/Mater" as "ecclesiastical," when Beckett, who knew Osler's *Principles and Practice of Medicine*, probably just meant the brain (p. 391). These are relatively insignificant inaccuracies in so vast a commentary. Some of the comparative material seemed to me unnecessary and occasionally remote. Did Beckett really have a poem by Joachim du Bellay in mind when, in a French poem, he wrote simply "il a fait un voyage"? In annotating the word "sorrow" in a poem called "To Be Sung Aloud," every use of the same word in other Beckett texts is adduced as somehow relevant for so common a word, pushing the commentary toward a concordance. Occasionally too, the interpretive annotations are somewhat *de trop*. The word "and" in "Saint-Lô" elicits this comment:

---

* *Collected Poems*, p. 331.

"and" is not merely the neutral connective it might seem to be, but in its "weak" way reinforces the feeling of one thing necessarily following hard upon another in a consequential chain impossible to break or escape from.

Fortunately this sort of philological gibberish is rare in Lawlor and Pilling's work, which on the whole provides all the assistance a dedicated reader of Beckett's poems requires, without overwhelming the texts.

If Beckett, especially in middle and later life, found it difficult to write literary and dramatic texts, letters seem never to have been a problem for him. The editorial team which has been working on an edition of a selection of his letters since as early as 1985 has located an astonishing 20,000 letters in public repositories and private collections all over the world, ranging in date from 1929 (when Beckett was twenty-three) to 1989, the year of his death. Beckett himself, despite his well-known reticence about his private life and his disinclination ever to comment on his own work or on the work of scholars ("I do not like publication of letters," he wrote to Alan Schneider in 1958), surprisingly gave his blessing to a letters project, provided that the letters chosen were devoted not to drinking parties and erotic shenanigans, but to his work. The editors, however, understand that even a modest non-literary letter can sometimes constitute a work of art in itself (as indeed some of them do). They have decided, wisely, that even an innocuous confession of a hangover or the lyrical narrative of birds in spring chattering outside the window of Beckett's cottage in Ussy-sur-Marne, about an hour from Paris in his day (in his Citroën *deux chevaux*), could have literary merit and textual significance. The project editors have chosen about 20 percent of the recorded letters to publish in an edition comprising four volumes, covering the years 1929–1940, 1941–1956, 1957–1965, and 1966–1989. The third volume has just appeared, and like its two predecessors, this book contains almost 800 pages.* The apparatus is truly astounding. All letters are located and extensively annotated, often with detailed notes that in themselves are minor models of detection and even scholarship. A reference in passing by Beckett to having heard Elisabeth Schwarzkopf sing in 1958 yields a footnote identifying the place and date of the recital; and a letter to Hugh Kenner primarily about a French cyclist named Roger Godeau provokes a longer footnote with a detailed identification of the man and his achievements. Few names have eluded the annotators' archaeological excavations, and many notes quote from letters not themselves printed in the volume to give context to those that are, as well as from other sources, Robert Pinget's unpublished "Journal" in the Bibliothèque Littéraire Jacques Doucet in Paris among them.

Perhaps the most striking characteristic of this third volume of Beckett's *Letters* is its continuous witness to a paradox: the writer's great public success during these years coexisted with unending self-doubt, even revulsion at his own work. The years 1957–1965 included the writing of texts that are part of his enduring legacy: the plays *Endgame*, *Krapp's Last Tape*, and *Happy Days*; most of the work he wrote for radio; his only film (*Film*, starring Buster Keaton); a first collection of his English poems; and the novel that followed his earlier trilogy, *How It Is/Comment c'est*. The creation of *How It Is* (written first in French and translated later) is intimately documented in his letters, and it was an astonishingly painful creative process. Over the two-year period of its gestation Beckett wrote constantly of his uncertainty about the book and his disgust at his own writing habits. The evidence is everywhere in the letters: "There are two worthwhile moments in my work: the opening up and the [waste paper] basketing" (to Jacoba van Velde). "I am in acute crisis about my work (on the lines familiar

---

* *The Letters of Samuel Beckett. Volume III: 1957–1965*, ed. George Craig, Marth Dow Fehsenfeld, Dab Gunn, and Lois More Overbeck (Cambridge: Cambridge University Press, 2014).

to you by now) and have decided that I not merely can't but won't go on as I have been going more or less ever since the Textes pour Rien" (to Barbara Bray). "Relief to fly from this Pim hell" ("Pim" being an early provisional title for How It Is; again to Barbara Bray). "I have just finished [my book]. Stopped it, rather. It is no beauty" (to Jacoba van Velde). *Je crois que cette fois je me suis à peu près coupé la gorge enfin. J'hésite encore à le rendre public* (I believe that this time I have finally just about cut my throat. I still hesitate about making it public; to Robert Pinget). When the book was finally published in early 1961, Beckett's reaction seems to have been one of absolute apathy: "Total indifference to its coming into world and reception, never look at it again" (to Barbara Bray). In fact, Beckett was not entirely indifferent. He followed the reviews, and was rather pleased to be told that a first printing of 3,000 copies of Comment c'est sold out and a second printing had to be ordered only two months after publication.

Along with many specific *cris de cœur* about his work in this volume are many other generally bleak comments about life and letters. The earth itself is a "bitch" and a "turd" and, in response to news that a good friend was dying of cancer, it's finally the "fucking fucking earth." More than once he writes that it would give him pleasure to have a full day to spend digging a series of holes in the ground, filling each with the dirt from the subsequent one as he went along. He confesses to lassitude, to sheer laziness, to drinking too much, to "[feeling] utterly abolished," to a conviction that attention to his work is "unmerited" and that "people keep giving me money for vinegar." Productions of his plays annoy and disappoint him more often than not, with actors, designers, technicians, and directors taking their portion of the blame for a failure to bring his plays alive in the way he envisions them. But at the same time, Beckett shows other sides of his sensibility in his letters. He can be funny, consolatory, and brilliantly critical of other writers' work in a helpful manner. The ex-husband of Barbara Bray, his lover or mistress or second partner (the editors admit to the usual uncertainty with the terminology for relationships outside marriage), died in 1958, and Beckett's letter of condolence is touching and beautiful. While in it he claims that he is "not a one to turn to in time of trouble," the final sentence that follows demonstrates the opposite and deserves to be quoted for its beauty and feeling: "Work your head off and sleep at any price and leave the rest to the stream, to carry now away and bring you your other happy days." His sense of humour is largely self-deprecating, but occasionally is directed elsewhere, as when, for example, he writes to Roger Blin about a "Big article on My Nibs" in a scholarly journal that is "in the schullarly style, with links and parallels that would give a dead man a wet dream." As for Beckett's critical acumen, one has only to read his long letter of April 22, 1958, to his South African friend Aidin Higgins, in which he comments on a story that Higgins had sent to him for forwarding to a literary journal. He first makes very specific corrections largely of a typographical sort before continuing on to characterize the story's central weakness as "a kind of straining towards depth and inwardness in certain passages." Higgins later acknowledged that Beckett's critical reading "was more helpful than publication," despite Beckett's avowal that it was "a terrible effort for me to write such stuff and I hope you disagree with it."

As Beckett's fame spread in the 1950s and 1960s his correspondence grew. In 1959 he complained of being "killed with fatuous mail and struggles to write," and the fatuous mail would only grow more onerous as the years wore on, despite the arrangement whereby his publishers in France (Jérôme Lindon), England (John Calder), and the United States (Barney Rosset) doubled as agents and looked after much of the everyday business of contracts and other arrangements. But he bears up and grows, if anything, more personal, open, even warm in his letters through the length and breadth of this volume, providing along the way tremendous grist for the mill of the Beckett scholar and much valuable context for the general reader of his works. The letters to Barbara Bray bulk largest here, and despite his constantly warning her not to expect too much from him (he was in a permanent relationship with Suzanne Dechevaux-Dumesnil at the same time), he gives a great deal of his feelings, while clearly benefiting in return from her emotional ministrations. ("You'd reassure a French horn on a winter Sunday.") When Beckett was in his late twenties and suffering from loneliness and the shock of his father's recent death, he moved to London to undergo psychoanalysis with Wilfred Bion, then a relatively young doctor but later a very well-known writer and analyst. Bion helped Beckett to "counter his self-immersion," as a biographer has put it, "by coming out of himself more in his daily life and taking a livelier interest in others."* The long-term effect of that psychotherapeutic counsel seems embodied most clearly not in Beckett's plays and novels, but in his letters, where it is plain for all to see that the man who wrote such seemingly *in extremis* works as *Not I* and *Play* also had a deeply humane and sympathetic face for his friends and loved ones.

---

* James Knowlson, *Damned to Fame: The Life of Samuel Beckett* (New York: Simon & Schuster, 1996), p. 174.

FULFILLMENT'S
DESOLATE ATTIC

PHILIP LARKIN'S COMPLETE POEMS

The vainglorious and self-congratulatory cynicism of Philip Larkin's poetry can quickly come to seem *de trop*. Life, it proposes, is equally divided between fear (childhood) and boredom (adulthood), and once grown up one is likely to be surrounded by loathsome or pitiful characters in the psychic mode of T. S. Eliot's Sweeney and Edwin Arlington Robinson's Richard Cory. The landscape of most of the poems is the England of the postwar period. Rationing and shortages are the order of the day ("butterless days"), and the country is littered with bad architecture, bad food, and bad lovers with imperfect teeth and National Health glasses who fumble the sexual embrace out of ignorance and embarrassment. ("In our family / Love was disgusting as lavatory. / And not as necessary.") The war had hardened the carapace of the typical Little Englander, and his characteristic xenophobia, racism, and misogyny, all of which Larkin shared, was very much abroad in the land. For Larkin, the prospect of death reigned over all. At only thirty-two, he was already telling a friend in a letter that "the approach and the arrival of death [...] seems [sic] to me the most unforgettable thing about our existence," and at fifty, a short poem entitled "Heads in the Women's Ward" would conclude this way:

> *Sixty years ago they smiled*
> *At lover, husband, first-born child.*
>
> *Smiles are for youth. For old age come*
> *Death's terror and delirium.*

In other words, when he was not being cynical and rather grim, Larkin was usually being pessimistic and rather grim. Grimness pervades his poetry from beginning to end. His dominant theme, he once said in a letter, was "that people will never be unhappy again as we are unhappy— we were born in the very tip of the shadow—Everything I write now seems to come back to this."

Of course if that were the whole story, Larkin would have relatively few readers and could not have attracted the friends and admirers, including scholars, whose devotions have produced the steady stream of studies, editions, collections, and Larkiniana that have appeared since his death in 1985 from esophageal cancer. There are moments in his poems, then, of heart-rending consolation and emotion. Most famous is the concluding line of "An Arundel Tomb" ("What will survive of us is love"), but an uncollected poem entitled "The Mower" ends with advice, unusual for Larkin in being a little maudlin, to be nice:

> *The first day after a death, the new absence*
> *Is always the same; we should be careful*
>
> *Of each other, we should be kind*
> *While there is still time.*

Most people, when they think of Larkin's poetry, tend to think of the infamous opening lines of pieces such as "This Be the Verse" ("They fuck you up, your mum and dad") or "Annus Mirabilis" ("Sexual intercourse began / In nineteen sixty-three"). Yet these deliberately provocative poems, often employing a vocabulary that had only recently been made available to English poets by the lifting of the publication ban on *Lady Chatterley's Lover* in 1960, while they may represent a lifelong strain in Larkin's thinking and talking, again do not tell the whole story. He can be tender in his poems too. He can write prospectively of "the million-petalled flower / Of being here," and realistically if a bit glumly that "Death is no different whined at than withstood." He can also be funny ("'My wife and I—we're pals. Marriage is fun.' / Yes: two can live as stupidly as one"), although too much of the humour in his lesser poems, admittedly not meant by him for publication, is based on racial and gender stereotypes. Some of his grumpiness and misanthropy arose from what he memorably called in an early poem "the instantaneous grief of being alone," a state he clearly associated with death.

Philip Larkin was born in 1922 in Coventry, a medium-sized city in the middle of England. Despite later objecting to a critic's description of his family life as "joyless," he seems to have remembered his childhood with little pleasure. A poem from his second collection, *The Less Deceived*, in which he finds himself unexpectedly driving through the city of his birth, ends dismissively with the line "'Nothing, like something, happens anywhere.'" His father, who was the city treasurer of Coventry, was a supporter of Nazism in Germany (he took the young Larkin there twice for visits in the 1930s), and apparently a small statue of Hitler stood on the Larkin family mantel during the poet's childhood. But the elder Larkin was also an avid reader of modernist poets such as Lawrence, Eliot, and Pound. After reading English at Oxford, Larkin fell into a job as the town librarian in Wellington in Shropshire (A. E. Housman country, happily enough for him), and

subsequently into a lifelong career in librarianship, for which no particular training was then required, that eventually led him to the
University of Hull where he was the head librarian from 1955 until his
death. In all of his jobs (he also held posts at the University College of
Leicester and at Queen's University in Belfast before landing in Hull),
he seems, somewhat surprisingly, to have been an effective adminis-
trator and a pleasant colleague, despite his frequent characterization
of work as "the toad" in his poems. (A job, one poem typically suggests,
helped him "down Cemetery Road.") Larkin never married or fathered
any children, but he had a series of lovers (often at the same time) and
clearly was dependent on women for emotional support, however he
may have dismissed them crudely in letters and minor poems. In an
uncranky mood he could write rather movingly of "How separate and
unearthly love is, / Or women are, or what they do," but one's main
impression from his letters, which Anthony Thwaite edited and published in 1992, is that, while Larkin indisputably inspired devotion in
women, they largely inspired his contempt.

Larkin published just four slim volumes of poetry during his lifetime, five if one counts a privately issued pamphlet. Although he died
at only sixty-two, he wrote very little after his last book, *High Windows*,
appeared in 1974, when he was fifty-two. His debut collection, *The
North Ship* (1945), is highly accomplished prentice work. The influence of Yeats, Hardy, and Edward Thomas is everywhere, Housman
too, and the atmosphere is one of largely unrelieved gloom and grimness. He confronts his own deeply pessimistic acceptance of human
limitations ("knowing that I can / Never in seventy years be more a
man / Than now—a sack of meal upon two sticks") and characterizes
love as little more than regret. With a residual adolescent relish he will
describe the waning of summer as a broken boil ("Summer broke and
drained") and the individual's life as a wholeness that is gradually
chipped away and eroded to nothing ("Time is the echo of an axe /
Within a wood"). The poems reflect little of the enormous change in

formal metrics effected by Eliot, Pound, and even the late Yeats, and are composed in a very conservative music. *The Less Deceived* (1955) shows some progress in acquiring the vernacular poetic language that would come to be closely identified with Larkin's mature work, but it still descends too often to conventional tricks like inverted word order ("With your depreciating luggage laden") and an almost sclerotic jumbling of sounds into a line ("That we insensately forbore to fleece"). The poem "Deceptions," in which the title phrase appears, contains one of Larkin's earliest memorable images, when he says of a young woman in the aftermath of her being raped, that "All the unhurried day / Your mind lay open like a drawer of knives," a line that Margaret Thatcher much later quoted to him when they met and he challenged her to cite something from his work. Larkin was a big admirer of Mrs. Thatcher.

With *The Whitsun Weddings* (1964) Larkin published his most accomplished book. His now familiar themes of loss, failure, and how the world is going to hell in a handcart are prevalent, and a pervading sarcasm does little to persuade the reader that such poems as "Naturally the Foundation Will Bear Your Expenses" should have got beyond the poet's notebook ("It used to make me throw up, / These mawkish nursery games: / O when will England grow up? /—But I outsoar the Thames"). More serious satire like "A Study of Reading Habits," while effective and somehow typically Larkinian (its speaker, while clearly not Larkin himself, counsels us to "Get stewed: / Books are a load of crap"), seems mistakenly placed in a book that also contains such accomplished and moving pieces as the title poem and "An Arundel Tomb." Ten years later, *High Windows* embodies a falling-off, although it follows its predecessor's mix of high seriousness and low satire. "This Be the Verse" and "Annus Mirabilis" are collected in this book, and both are among Larkin's most famous poems. (He once said, referring to the former piece and to a well-known poem of Yeats, that "'They fuck you up' will clearly be my 'Lake Isle of Innisfree.' I fully expect to hear it recited by a thousand Girl Guides before I die.") But

188 WORK TO BE DONE

the poems whose length and gravity suggest that they were meant to be major accomplishments, such as "The Building" and "Show Saturday," if not failures are somehow unimpressive. An attempt to compose a political poem ("Homage to a Government") is rather embarrassing, and an *ubi sunt* entitled "Going, Going," about the supposedly inevitable deterioration of the England Larkin admired, is tiresome:

> For the first time I feel somehow
> That it isn't going to last,
>
> That before I snuff it, the whole
> Boiling will be bricked in
> Except for the tourist parts—
> First slum of Europe: a role
> It won't be so hard to win,
> With a cast of crooks and tarts.

("The whole boiling" is slang for "the whole thing.") After the publication of *High Windows* Larkin wrote relatively little and published poems only sporadically. A poem called "Aubade," printed in the *Times Literary Supplement* in 1977, might have anchored a fifth collection had he lived to complete one. It is about death, Larkin's lifelong subject ("The anaesthetic from which none come round"), and it is frankly terrifying until its final paragraph. "Not to be here, / Not to be anywhere, / And soon; nothing more terrible, nothing more true," he acknowledges, before stating that only "people" and "drink" can accommodate us to the thought of dying. Yet in the concluding stanza, the world, though it may only be "rented," does go on in some consolatory way. "Work has to be done. / Postmen like doctors go from house to house."

Anthony Thwaite, one of Larkin's three literary executors, edited and published the *Collected Poems* in 1988, and a corrected edition appeared in 2003. Thwaite added substantially to the corpus that had previously appeared in book form by collecting poems that had only been published in periodicals and by digging out poems from Larkin's letters and papers. Now *The Complete Poems* have been published,* edited and with a commentary by Archie Burnett, an English professor at Boston University. This book is almost exactly three times as long as the earlier collection (730 pages of text plus 30 pages of introduction, compared to 240 pages), not because Burnett has discovered a trove of uncollected or unpublished Larkin, but because he has written an extensive commentary that discusses every poem, some at great length. He does have a few minor squibs and fragments to add as well, and he does make some corrections to Thwaites's text, again mostly of a minor nature. But the commentary (over 300 pages) is what justifies this new version of Larkin's oeuvre. It is well done and shows the results of extensive research, and its bibliographical underpinning is precise and useful to any reader who wants the minute details of Larkin's largely straightforward writing and publication history. Sometimes Burnett supplies too much of a good thing, as, for example, when he quotes numerous similar passages from the poet's letters to justify the identification of the speaker in a poem called "Self's the Man" or when the use of a double exclamation point in "The Card-Players" is said to be analogous to similar use in poems by Rimbaud and Whitman. Citing a critic who discusses the importance of the word "void" in symbolist aesthetics when Larkin has merely if cleverly employed the verb to mean "empty" (specifically to empty a can of tonic water into a gin glass) is more exasperating than helpful. Burnett evidently had some difficult decisions to make in choosing whether to define certain words which conceivably would be unfamiliar to either a British or an American audience, but usually not both, and while one sympathizes with the difficulty, I wonder whether anyone on either side of the ocean really needs to be told what a "Freshman" or a "quim" is (the latter, incidentally, being not just

* Philip Larkin, *The Complete Poems*, ed. Archie Burnett (New York: Farrar, Straus and Giroux, 2012).

"British vulgar slang" given that Henry Miller used the word many times in the "Tropic" novels), much less a "titman" (as Larkin humorously improvises in a short couplet about Whitman). Burnett, who has also edited A. E. Housman's poetry, is learned and rarely to be caught out in a mistake, but I think he gets it backwards when he annotates the word "scored" in a poem entitled "For Sidney Bechet." Larkin's phrase is "scored pity," and Burnett notes that "Bechet was a celebrated improviser." But surely the poet's point is that it is in classical music that pity is scored, not in jazz improvisation.

On the whole, Burnett's commentary is admirable, although in one sense it has to be admitted that Larkin may be one of the twentieth century's poets least in need of scholarly demystification. "Discursive he is and sometimes vagrant," then, as Housman said of Joseph Scaliger, his predecessor as editor of the Latin poet Manilius. And yet Burnett could counter by quoting Larkin himself, who once wrote: "There's nothing like writing poems for realizing how low the level of critical understanding is." Burnett is clear that his goal was to provide documentation about the poems and not critical interpretation or evaluation, much in the way that Housman himself prepared his edition of Manilius largely without revealing his own views as to whether the poet was any good. (He was not any good, despite the single personal opinion that Housman allowed himself in his introduction, that Manilius was "the one Latin poet who excels even Ovid in verbal point and smartness.") "The editor's duty," Burnett intelligently proposes in his introduction, "ends with providing the reader with information that has some bearing on the poems, and it is for the reader to assess the pressure of that bearing." I suspect that most readers will consult Burnett's commentary only sporadically as they read the poetry, but when help is demanded, Burnett is there at one's beck.

Richard Bradford, an English scholar and critic, claimed in the last sentence of his biography of Larkin that his poetry constituted "the

twentieth century's most outstanding body of English verse."* This is
surely a monstrous case of special pleading for one's subject, and not
to be deemed plausible. Even if "English" here means not the language
but the country, a picayune and misleading distinction if Bradford
intended it, and thus excludes Yeats, Pound, Eliot, Williams, et al. from
the competition, it still remains an indefensible contention. More
outstanding than, say, Auden, or D. H. Lawrence, or Ted Hughes, one
wants to ask? Certainly at his best and least cantankerous, Larkin was
a very accomplished poet. The difficulty, I think, is that he was rarely
both at his best and not cantankerous, with the result that famous
poems like "This Be the Verse" made and even continue to make an
impact, but it is a slightly specious one. Crankiness and satire are often
difficult to sort out in Larkin's poems, and his deft cleverness at traditional rhyme and meter, while equally suited to expressing both,
sometimes created such a guarded emotion that the centre of a poem
is too uncertain to be true. For example, in "Vers de Société" from *High
Windows*, Larkin begins unpromisingly by imagining a written invitation to a cocktail party from a certain Warlock-Williams (the name
itself makes one start to smirk):

> *My wife and I have asked a crowd of craps*
> *To come and waste their time and ours: perhaps*
> *You'd care to join us? In a pig's arse, friend.*

This satirical opening, however, soon modulates to a much more serious meditation on the value of aloneness. But then the image of
solitude and its utility for reflection and work (writing poetry, presumably) shifts to one of "other things," especially failure and remorse, and
the poem ends with the opening words of the poet's assumed reply to

---

* Richard Bradford, *First Boredom, Then Fear: The Life of Philip Larkin* (London: Peter Owen, 2005), p. 263.

the invitation (*"Dear Warlock-Williams: Why, of course—"*). The tidiness and the reversion to satire only succeed in blurring or even cancelling the felt seriousness of the poem's centre. The adolescent high jinks function best perhaps when unalloyed, as in a sonnet entitled "The Card-Players," which manages to be a kind of live-action seventeenth-century Dutch genre painting in which the figures at cards have names like Old Prijck and Dick Dogstoerd. The scene it limns and its unabashedly obscene vocabulary force one to sit up and take notice, and its sprezzatura makes one laugh. Yet it does not stay in the mind as a memorable poem. This is sadly true not only of Larkin's amusing poems but often of his serious ones too, at least in his earlier work. The great exceptions such as "The Whitsun Weddings," "An Arundel Tomb," and perhaps "Aubade" are just that: exceptions. They are wonderful pieces, but not enough to constitute the centre of the supposedly most "outstanding body of English verse" of the twentieth century.

At the Booker Prize ceremony in 1975, a year when he was the chair, Larkin said in his speech that the poem, "or the kind of poem we write nowadays" at any rate, "is a single emotional spear-point, a concentrated effect that is achieved by leaving everything out but the emotion itself." This is a wise and workable definition of poetry, or of one kind of poetry, and it makes one regret that Larkin himself did not follow his own conviction more often and more convincingly.

FOUR

CANLIT

SET APART FOR
A REAL MINISTRY

The heads of the three major Canadian publishing houses in 1950 comprised an odd and ill-assorted trio. Jack McClelland, of McClelland and Stewart, not quite yet the inheritor of his father's company (he would take over in 1952), was suave, hard-drinking, and full of unusual and even lunatic ideas for the house that would come to be identified with the best of Canadian literature in the 1960s and 1970s. John Gray, suave too, but more debonair, highly intelligent and a veteran of World War II, a survivor of his company's Education Department, was at the helm of Macmillan of Canada, an important publisher of Canadian books but still a firm to some degree in thrall to its London parent. And finally Lorne Pierce, not in fact the actual head of Ryerson Press (the so-called Book Steward was his boss), but its literary editor and titular head, was the eldest of the three, an ordained Methodist minister, anti-smoker and temperance advocate. He was profoundly deaf in a business which even then depended on schmoozing and speaking on the telephone, two activities of which he was incapable for much of his career. Pierce had also been ill for most of his adult life. Various ailments were eventually diagnosed as systemic lupus, incurable then as now, and he seems to have accomplished a mountain of work in the face of frequent medical crises, doctor-ordered bed rest, and holidays in warmer climates than that of Toronto.

Pierce was appointed the editor at Ryerson in 1920, when he was thirty years old and the company itself, founded in the early nine-teenth century, had just been reorganized and the Ryerson imprint founded to keep distinct the firm's trade list from its activities as a religious printing and publishing concern. Based on Sandra Camp-bell's in-depth portrait, there was much about him as a person then that seems frankly unattractive from our vantage point. Smart he was, and well educated (he had a BA from Queen's University, as well as graduate degrees from the University of Toronto and Union Theologi-cal Seminary in New York), but his literary opinions were already somewhat fusty (they would grow fustier as he aged), his views of women were Victorian to say the least, and his moralistic streak man-ifested itself in a general view of literature as uplift and a specific distaste for anything that smacked of sex. This priggishness is not sur-prising perhaps in a man who grew up in small-town Ontario in the late nineteenth century under the watchful eye of a mother whose favourite reading (apart from the Bible) was the work of John Ruskin. A quote from Goethe (misidentified by Sandra Campbell as coming from Ruskin) was posted over the kitchen sink during Pierce's boy-hood: "We ought to acquaint ourselves with the beautiful. We ought to contemplate it with rapture, and attempt to raise ourselves up with its height." This sentiment remained part of Lorne Pierce's aesthetic ideal throughout his life, and while admirable in its way, it did not prepare him well for the developments in poetry and fiction would come after World War I. Increasingly Canadian literature embodied political rad-icalness, sexual frankness, and an obsession with the seamier side of life, and Pierce disliked all of those tendencies. His distaste did not prevent him from publishing Frederick Philip Grove's *Settlers of the Marsh* in 1925, a novel that got him into a lot of trouble and that seem-ingly went against his literary instincts in many ways. But such an exception does not disprove the general rule that Pierce really was not a modernist in sensibility, and he was in charge of the trade division of a major publishing house at a time when modernism was the reigning aesthetic in Canadian literary culture. Pierce would champion Charles G. D. Roberts and Bliss Carman all of his life, and when an older-fashion writer like Marjorie Pickthall or Audrey Alexandra Brown surfaced, he would throw his considerable weight behind their work too. Campbell rightly points out that Pierce has not had sufficient credit for publishing young and experimental poets such as Louis Dudek, P. K. Page, Raymond Souster, and others, but while he deserves acknowledgement for doing so, the fact remains that his real interests lay with the Confederation poets and their progeny, poets like Wilson MacDonald and Albert Durrant Watson in addition to Carman and Roberts.

Lorne Pierce was in charge of Ryerson's trade list for forty years, from 1920 until his retirement in 1960. He was also the chief editor of Ryerson's schoolbooks, and the success of such projects as the Ryerson-Macmillan Readers gave him the financial flexibility to publish such unremunerative projects as the Makers of Canadian Literature series and the Ryerson Poetry Chapbooks. Pierce seems to have had endless unhappy conversations with the Ryerson accountants since, apart from the educational books he published, his list was usually a money-loser, while Ryerson's real money was being made in agency publishing and the printing of books for other publishers, sectors of the company over which he had no administrative control. Profit and prestige rarely went together, as has so often been the case in the history of publishing in Canada. We remember Pierce for publishing such books as E. J. Pratt's first collection, *Newfoundland Verse* (1923), Grove's *Settlers*, Harold Innis's *The Fur Trade in Canada* (1930), critical books by E. K. Brown and Desmond Pacey, A. M. Klein's *The Rocking Chair and Other Poems* (1948), Al Purdy's first commercial book, *Pressed on Sand* (1955), and a few other significant books by poets such as Dorothy Livesay. Almost none of these books made any money, and they had always to be propped up by books like Evelyn Richardson's *We Keep a Light* (a memoir of living in an East Coast lighthouse,1945) and similar titles. The books that Pierce would have thought of as his monuments, such as the *Collected Poems of Duncan Campbell Scott* (1951), were not titles that were supported by sales, and virtually all of Pierce's publishing career took place before the founding of the Canada Council (1957) and the support it would eventually proffer to the publishing of literary books without a large sales potential.

Sandra Campbell has had both the advantage and the curse of a huge archive to work with in researching her biography of Pierce, and in addition to the vast records at Queen's University Library (his diary, his correspondence, and his Ryerson business records among other material, including a childhood record that his mother kept and gave him when he was fifteen), she has not hesitated to trace his leavings among the archives of many other writers, colleagues, and friends when necessary. The result is a highly detailed life story; Campbell's source material has given her a rich opportunity to delineate not just the facts of Pierce's life and career, but his inner life as well, and both are interesting. One may not respond particularly warmly to the spiritual directives that drove Pierce, and his highly developed sense of public service, nationalistic pride, and moral purity may all to some extent seem more to be admired than emulated, while the threadbare commands of Methodism in particular appear sometimes regrettable and occasionally deplorable. This is true despite the fact that Methodism's hold was sufficiently imperfect to allow him to stray into some weird and wonderful territory such as Theosophy, a nut-bar pseudo-spiritualism that was surprisingly popular in early-twentieth-century Toronto. It counted the Group of Seven artist Lawren Harris, for example, among its adherents, as well as F. B. Housser, a journalist who wrote the first important book on the Group of Seven. (Albert Durrant Watson, a medical doctor and poet with lunatic spiritualist affiliations that included a passion for seances in which he communicated with

Christ and Coleridge, to name just two, was a mentor and a significant influence on Pierce's thinking.) Pierce always thought of his ordination in 1916 as one of the high points of his life. He was twenty-six years old then, and his mother had prepared him for it virtually from birth. When he agreed to become the editor at Ryerson four years later, he was already married, had an infant daughter, and had contributed to the Canadian war effort (though not in France), but as his hearing was already becoming a problem, his future as a Methodist minister was in question. (He would later call it "the tragedy of deafness.") While he was never again to have charge of a parish, his religious training and moral upbringing both played key roles in his work as a publisher. They combined to give him an instrumentalist view of literature, and that, combined with a profoundly nationalistic devotion to Canada, was at the root of much of his publishing activity. So the inner life and the outer achievements were inextricably intertwined.

*Both Hands** is richly documented, then, and little about Pierce's life has had to be passed over lightly for lack of primary research material. At times the book is almost overwhelmingly detailed, but while in the general scheme of things a publisher may not seem to deserve almost 700 pages of readerly investment, Pierce was so much at the centre of the development of Canadian literature during a crucial period that one's interest rarely flags. What other cultural figure in Canada in the period from 1920 to 1960 was more involved in literature, politics, history, art, education, religion, and scholarship and knew so many important writers and artists? Pierce may not have liked all of his friends (he was intensely critical of Pratt, Roberts, and Carman for their propensity to debauch, for example, and it was this lack of sympathy that prevented him from writing Carman's biography, an almost lifelong backburner project), but they liked and respected him,

---

* The title will seem unfortunate to anyone who is familiar with Rousseau's infamous reference in his *Confessions* to books that "can only be read with one hand." "Two Hands" was Pierce's habitual invocation at the end of letters.

and he managed to impress creative people so utterly different as Audrey Alexandra Brown (whom Campbell is convinced he oppressed because she was a woman) and Wyndham Lewis, of all people, who drew his portrait and whose pamphlet *Anglosaxony* Pierce published in 1941. (Campbell says that it got no reviews and sank without a trace.)

As detailed as Campbell's book is, and as lengthy, there are two aspects of Pierce's life where I believe she stints. The first is sex. While she is able amply to document his aversion to explicitness in literature, and his antipathy for the sexually liberated side of some of his literary friends, we learn nothing about his own sex life. Perhaps there is nothing to be learned, and one can imagine that, as detailed as the Pierce diary is (it covers the period from 1915 to 1945, which includes his wedding day), he may well have been completely reticent about his own feelings where sex is concerned. I don't think it is merely to give in to a proclivity for luridness to want to know how a young man brought up in a religious household and ordained as a Methodist minister dealt with the *vita sexualis*. Then there is money. Campbell frequently mentions the financial problems that Pierce and his wife, Edith, experienced, and how this shortage caused friction in their marriage. Yet Pierce managed to be a major philanthropist throughout his life, supporting causes that were dear to him, donating hundred of rare book and manuscripts to Queen's, owning pictures by the Group of Seven (though his major Group painting, MacDonald's *The Elements*, was a gift from Thoreau MacDonald, but it was recompense for a financial favour), as well as owning a house in Toronto and a cottage. How he supported all of these things is only vaguely documented in the book.

Was he "the most influential publisher and editor of his era," as Campbell claims in her summation? Yes, I think so. Had Hugh Eayrs lived longer and been able to direct Macmillan of Canada through the 1940s and 1950s, he might have surpassed Pierce's achievements, but he died young in 1940 with an impressive but limited legacy. And at McClelland and Stewart, a house directed editorially by John

McClelland Sr., a man of religious principle and a strict teetotaler, while many important books were being published throughout Pierce's period of activity, there was perhaps a less panoptic view of what mattered to Canadian writing, and no real interest in educational books with their lasting aesthetic and nationalistic influence on the young. Pierce's own voluminous writings are perhaps not scholarly enough or too much a product of their time to be worth reviving, but his greatest influence was not in writing itself, but in making the writing of others available in the marketplace, and that he did for forty years with dedication, incredible hard work, and, finally, love. Only someone who really loved literature, and damn the balance sheet, would do what Pierce did for John Sutherland, for example, getting his (admittedly imperfect) book about E. J. Pratt rushed into print in only six weeks, from manuscript to printed book, so that the author could hold a copy in his hands before dying of cancer at thirty-seven. Pierce wanted to support Sutherland's religious reading of Pratt's poetry, so in that sense he had a critical investment in the book. But that takes nothing away from his generosity and affection in publishing what he also knew was a book that needed revision. Is there a publisher alive today who would do the same?

—

Sandra Campbell, *Both Hands: A Life of Lorne Pierce of Ryerson Press* (Montreal: McGill-Queen's University Press, 2013).

JOHN SUTHERLAND,
1919-1956

... so will you lie,
While we who are intent on sorting stones
Still seek to classify each one anew.
This is our fashion, yet if our hands should stray
To touch a stone incuriously or lay a weed
On water, we'll owe that gentle move
Not to ourselves, but to the death of you.
MIRIAM WADDINGTON, "AN ELEGY
FOR JOHN SUTHERLAND"

S ince its inception, this column has dealt solely with poets. I have
tried to give some sense of the nature of their work, and more
particularly to set that work in its historical context—not (I hope it has
been clear) out of any inkhorn obsession with the facts of our literary
history, but on the assumptions that the historical context can help to
illuminate the poems themselves, and that the more a poet knows
about the history of Canadian poetry, the clearer will the contemporary scene become. These generalizations naturally beg a formidable
number of philosophical questions about critical interpretation, the

nature of history, et cetera; but as W. W. E. Ross once put it, "This form seems effective now; / It is monotonous, crude. / It may be called 'primitive'. / . . . / Nevertheless it expresses."

John Sutherland did write poems, but they are minor and incidental to his achievement. In a letter to Earle Birney, who had asked to use one of his poems in his anthology *Twentieth-Century Canadian Poetry*, Sutherland defended his refusal in these words: "I dicker with verse from time to time, am willing to make the occasional flight in a magazine, but I don't consider myself a poet." Nevertheless, his importance as an editor, publisher, critic, and *animateur* of the literary scene during the period from 1942 to 1956 makes his appearance in this column almost an inevitability. He was, for ten years at least, at the very centre of the modern movement in Canadian poetry, as midwife and conscience, as psychopomp, interpreter, and disciplinarian.

Sutherland was born and grew up in the Maritimes, first Nova Scotia and then New Brunswick. His mother died when he was young, and his father remarried. (Donald Sutherland the actor is his stepbrother.) When he was eighteen, it was discovered that he had tuberculosis, and he spent most of the following three years in bed. A. G. Bailey remembers reading *The Waste Land* to Sutherland during one of the periods he spent in the sanatorium in Saint John—Bailey at that time was the curator of the Saint John Museum—and this may well have been Sutherland's earliest contact with modern poetry. He also met P. K. Page around the same time. An unpublished autobiographical fragment among Sutherland's papers, entitled simply "Myself," shows how strongly these childhood and adolescent experiences affected his character and contributed to the drive that animated his literary activities. "The loss of freedom, during the period that I spent in bed, convinced me that I had a special niche all my own." Equally important, and not usually remarked on because he spent most of his adult life in Montreal, was the fact that his childhood was passed near the ocean. In a commentary on one of his own poems, also unpublished, he wrote: "From the age of eight to twelve, I lived in a little sea town, and now, more than ten years later, I find myself in my writing constantly making images and symbols of the sea."

Before his illness, Sutherland had started a degree at Queen's, and after recuperating, he went back to school, this time to McGill. Before the year was out, he left McGill, and with some friends published the first issue of *First Statement* in August 1942. It was an inauspicious debut—small, mimeographed, and made up largely of the group's own work—but the magazine appeared at a crucial time in the history of Canadian poetry. Ralph Gustafson's Pelican anthology had come out in North America only two months earlier, and A. J. M. Smith's *Book of Canadian Poetry* would appear the following year. Alan Crawley had founded *Contemporary Verse* in 1941, and Patrick Anderson's *Preview* had begun a few months before *First Statement*. Despite its unpretentious look, *First Statement* from the beginning was intended by Sutherland to be an important magazine. To Earle Birney, he wrote: "We want to serve as an outlet for writing of all kinds, and become the mirror of variety in the Canadian scene...Our intention is to develop *First Statement* into a lucid and well-defined medium for representative styles and types of writing as they exist in Canada." This was an ambitious program, but by the spring of 1943 the group had bought a printing press and type, which was installed in an office at 207 Craig Street (now St Antoine—the office was later destroyed and there is presently a fast-food restaurant on the site), and the magazine was solidly established.

From the first, Sutherland was interested in a kind of poetry that would deal realistically with the experience of Canadians in the world of the time. He recognized the value of earlier Canadian poetry— recognized it but rejected most of its assumptions as incommensurate with the world he knew. Magazine editors, he felt, must work "on the assumption that a fundamental realism is lacking in Canadian writing." They should "endeavour to encourage those writers who show themselves capable of a critical awareness of the individual and society." Many of the writers with whom Sutherland became associated, and who published in the pages of *First Statement*, were also dedicated to adopting a poetic language that would be equal to the expression of this poetic aesthetic. Louis Dudek, Raymond Souster, Miriam Waddington, and others (including Layton, whom Sutherland thought of primarily as a short story writer, and who married his sister, Betty) all became friends and all first found a sympathetic reception in his magazine. In 1945, Sutherland branched out into book publishing with the New Writers Series, which issued the first book of the last three of those poets, as well as the first "commercial" collection by Patrick Anderson. Anderson was another galvanizing force on the Montreal poetry scene, and the editor of *Preview*, which critics have described as a rival of *First Statement*. One need only look at the lists of contributors of the two magazines for a qualification of that view. Many writers published in both, and if anything is to be made of the difference in the two magazines, it will have to be based on the more obviously North American outlook of *First Statement*. Furthermore, as the scholar Neil Fisher has pointed out, *First Statement* published much more critical commentary. Sutherland was anxious to provide a context for the new poetry, as well as an outlet and an audience for it.

In 1945, *First Statement* and *Preview* amalgamated to form a new magazine. The first issue of *Northern Review* appeared in December of that year, and for the next ten years it was the major literary magazine in Canada. Members of the editorial board changed a good deal over the decade. Several members resigned in 1947, when Sutherland published a no-nonsense review of Robert Finch's *Poems* (which had won the Governor General's Award), and Sutherland's plain-spoken introduction to the anthology *Other Canadians*, which appeared at about the same time, also caused some indignation. Changes in Sutherland's own thinking, which crystalized in part in an essay called "The Past Decade in Canadian Poetry" (1950), also lost him the support of poets like Dudek and Souster, and gradually *Northern Review* became more and more a one-man operation. It was almost a full-time job for Sutherland, as his letters attest; they are rife with requests for support and continuing concern for the magazine's existence. In the absence of a body like the Canada Council, Sutherland had to depend on funds provided by guarantors, in addition to subscription sales and advertising. He sold his press in the summer of 1950 in order to free up some of his time for other work, but aside from a few months in 1954, when a grant from the Humanities Research Council gave him the time to write his book on E. J. Pratt, he was never free from the constant economic struggle that the magazine entailed.

The list of contributors to *Northern Review* is a formidable one, and it is hard to think of any significant Canadian writer of the period who did not publish in its pages. From Livesay, Gustafson, and Ross, to Pratt, Klein, F. R. Scott, and A. J. M. Smith, to Layton, Souster, and Dudek, to Wilkinson, Reaney, Page, Norman Levine, Hugh Garner, and many others, the magazine was their major outlet for their critical and creative work. Articles and reviews dealt not only with literary subjects, but with all the arts: music, radio, film, visual art, and so on. Sutherland's own commentary and essays were rarely absent from an issue, and on the whole form the most important body of critical work of their time. (Some of them have been gathered together by Miriam Waddington in a collection called *Essays, Controversies, and Poems.*) As Waddington has observed, Sutherland managed always to maintain a balance between a theoretical approach to reading and a close reading of individual poets and poems undertaken without the enormous battery of critical prejudices that too often mar much academic criticism.

Toward the end of his life (he died in 1956 at thirty-seven), Sutherland's views changed significantly, and with this evolution of outlook came a change of direction in *Northern Review*. His excitement of the early 1940s ("Perhaps there was never a time in Canada when so many poets of promise appeared simultaneously or when, within the general pattern of the movement, there was so much creative variety") gave way to disappointment by 1950 (he speaks in the same article of "the poor durability of the poetic talents") and a gradual retreat into religious conservatism. His developing religious convictions led him into the Catholic Church in 1954, and a concomitant unhappiness with Canadian modernism gave rise to critical views which, in retrospect, were far off the mark. The religious tendency which he divined in contemporary poetry was more detached and sporadic than he thought, and his confident obituary for modernism—"There is not the slightest doubt that modern literary decadence is now on its death-bed. All that was fathered by Joyce and Pound is obviously on the verge of complete extinction"—seems from our vantage point over-hasty to say the least.

But none of this detracts from John Sutherland's importance. *Northern Review* was for a time at the very centre of the literary scene, but certainly that could not last forever, irrespective of the editor's views. Sutherland's legacy—his own work at its best, as well as the work to which he gave print—is a large and permanent one. It is hard to think of a comparable figure in the thirty years since his death, and no single magazine has had the importance and the influence on Canadian writing that *Northern Review* exercised in its heyday.

HER LONG DUTY
CUT SHORT

ON ANNE WILKINSON

> The poet's daily chore
> Is my long duty;
> To keep and cherish my good lens
> For love and war
> And wasps about the lillies
> And mutiny within.

ANNE WILKINSON, "LENS"

Anne Wilkinson's literary legacy is small: a book about the Osler family, *Lions in the Way* (1956), a children's book, *Swann and Daphne* (1950), and the posthumously published *Collected Poems* (1968), which A. J. M. Smith edited. The latter, a book of some 200 pages, includes the two small collections that she published in her lifetime (*Counterpoint to Sleep* and *The Hangman Ties the Holly*), some uncollected poems from magazines and anthologies, poems that Smith culled from among her papers, and finally a prose memoir entitled *Four Corners of My World*. A small output this, though virtually all of it was written during the last twelve years of her life (she was forty-one when her first book was published); but size is an over-rated factor, and Anne Wilkinson's work deserves an important place in the history of Canadian poetry since World War II. It also deserves to be reprinted.

It was on her mother's side that Wilkinson was related to the house of Osler, and *Four Corners of My World* bears witness to her monied upbringing. This autobiographical fragment has little to say about her literary beginnings, but it was not until the late 1940s that her poems began to appear in print. (She was born in 1910.) Appearances in *Reading, Here and Now*, and in Alan Crawley's *Contemporary Verse* brought her to the attention of John Sutherland, the editor of *Northern Review*. In the summer of 1949, he wrote to her, asking for contributions to his magazine and proposing that she send him a manuscript for publication in the New Writers Series that his First Statement Press was issuing. Sutherland became a warm supporter of her work, and the manuscript (with her financial help) was eventually published in 1951 as *Counterpoint to Sleep*, though the poem of that title had been dropped. Unlike many first books, which subsequently prove an embarrassment to their authors, this chapbook was a remarkable debut. Though conservative formally and very much *à rebours* of the kind of American-influenced modernism that Souster, Dudek, and Layton were about to introduce into Canada with the founding of *Contact* magazine, *Counterpoint to Sleep* displays a poet very much in control of her work. The poems show influences but are not derivative, and above all Wilkinson is able to transpose into language that fresh and sensual apprehension of the world which she so richly possessed:

> My blood is a clot in the stone,
> The blood of my heart is fused to a pit in the rock;
> The lips of my lover can wear away stone.
> My lover can free the blocked heart;

> *The leaf and the root and the red sap will run with lake water,*
> *The arms of my lake water will carry me home to the sea.*
> *(From "Lake Song")*

Sutherland wrote to her a few months after *Counterpoint to Sleep* appeared: "I think you are doing more promising work than almost anyone else in Canada." In hindsight this may seem an extravagant claim—Souster, Dudek, Reaney, Layton, and Page were after all then still in the early stages of their careers—and it may say as much about Sutherland's changing taste as about Wilkinson's poetry. There is no gainsaying, however, the fact that she was publishing some fine poems.

The Hangman Ties the Holly (1955) confirmed Sutherland's prediction, and it contains several of the poems by which she is usually represented in anthologies ("Lens," "In June and Gentle Oven," and "The Red and the Green"). The book embodies a kind of aloof mastery which Sutherland recognized as a double-edged sword. "Your technical virtuosity," he wrote to her in early 1953, "is the outstanding thing about your work as a whole, but it may also have the effect of making the emotional statement seem rather specialized and even unreal." But balanced against this element in the collection is a sensuousness and what one can only call a knowledge of being human that are developed much beyond what one finds in her earlier book. As in the poems written nearer the end of her life, and as the title indicates, death is very much a presence in the book, but not in a macabre or pathological sense. Critical dogma to the contrary, and for all that *Hangman* is full of poems with titles such as "Dirge," "Little Men Slip into Death," "On the Death of a Young Poet," et cetera, it is the presence of a warm, green world that is evoked most powerfully. The one commandment in "Letter to My Children" is this: "Mind the senses and the soul / Will take care of itself, / Being five times blessed." Her advice is practised most lyrically in what is probably her best-known poem, "In June and Gentle Oven," of which—it being too long to quote in full—I give the first four verses:

In June and gentle oven
Summer kingdoms simmer
As they come
And flower and love
Release
Their sweetest juice.

No wind at all
On the whole green world.

Where fields go stroll-
ing by
And in and out
An adder or a stream
Parts the daisies
On a small Ontario farm.

And where, in curve of meadow
Lovers, touching, lie,
A church of grass stands up
And walls them, holy, in.

The conventional aspects of this poem—its patently traditional symbols and its quasi-seventeenth-century music—do not at all detract from what is a perfectly written celebration of love and its consummation inside the tangible world.

Many of the poems written between the publication of *The Hangman Ties the Holly* and Wilkinson's death in 1961 are, not surprisingly, darker and more troubling. "When a body breaks or is / Cast off from its hemisphere / Something grave has gone amiss, / Danger, danger, everywhere." Though often moving and technically accomplished, none of these poems stands out as quite so evidently a masterpiece as

"In June and Gentle Oven." The longest of them, "Notes on Robert Burton's *The Anatomy of Melancholy*," which Smith liked a good deal, seems
to me rather circumscribed and artificial. And yet there is no denying
the effect of the poems of pain, such as the untitled one that begins
"Accustom the grey coils / Locked in the skull," and ends this way:

> *Listen, you grey coils*
> *Locked in the skull,*
> *To the pounding; it's growing*
> *As fontanelle shuts*
> *On the silence; the swelling*
> *Predicts at its pressing point*
> *Hoarded nights bursting, the*
> *Black sky, unloading*
> *Its stars until the skull is alight.*

It does not seem that Wilkinson took a large part in the literary
scene, though she worked for a time on an anthology and was the self-
styled "sports editor" of *The Tamarack Review* (as reported by W. W. E.
Ross). Her poems have not had a wide influence or readership, which
is surprising in light of the fact that she was the first to give expression
to certain aspects of a woman's consciousness and experience of the
world. Her early death no doubt contributed to this neglect; it does
not seem unlikely that if she were alive today, she would be as celebrated as, say, Dorothy Livesay or P. K. Page. The poems remain of
course, and though out of print, they are not that difficult to search
out. The vigilant and the curious, as the vigilant and the curious
always are, will be rewarded.

WHATEVER HAPPENED
TO THE AVANT-GARDE?

t is an interesting fact that Canadian poetry in the twentieth century has gone through a regular cycle of advance and assimilation. Beginning in the 1920s, every second decade has been a period of experimentation and iconoclasm, followed by a period of retrenchment and formal conservatism. In the 1920s, W. W. E. Ross, Dorothy Livesay, and Raymond Knister brought the imagist aesthetic to bear on Canadian poetry and thereby produced the first genuinely modern work in the country. In the 1940s, the poets who published in *First Statement* and *Contemporary Verse* gave common coin to a poetry that was close to speech and concerned with the quotidian. Their influences were more American than British, and thus they helped to prepare the way for the generation of the 1960s, whose postmodern models were almost exclusively American. At the same time, the North American context in which the '40s poets worked was a kind of forelighting to the re-emergence of literary nationalism twenty years later. One night grossly chart this every-twenty-years phenomenon with four representative occurrences: T. E. Hulme's trip across Canada (1906), the publication of Dorothy Livesay's first book (1928), the appearance of John Sutherland's anthology *Other Canadians* (1947), and—unavoidably—the centenary of Confederation in 1967.

214 WORK TO BE DONE

The 1920s, '40s, and '60s were lively periods for Canadian poetry, when young writers made a good deal of useful noise about the stuffiness of their elders and when they actively sought contemporary alternatives for what struck them as outmoded approaches to the poem. All three decades showed a concern for the formal renewal of poetry, an obsession which is a *sine qua non* for any genuine avant-garde. The 1930s and '50s were by comparison a time when, for different reasons, poetry was in retreat. Avant-garde literature always struggles against the economics of publishing, but the Depression predictably made the context a hopeless one. The social conservatism of the '50s had something of a similar effect on poetry, though increasing use of the mimeograph machine, which Edison had invented as long ago as 1876, made poets less dependent on mainstream publishing, and/or the time-consuming technology of printing by hand, and thus freer and more able to experiment.

Had this pattern continued, we should, in the 1980s, be in the midst of another revolutionary rethinking of our poetry. Instead, we are surrounded by schools of content and an old avant-garde that has been incorporated into the mainstream. The title of Dennis Lee's anthology, *The New Canadian Poets 1970–1985*, is strikingly reminiscent of Donald Allen's epoch-making *The New American Poetry 1945–1960*, but with the title, any resemblance ends. Where Allen's book introduced to a larger public a genuine avant-garde, Lee's simply chronicles the coming of age of a generation. Poets like Roo Borson, Lorna Crozier, Pier Giorgio DiCicco, Susan Musgrave and Bronwen Wallace are competent, at times even brilliant poets; but no one would claim that their poetry in any way advances the frontiers of the art. In each case, the work as a whole is more attractive to readers through the force of a personality than by its technical originality or its innovation of subject. Chris Dewdney alone among Lee's choices is a genuinely innovative writer, but his meteoric rise in a few short years from just another marginal Coach House writer to a poet with two Governor General nominations, an impressive McClelland & Stewart selected poems, and an already lengthy list of critical articles about his work, is symptomatic of how quickly the avant-garde is assimilated now. Dewdney is so extraordinarily talented and his material is so *sui generis* that he can probably withstand the secondment. But whatever dangers may present themselves to the poet who becomes a star, the potential loss of the freedom that obscurity or neglect allows is by no means the least.

The avant-garde has traditionally had to publish its own work, and the profound changes in poetry brought about by poets like Souster, Dudek, George Bowering, bpNichol, Daphne Marlatt, and others would have been impossible without such presses—poet-founded and poet-run—as First Statement Press, Contact Press, blewointment press, Coach House Books, and others. But now the presses too are part of a lack of animation and a disinterest in—or inability to find—the new writers with an interest in restructuring language and poetic form. Coach House still publishes good new writers, Anne Michaels and Kate Van Dusen, for example—poets with skill and confidence, but not poets with any detectable need to start from a clean slate. Coach House has, furthermore, branched out into publishing more established writers like D. G. Jones, Phyllis Webb, and Dorothy Livesay, as well as more fiction and even criticism. This is all well and good; but the house's earlier function as printer-in-ordinary to the avant-garde has not been taken up by anyone else. jwcurry's Curvd H&Z Press operates somewhat in the manner that bpNichol's Ganglia Press or Nelson Ball's Weed Flower Press once did, but so far at least, jwcurry has not created a list of important writers on the scale of these former presses.

Where does the explanation for the disappearance of the avant-garde lie? Is Canadian poetry merely suffering a period of conservatism concomitant with the political conservatism resident now in much of the Western world? Has the easy access to money for readings and grants and publishing projects (from the Canada Council and the provincial councils) blunted the younger writers' devotion to the unpopular and the *outré*? Has the whole idea of the avant-garde, from the generation of 1910 on (I think of Pound's remark in his 1914 essay "The Renaissance," that "a sound poetic training is nothing more than the science of being discontented"), finally worn itself out? Has the creeping influence of literary theory on poetry—surely a case of the tail wagging the dog—domesticated the avant-garde impulse by leasing it to academic, reductivist systems of language that tend simply to remove writing from the open arena where experiment at its most productive thrives? (George Bowering claims that "once the writers were the avant-garde, now the critics are.") Or are we, as David Solway suggested recently in an article in *Canadian Literature*, "witnessing the end of poetry as a form of artistic response to the world"?

The impulse to poetry is fundamental to human consciousness, and any conservative view of its history, like Solway's, which proceeds from a pessimistic, *ubi sunt* point of view, must come to grief if it neglects this fact. Of course there are dark periods and bright periods, periods of desuetude and periods of grace. None of the other reasons which I have suggested in and of itself adequately explains the "quiet period," as George Butterick, referring to American poetry today, described it in the last issue of *Brick*, which Canadian poetry is experiencing now.

Perhaps Butterick's observation that this quietude is "not dormancy,...as much as a taking stock, deliberating, tolerating" applies not just to the United States but to North America as a whole, even to English-language poetry in general. The periodicity of avant-garde activity which I have observed may be more of an accident than a law; doubtless the 1990s will see the recrudescence of an avant-garde spirit whose proponents will be prepared to fight the views of Nichol, Steve McCaffery, Marlatt, Nicole Brossard, et al. as so many *idées reçues*.

LOUIS DUDEK AND
RAYMOND SOUSTER

O f Dudek, Souster, and Layton, the three poets whose work, in both poetry and the "poetry business," dominated Canadian literature in the period from roughly 1950 to 1960, it is Dudek to whom plaudits and recognition have been slowest in coming. His work as critic, intellectual historian, editor, and publisher has been the farthest ranging of the three, and consequently, in terms of sheer quantity, he has published less poetry. His style is also less immediate and accessible than that of his *confreres*, although it is certainly not as difficult as that of some of his models, Pound in particular. Perhaps these facts help to explain why he is not as widely read or taught as the other two founding editors of Contact Press. All along, of course, the poems— *Europe, En Mexico,* and *Atlantis* especially—have been there, and they have had an important poetic influence, if only modest public acknowledgement. In any case, Dudek is now gaining a greater measure of recognition, and the past year, as Frank Davey points out, has been an important one for him. The first critical study of his work has appeared, a selection from *Delta* is due, and three books by Dudek himself have been issued: the first part of his long poem *Continuation,* a selected *Atlantis,* and the double issue of *Open Letter* under review here.

Louis Dudek: Texts & Essays is comprised of three sections: an interview by correspondence, reproductions of some of Dudek's manuscripts (with the corresponding text from the published editions *en face*), and a group of essays and notes, about half of which are published here for the first time. It is the essays, to which the interview acts as a kind of expansive footnote, which command the most attention, and I would like to concentrate on them.

Dudek's interests as a critic and intellectual, which of course have also been reflected in his poetry, have been remarkably consistent over the years. He himself puts it succinctly in a sentence that appears toward the end of the introduction to *Literature and the Press*: "My purpose in writing this history is to understand the present; to reach to the roots of the now precarious position of literature in our society, and to clarify the condition of the artist as writer in a world of mass audiences." It is for this purpose that he has undertaken the bulk of his critical writing, and not a small proportion of his poetry. And it is a poem called "For Jon Stallworthy" (*Cross-Section*, p. 89) which to my mind best encapsulates the stance he has taken as a man of letters:

> *We survive by being, whatever we are,*
>> *human*
>
> *by holding on*
>> *to the small few essentials—*
> *a lifebelt, an open simile,*
> *the insistence that rational good sense*
>>> *comes first,*
> *fanatic impulse after—*
>>> *that even when we lack*
> *the mind, for clear thinking, we must*
>>>> *by a kind of act of*
> *sanity, try to honour*
>>> *the better reason.*

Dudek's poetry has sometimes been criticized for its strong Poundian cast, and there is some justification for this complaint. But it is one of Pound's less frequently remarked enthusiasms—the Enlightenment—which, whether by direct influence or not, most crucially informs Dudek's views. He is a man of reason (as he himself attests), an avoider of extremes, a defender of conscious craft and the centrality of the great tradition. While he neither deplores nor eschews experimentation, he is insistent that the future of poetry lies in a conscious and reasoned extension of mainstream modernism and not in an exploitation of its more extreme (and to him failed) characteristics. Parts of Joyce, Eliot, and Pound show the direction. Olson, Louis Zukofsky, and the more egregious manias of *The Cantos* are dead ends.

One of the articles in the *Open Letter* collection is entitled "Middangeard: The Middle World," and it is a phrase which accurately could be used to characterize the issue as a whole. Dudek abhors the uses to which the formal freedom of the modern poet has been put and labels much of the resultant poetry barbaric. (He does not quote Rémy de Gourmont's phrase "*Écrire franchement ce qu'ils pensent: seul Plaisir d'un écrivain*," so often quoted by Pound, but well he might, as he sees this as one of the keys to modernism.) Barbarism, says Dudek, in "Whatever Happened to Poetry?," "refuses to discriminate"; in fact it sets out purposefully to subvert the progress of civilization. "I do not think it [this progress] has been a tragic desiccation and deterioration of art and poetry," Dudek writes in "The Poetry of Reason," "but an intellectual conquest and advance. And this is my difference from the whole tribe of nature-boys and primitivists on the literary scene today. They are going back, when they should be going forward." Dudek is the Dr Johnson of Canadian letters.

Dudek's conservatism is temperate, however, and he is willing enough to reserve final judgment on those aspects of contemporary poetic practice which his inclination is to reject as barbaric because, basically, his interest is in good poetry, not in critical systems or in *ex cathedra* evaluations. Pound once quoted Yeats as remarking that "the highest poetry is so precious that one should be willing to search many a dull tome to find and gather the fragments." It is such an impulse, I think, that lies behind most of Dudek's essays and notes, and which also informs his longstanding arguments with Frye, McLuhan, and other critics who, in his view, interest themselves in poetry to the extent that it fits into their systems. There is nothing reductive or systematic about Dudek's criticism, though this is not to say that he lacks a defined point of view. Far from it. He is a rationalist, a realist (in the philosophical sense), and an immensely well informed historian of literature in general and Canadian literature in particular. His criticism, though we may disagree with some of it, always shines a light in a direction we had not previously thought to follow. To quote Pound once again, "All that the critic can do for the reader or audience or spectator is to focus his gaze or audition." This Dudek does almost unfailingly.

—

The period covered by the second volume of Raymond Souster's *Collected Poems* (1955–1962) is an interesting one, though it remains relatively unstudied. The decade of the 1950s has attracted a myth of barrenness. That it is a myth becomes apparent if one thinks of the "first books" which appeared then: Cohen's *Let Us Compare Mythologies*, Nowlan's *The Rose and the Puritan*, Acorn's *In Love and Anger*, D. G. Jones's *Frost on the Sun*, and so on. And there were other important and lasting books beyond these auspicious debuts: selected volumes by Souster and Livesay, collected volumes of Layton and Pratt (second edition), and two of Dudek's book-length poems with their auguries of books to come. The small-press boom of the 1960s has obscured the fact that a number of poets' presses were active during the previous decade: First Statement Press issued its two last books in 1951, Contact Press began the following year with *Cerberus*; later in the decade Fiddlehead published its first books, and John Robert Colombo inaugurated the Hawkshead Press which would issue Atwood's first chapbook. The little magazines had begun to flourish, and poetry readings, if not as ubiquitous as they now are, nonetheless took place. All this ferment has been lost sight of to some extent behind the smoke from the explosion that followed it—the 1960s—but that explosion did have a quite definite cause. It was prepared. In its preparation, Souster had an important part to play.

Of the four books which comprise this second volume of what will eventually constitute Souster's *monumentum aere perennius*, three were first published by Contact Press. The fourth, *Place of Meeting*, was a collaboration between Souster and Michael Snow and was the second of three books issued as "Gallery Editions" by the Toronto art dealer Avrom Isaacs. This was also the last of Souster's small-press books. With the subsequent publication of *The Colour of the Times*, he was finally an established poet. The days of paying for five hundred, or one hundred, or twenty-five copies of his own books were past. *Collected Poems II* thus represents Souster on the brink of a truly public career; since these books, he has in many ways rather elaborated and expanded on the work contained in them than moved in a new or experimental direction. The exception to this generalization is the series of poems entitled "Pictures from a Long Lost World" which has been appearing in recent years.

The four books brought together in this volume—*Walking Death, Crêpe-Hanger's Carnival, Place of Meeting*, and *A Local Pride*—show Souster in full command of what became his dominant mode. The content owes much to the example of Williams, as many readers, and Souster himself, have remarked. One influence which to my knowledge has not been noticed is that of Winfield Townley Scott, an American poet who died in 1968. Scott was for a long time the literary editor of the *Providence Sunday Journal*, and he published some of Souster's work in its pages during the 1940s. Scott's approach to the poem—his use of the flat inflections of colloquial speech and his avoidance of the high modernist style—corresponds closely to Souster's practice. Both men were also admirers of Williams. This second volume of the *Collected Poems* is dedicated in part to the memory of Winfield Scott, and this suggests that the relationship between the two bears investigation.

Souster's remark that he writes poems in the way that an amateur photographer takes pictures tells some of the truth about his manner and his intentions. The poems of this book are intensely visual, and this is true irrespective of whether the particulars presented arise from memory or the present. In his best poems, Souster allows the details of the world to shine forth, to speak for themselves, as in the well-known poem "The Six Quart Basket" or in "Cobweb":

> *This one*
> *only cobweb*
>
> *hangs from a corner*
> *of our room*
>
> *still waiting*

This kind of poem bulks large in Souster's work, and each of them adds to the composite picture of the world he presents to us, like bits in a mosaic. A mosaic, with its suggestion of objectivity and the agglutination of the very small, is not an inappropriate word for the whole that emerges from Souster's books. He is a poet who needs to be read in the depth this ongoing collected edition permits.

Where Souster differs from a photographer is in the way that his responses to the world enter the poems. This happens in two ways. The first is via a belittlement of himself in which his self-satisfaction is undercut or mocked. The second and more irritating access we have is by way of Souster the commentator as distinct from the observer. Not infrequently the poet cannot resist underlining in red a point that might better have been left implied from the particulars of the poem itself, as in "Our Snowman":

> No doubt because
> of last night's warm rain
> the old grey fedora
> our snowman is wearing
> this morning has
> a slight forward tilt,
>
> which, when compared
> to that very debonair
> off-the-forehead look
> he sported yesterday,
> makes him look very old,
> a very tired man,
> not long for this freezing melting world.

The last line of this poem strikes me as too deliberately pointed, as though there is a scholiast inside Souster longing to get out. This is a less egregious example of an impulse that sometimes mars a Souster poem.

Notwithstanding this complaint, one cannot but be grateful for and admiring of the body of work which the Collected Poems is making available. Souster almost single-handedly brought a clarity and directness of language and perception into Canadian poetry. He had Canadian predecessors—W. W. E. Ross among them—but he has had many more successors.

RAYMOND SOUSTER
AND POETRY IN THE 1950s

R aymond Souster must surely rank high among those twentieth-century poets whose "work," in the largest sense, has been tremendously influential on the poetry scene in Canada. At one end of the spectrum are the hordes of high school students who, if they have read any Canadian poetry at all, will have studied one or more of his poems in an anthology; at the other end are the many poets of his and the succeeding generation who learned from his work and benefited from his boundless enthusiasm as an editor, publisher, organizer, and proselytizer. Souster has been writing and publishing for almost half a century now, and although his style has changed during that time, it has not changed radically. The result is that we tend to take him for granted, and to forget the multi-faceted transformation that he helped to bring about in Canadian poetry during the 1950s.

The late 1940s and early 1950s were not a propitious time for poetry in Canada. There were few magazines and few publishers willing to issue poetry, and the audience, for new work especially, was very small. Souster remarked to Charles Olson in a letter in 1952 that "this damn country right now is deader than ever as far as creative work goes." Two years later he wrote to Robert Creeley in a similar vein: "No doubt about it that the state of literary health has never been lower this side of the Atlantic." Souster saw this state of affairs not just as a gulf between a younger generation of writers and an older generation of readers, but as, more generally, a cultural conservatism that extended even to many of his contemporaries among the poets. "Our fellow litterateurs just don't give a damn for anything new or exciting," he complained to Irving Layton in 1952. "How are we going to wake them up?"

The "how" in that question would be answered in part by Souster's own poetry, which slowly gained him a reputation through the course of the 1950s and culminated in his winning the Governor General's Award in 1964 for *The Colour of the Times*, the closing poem of which ("Be the Weed-Cutter") cuts a number of ways:

> *Be the weed-cutter*
> *steaming slowly the lagoons,*
> *working quietly, well,*
> *your blades searching out*
> *a clearer, deeper channel*
> *than has been before.*

But equally that "how" was answered by the parallel thrust of Souster's other work as editor, publisher, and *animateur*. Souster had edited his first poetry magazine during the war years, when he purloined paper and time at a mimeograph machine to produce *Direction* from the air force camp in Sydney, Nova Scotia, where he had been posted. With *Contact*, which first appeared in January 1952 in a press run of only a hundred copies (it was never more than two hundred), Souster began to make public his commitment to a renewal of Canadian poetry. That renewal was to be fostered largely by experimentation along international modernist lines, and along with Canadian work, *Contact* published a good deal of American writing and contemporary non-English-language poetry in translation. Souster was in touch with Olson, Creeley,

Cid Corman, and other American poets in the Pound-Williams-Zukofsky line, and *Contact* introduced their work to the Canadian scene. Souster also arranged for these and other American poets to read in Toronto in the Contact Poetry reading series which began in 1957.

Like many mags before and since, *Contact* gave rise to an eponymous small press, and it was through Contact Press that Souster's most enduring contribution to the development of Canadian poetry was made, apart from his own work, of course. The Contact imprint was attached almost as an afterthought to the first book of the press. Souster, Layton, and Dudek had been talking about a group book for some time before *Cerberus* (1952) was sent to press, and the three poets, independently it seems, thought it a good idea "to tie the thing in with the work we're trying to do in *Contact*," as Souster put it. Layton and Dudek mostly ran the press in the early years ("the press is strictly a twin baby between you and Louis," Souster told Layton in 1954), but Souster was deeply involved in the editorial process as well as in everything from publicity to records-keeping. His involvement increased over the years, particularly after Layton lost interest in the mid-1950s, and some of the more important books published in the 1960s were brought in by Souster. One of his last gestures as a part of Contact Press was to edit and publish *New Wave Canada* (1966), the important anthology that brought together the poetry of the 1960s generation (Michael Ondaatje, Daphne Marlatt, David McFadden, Victor Coleman, bpNichol, Fred Wah, et al.) for the first time. It is characteristic of Souster that the book was his centennial project, and that the 1,000 copies of it were collated in his basement on several doors from his house, removed from the hinges for the purpose. (What a wonderfully literal way to carry out Whitman's injunction to "Unscrew the locks from the doors! / Unscrew the doors themselves from their jambs!," quoted by Allen Ginsberg as the epigraph to *Howl and Other Poems*.)

In late 1952, when both the magazine and the press were still quite new, Souster reminded Layton of their difficult position vis-à-vis the established standards and traditions. "And let's not lose sight of the fact that we're a few isolated guys in a nation of 12,000,000 trying to put something we think is important over." The print runs of most of the Contact Press books were soberingly small, from as few as 25 up to only 500, the single exception being the historical anthology *Canadian Poems 1850–1950* prepared by Dudek and Layton and which sold well as an introductory text for university courses and was the only Contact Press title to appear in a second edition. The strain of quasi-anonymity sometimes told on Souster during the 1950s. Of his own collection *Shake Hands with the Hangman* (1953) he admitted that the reaction was "not very favourable... and I can perhaps see why. But a few have liked it and I don't give a damn anyway. More and more I am caring less and less about who cares about what around here." Of *Walking Death*, published the following year, he wrote glumly to Creeley that "after considerable experience I've decided that 25 copies is my present active audience and that to waste paper and the time doing more is just not to face the facts. Which are—who the hell cares about poetry?"

All the same, through *Contact* and Contact Press, and later through *Combustion* (1957–60), Souster was laying the groundwork for the efflorescence and the broader-based experimentalism that would occur in Canada in the 1960s. It is hard to imagine the poetic activity that included *Tish* on the West Coast and Coach House Books and House of Anansi Press in Toronto coming to pass if Contact Press and the work of Souster, Dudek, and Layton had not prepared the way. Aesthetically, Souster's own poetry bears the imprint of the American postmodernists in only the most marginal fashion, though he once admitted in the mid-1950s to having a notebook full of poems written à la Creeley. Souster's encounter with the work of William Carlos Williams was probably the last major formative influence on his style; the risks he took as a poet ("My problem is, as you may know, to make the most open statement possible and yet at the same time to strive to keep it from being too flat, too banal," as he wrote to Creeley) were the risks run by the poet in the Williams mode. Dozens of later poets, devoted to the same vernacular and phenomenalist approach, have run the same risks; few have been as consistently successful as he in achieving the kind of poem which might deservedly be called Sousterian:

THE SIX-QUART BASKET

The six-quart basket
One side gone
Half the handle torn off

Sits in the centre of the lawn
And slowly fills up
With the white fruits of the snow.

A GENTLEMAN
OF PLEASURE

ONE LIFE OF JOHN GLASSCO

To call the Canadian writer John Glassco (1909–81) a late bloomer would be a vast understatement. Apart from a single contribution to *This Quarter*, the 1920s Paris-based literary magazine edited by Ernest Walsh and Ethel Moorhead, Glassco published almost nothing until the 1950s. When he was paid five dollars for a poem read on CBC Radio in 1956 it was the first money he had ever made from his writing. During his rather ignominious career as an undergraduate at McGill University in Montreal in the 1920s he published a few brittle and cranky pieces in the student newspaper, but if they were the harbinger of more serious future work, it lay a very long way off. Glassco quit without graduating in 1927 and with an allowance from his father headed to the Paris of Joyce, Hemingway, and Gertrude Stein where, along with his friend and lover Graeme Taylor, he became well known rather quickly among the expatriate set. They saw a lot of Robert McAlmon and Kay Boyle, drank and giggled and postured and made a little extra money from various *sub-rosa* activities, and stored up memories for future possible poems, stories, novels, and memoirs. They were too busy living as writers actually to write much, however, and when Glassco was forced

to return to Canada because he contracted tuberculosis from a lover—
she also gave him a sexually transmitted disease for good measure—he
had little to show for his months in France. Among the many lies told by
Glassco during his lifetime, one was the claim that he had had a small
book of pornographic stories published in Paris in 1929 entitled *Contes
en crinoline*, but no copy has ever been traced by any Glassco scholar, and
Brian Busby, like his predecessors, is forced to admit that the book is
likely a ghost, or more possibly a simple fabrication.

Glassco is nevertheless best known to readers for his startlingly evocative and charming memoir of the Paris adventure, a book called *Memoirs
of Montparnasse*. It was first published in 1970, and many people, myself
included, think it the best of all the expatriate memoirs from that period
when a number of Canadian and American writers lived in Paris. Hemingway, Robert McAlmon, Kay Boyle, and Morley Callaghan among
others wrote memoirs too, but none is as compelling as Glassco's wonderful book. It is partly a matter of style and partly a matter of the good
stories recounted. After Glassco's death, Canadian scholars discovered
that his account of the book's genesis—he said that it was drafted in the
early 1930s when he was back in Quebec recovering from TB—was a lie,
and they also proved that many of the incidents in the book were either
invented, misdated, massaged to make the author look better, or otherwise altered. To my mind this caused a good deal of unnecessary
revaluation of the *Memoirs*, as though somehow Glassco's inventions
made the work any less worthy, and as though every memoir other than
his is rigorously truthful.

I say this despite the fact that Glassco's routine exaggerations and
distortions of the truth throughout his life are in fact troubling. He lied
almost as a matter of course, often about trivial matters and for little
apparent gain. Busby makes it clear that this character flaw had psychological roots in Glassco's childhood, for his father routinely beat
him and was in every way an unsympathetic character. An artistic son
was evidently the last thing he wanted, and from an early age Glassco

began keeping things from his parents and transmuting the truth to avoid confrontations. The physical abuse was also at the core etiologically of Glassco's sex life. He was bisexual, but also given to sadomasochism and several fetishistic compulsions. His pornographic books (he wrote many) largely deal with punishment and rubber fetishism and rarely exploit normative sexual pleasure with either sex. On the whole the texts are rather maidenly by today's standards; and although Busby claims to be surprised and depressed on Glassco's behalf that none of the books ever had a Canadian edition, despite their popularity elsewhere in the English-speaking world, they have surely all had their day in the era of the thousands of websites now servicing every paraphilia found in DSM-IV.

Lying became rote for Glassco, and that is the disquieting thing. He once claimed to have been the mayor of his town when he was only a member of the town council. His self-composed bibliographies are rife with invented entries and pseudonymous items. He stole books from libraries and faked at least one inscription to increase the value of a book. He was regularly unfaithful to all of his lovers (some of them his life partners, some not), and he even published stories under his name that had been written by his (then dead) partner Graeme Taylor. He more or less abandoned both Taylor and his own wife Elma as they lay dying, writing on one occasion: "But oh how I have deserted all those who once loved me—so many." One understands this kind of emotional infidelity, and in Glassco's case one sympathizes with it given his childhood experiences. All the same, the man as an adult, now that we have him fully described and explored by a competent biographer, seems rather a nasty person. His need to present himself as someone else and his ability to assume variant personalities certainly did not serve his work well in my opinion, although Busby thinks otherwise. He begins his biography with the statement that these "talents, cultivated at an early age, served well his art and public persona." Glassco's expert completion of Aubrey Beardsley's unfinished *Under the Hill* supports this contention, but in general I think those "talents" led him astray more often than they stood him in good stead.

In addition to the pornographic books and the *Memoirs of Montparnasse*, Glassco was a well-known poet and translator. The poetry is difficult to characterize and to place. It is not particularly modernist in tone or technique, and its frequent rootedness in a rural setting (Glassco lived much of his life after Paris in the Eastern Townships of Quebec on or near a farm) evokes not so much the tradition of Baudelaire and Huysmans (a tradition he claimed to be part of) as that of poets like John Clare and Francis Jammes. Pastiche and imitation he thought worthy of incorporating into his work, and the poetry often braves an *ubi sunt* self-indulgence that seems very much at odds with his sophisticated dandyism of spirit. As a translator, Glassco focused on what he would have called French-Canadian literature, and he was an accomplished practitioner in this field, in both poetry and fiction. His versions of the poems and the private journal of Hector de Saint-Denys Garneau, Quebec's first major modernist poet, are exquisitely done, and his anthology entitled *The Poetry of French Canada in Translation* (1970) was crucial in introducing the francophone poetry of Quebec to English readers. Glassco did not sympathize with the nationalist aspirations of most of the younger Quebec writers, and they for their part were rather contemptuous of his opinion that political posturing made for bad verse. All the same, his contributions to the profile of French-language Canadian poetry and prose were and remain deeply admirable and durable.

Brian Busby's biography—"one" life he deliberately calls it, although the specificity seems unnecessary to me—is solidly researched and mostly well written. He has interviewed many people who knew Glassco (though many of his closest friends had already died when Busby began his project), and he has made good use of archival material, especially Glassco's so-called Intimate Journal, an unpublished record which, while it needs to be read with a keen and critical eye (as does everything Glassco ever wrote!), is of tremendous biographical value. He navigates expertly through Glassco's pseudonymous writings and inventions, and he has consulted widely in the literary, bookselling, and horsey sets. (Glassco started and ran the Foster Horse Show for several years.) He is sometimes unforthcoming about where certain supporting evidence has fetched up (two important copies of the *Memoirs of Montparnasse*, for instance), and he makes a few mistakes, missing, for example, the fact that Glassco is parodying Keats when he writes about "a season of feasts and hallow frightfulness" (p. 292), and taking "Fecit" as an artist's surname, when it is of course the standard Latin indication of authorship for painters and engravers ("Leonardo *fecit*" equals "Leonardo made it"). The painter Marian Scott's given name is consistently misspelled with an *o*, and Busby has an odd way of referring to certain editions of books, for example calling one "the 1934 the English house Herbert Joseph edition."

This is on the whole a fine book, then, about a less than fine man. Glassco characterized himself in 1934 as a "trifler, dilettante, *petit-maître*," and although Busby takes issue with that self-appraisal, I think Glassco was essentially right. There is nothing wrong, after all, with being a *Kleinmeister*. Many writers, painters, and composers whom we value were exactly that. The history of the arts would be much the poorer without the work of Aloysius Bertrand, Ernest Chausson, and Henri Rivière, just to name three nineteenth-century French minor masters. By virtue of one imperishable book, some good poetry, and some excellent translations, not to mention his many famous friends and acquaintances, John Glassco deserves a biographer as accomplished as Brian Busby and a book as compellingly readable as *A Gentleman of Pleasure*.

—

Brian Busby, *A Gentleman of Pleasure: One Life of John Glassco, Poet, Memoirist, Translator, and Pornographer* (Montreal and Kingston: McGill-Queen's University Press, 2011).

THE IMPOSSIBLY/
BEAUTIFUL

PHYLLIS WEBB

I don't know whether there is any such thing as a "normal career" among Canadian poets, but if there is, Phyllis Webb has not had one. She is approaching ninety now and has not published a book of new poems in twenty-five years. She experienced silences in the past too—a highly critical article about her poetry by John Bentley Mays published in *Open Letter* in 1973 drove her into years of retreat—but it now seems safe to say that she abandoned poetry two and a half decades ago for painting. All along the way, even for those (like me) who knew her only from her work and not as a friend or colleague, there were signs aplenty that she found writing difficult, suffered from various kinds of anxiety and despair, and often thought poetry a command, not a choice, that might not be worth the psychic displacement, the writhing in public, as it were. As early as 1954 (she was twenty-seven) in a poem from her first book, she envisioned a future "where pain / is a lucid cargo." Eight years later, in "Countered" from *The Sea Is Also a Garden*, the world is said to "tether joy," a joy she defines powerfully, if sadly, as "creation's sweet pathetic trust." The poems in that book are full of the "anguish of being," and its contrary moments of comedy and high spirits are more than overwhelmed by images of the "only / remotely human," and statements such as that thinking about the various manners of suicide constitutes "surely the finest exercise of the imagination." *Naked Poems*, published in 1965, embodied a different affect. Minimalist utterances that feel barely articulate in a way, the poems nevertheless seemed to embody the emotions of a sometimes joyful lover, not a poet constantly under threat of erasure or at least of silence. The final section, which as Mays suggested appears to be organized like a psychotherapy session, with questions and answers, reveals some of the dread underlying the love poems and culminates in the interlocutor, whoever that is, saying, merely, "*Oh?*" And with that, Webb did not publish another book for fifteen years, including the time when she was, as she admitted, licking her wounds after the publication of the Mays article.

With *Wilson's Bowl* (1980), Webb seemed to rediscover her creative direction, and even if many of the poems in that book derived from a separate book about Peter Kropotkin that never cohered and was never published as such, and even if she talks quite openly about failure in many of the poems, the poetry itself demonstrated a greater technical sophistication and a broader range of emotion and music than her earlier books. *Water & Light* followed in 1984. A friend had introduced Webb to the Persian poetic form known as the ghazal (memorably brought into Canadian poetry by John Thompson in his book *Stilt Jack*). She clearly found the ghazal's typical combination of dislocation and emotional power congenial. To my mind, *Water & Light* contains her best poems, while *Hanging Fire* (1990), her final collection, embodies a less focused poetic intelligence and feels emotionally more decentred. Webb herself is on record as saying that *Hanging Fire* contains poems that she thought of as "my uglies," and while every poet deserves readerly latitude to publish "ragged" poems as well as polished work, nothing in Webb's final book is as beautiful and accomplished as the ghazals, particularly the so-called anti-ghazals in a section of *Water &*

Light entitled *Sunday Water*. John Hulcoop, the editor of *Peacock Blue*, includes a large group of uncollected and unpublished poems in a section following *Hanging Fire*. It is good to have these new poems to add to Webb's corpus of books, but they do not alter the shape of her lifetime's work in any surprising or unexpected way. With *Hanging Fire*, her work came to an end. *Peacock Blue* makes all of it available again in a well-edited text.

Phyllis Webb comes from a generation of modernist Canadian poets that begins with Irving Layton (born 1912) and includes P. K. Page (born 1917), Louis Dudek (born 1918), Raymond Souster (born 1921), and D. G. Jones (born 1929), among others. There is little similarity in the work of these poets, so while they are connected by generation, they do not share a common aesthetic in the way, for example, that Robert Lowell, Elizabeth Bishop, John Berryman, Anne Sexton, and Sylvia Plath—all born over a similar span of time as the Canadian group—more obviously do, whatever their dissimilarities. Phyllis Webb published her first poems in a group book called *Trio*, where she shared space with Eli Mandel and Gael Turnbull, a book published by Contact Press, which Layton, Dudek, and Souster had founded just two years earlier. Her early poems are formal, often rooted in discernible meter and with recourse to end-rhyme, as in these opening lines from "The Second Hand":

> Here, Love, whether we love or not
> involves the clock and its ignorant hands
> tying our hearts in a lover's knot;
>
> now, whether we flower or not
> requires a reluctance in the hour;
> yet we cannot move, in the present caught
>
> in the embrace of to be or not;

THE IMPOSSIBLY/BEAUTIFUL   237

This poem moves to a pleasant tetrameter music, and the rhyming, while not perfect ("hands" does not ever rhyme with another word), is well done, i.e., it has semantic as well as sonic significance within the poem. The work in *Even Your Right Eye* (1956), Webb's first solo collection, often moves with a similar formal grace, as one can hear in the first stanza of the wonderful "Lament":

> *Knowing that everything is wrong,*
> *how can we go on giving birth*
> *either to poems or the troublesome lie,*
> *to children, most of all, who sense*
> *the stress in our distracted wonder*
> *the instant of their entry with their cry?*

The repetition of "their" in that final line may represent a defect, but over all, this poem has a sad, tragic conviction that is utterly compelling. There are poems in that book, however, that dance to a different measure, and demonstrate that Webb will move beyond the poetic conventions she inherited. The opening piece, entitled "The Mind Reader," uses rhyme, but its musical pointing, set to a narrower and less predictable line (largely four, five, and six syllables), is delicate and elegant:

> *I thought,*
> *and he acted*
> *upon my thought,*
> *read by some wonderful*
> *kind of glass my mind*
> *saw passing that way*
> *gulls floating over boats*
> *floating in the bay,*
> *and by some wonderful*

> *sleight of hand*
> *he ordered the gulls to land*
> *on boats*
> *and the boats to land.*
>
> *Or, was it through waves*
> *he sent the boats*
> *to fly with gulls*
> *so that out of care*
> *they all could play*
> *in a wonderful*
> *gull-boat-water way*
> *up in a land of air?*

The Sea Is Also a Garden similarly contains poems in conventional form and line, but also poems that are less obedient to regularity. As the singularity of her music came to prominence, so too sometimes did the content of Webb's poems become more obscure, as her poet's ear, hearing music, cared less about semantic definition. "Why should we stop at all for what I think?," as Ezra Pound put it in an early sonnet.

Naked Poems marked a sharp change in Webb's work, but one from which, ultimately, she drew back. The emotions are rawer and the forms are extremely austere. In other words, the poetry is naked on every level. Critics have argued over the nature of the love affair that the poems encode, but in formal terms the poems constitute not so much a fruitful new development as an end point. Webb admits to "trying to write a poem" during the final conversation in *Naked Poems*, the one which sounds very like a psychiatric session; the sequence ends with nothing more than a single word, "*Oh?*," on one level nothing more than a vowel with a question mark. And so concludes the first half of Webb's career, with language seemingly disappearing into silence (as she had sometimes threatened that it would), and the lover in the middle of things, unshriven and somewhat unforthcoming, seemingly *in extremis* if rather cheerful at times about it ("I have given up / complaining").

With *Wilson's Bowl* began a ten-year period of great creativity for Webb, a decade in which she published three important new books and won the Governor General's Award for a fourth book, *The Vision Tree*, a selected poems edited by Sharon Thesen. *Wilson's Bowl* continued and ramified some of Webb's now well-established themes—the very first poem speaks of the fact "that / we are inconsolable," and another early poem allows almost casually that her decision about what to do next boils down to "Russia, Suicide or France"—but there is a breadth and richness in the poems that is new. She may, in a moment of her typical lack of self-assurance, feel that she'll "leave a legacy of buried verbs, a tight-mouthed treasure," but in fact she leaves much more. There is nothing "buried" about the music of lines like these, from the fourth of the "Poems of Failure":

> *Far out in the strait low star lights of the*
> *ferry boats follow a radar map.*
>
> *The cat jumps on my lap. She stares.*

Wilson's Bowl ends with a poem about "performing music and extinction," but Webb was far from finished then as a poet. Her take on the ghazal as collected in *Water & Light* was in a sense disrespectful of the traditional formal elements of the Persian poem, but indisputably regenerative for her own work. The "mellifluous / journey of the ten lines" with their "clandestine order" was seemingly highly congenial to her poetic instincts. She could even admit, contrary (or at least contiguous) to her usual lack of faith in the creative powers of nature and human realities, that "Everything is waiting for a condition of grace." With *Hanging Fire* she then went on to write more ghazals, prose poems, even visual and concrete poems (not her strength, per-haps), along with a sonnet, a poem in syllabics, and other experiments. And then she stopped. You can feel her stopping in that final book.

Peacock Blue is a huge book of poems. While inevitably in a poet's end-of-career *omnium-gatherum* there will be poems that go over one's head, poems that seem weak or failed, and poems that leave one impressed if unmoved—no one can write 500 pages of poetry without some slips and dips—Webb's life's work is a book to return to again and again for its virtuoso music, its philosophical breadth, and its moments of comfort and sanctification, oddly perhaps. The feeling is consis-tently one of struggle, psychically; she never gives in to a countervailing confessional voice, or at least when she does, she always holds things back. There is spiritual autobiography in *Peacock Blue* but seldom lit-eral autobiography. It is an impertinence to ask for names and times and dates from poetry anyway. When she says in the first line of the last poem in *Hanging Fire*, "Eye contact, and it's forever," you know she is not talking just about the Japanese print ostensibly the subject of the poem ("The Making of a Japanese Print"). She is evoking the poet and the poet's reader. With Phyllis Webb, that relationship, once estab-lished, is fated to last a lifetime.

—

Phyllis Webb, *Peacock Blue: The Collected Poems* (Vancouver: Talonbooks, 2014).

A SLAM-BANG
CASE OF EXTREMIS

K ingdom of Absence, Dennis Lee's first book of poetry, was published fifty years ago in 1967 and has never been reprinted, in
whole or in part. Its title announced a subject which Lee has been
exploring ever since; and despite the fact that his subsequent books
ostensibly focused on civic life, on erotic love, and on the perils of life,
especially urban life, in the twentieth century—getting and spending,
as Wordsworth put it, and the psychic dismemberment they can
cause—his real subject all along has been God. Several times in his
work Lee invokes the Latin word "*tremendum*," the theological concept
of awe and dread we feel when faced with the mystery of God. And
although he more often bemoans the absence in postmodernity of the
experience of *tremendum*, rather than adumbrating or even celebrating
it—it seems to have vanished just as civic order has disappeared, or as
the human respect and morality with which Lee grew up in 1940s and
'50s Toronto has gone—the need for it remains strong in his feelings
and in his search for a rich and reliable manner of being in the world.
Lee may claim in the third of his *Civil Elegies* that "it is two thousand
years since Christ's corpse rose in a glory, / and now the shiny ascent
is not for us, [Tom] Thomson is / done and we cannot / malinger
among the bygone acts of grace," but in truth that is exactly what *Heart*

Residence comprises: a malingering among the bygone acts of grace, an unceasing hunt for spiritual truth, for God. Lee never really left behind the pious Methodist teenager from Don Mills who aspired to be a man of the cloth.

The tessitura of Lee's language is unusually broad. He will use *logos* and *aevum* and, again, *tremendum*, while also overindulging in boyish slang words such as "hoo boy" and "awright" and "yippee." A typical Lee line will combine those two extremes of diction: "and snag apocalypse," for example, or "Lost in the dark, with a slam-bang case of extremis." The poems can sometimes sound like the equivalent of what an inexperienced duck hunter might do, filling the sky with shot in the hopes of hitting *something, anything*, metaphorically God or some sort of authenticity, even if it comes from trying to be someone you're not. The love poems gathered in *Riffs* aspire to the instantaneity of jazz or the blues, and celebrate the body of woman ("woman," "baby") as a substitute for the body of Christ. The ecstasy feels willed and self-conscious ("the onus of joy," "the / tasks of / passion"), too much a forced letting go that the poet is watching closely, like an observer rather than a celebrant:

> But if I gain
>
> beatitude galore, and lose the gift of
>
> moral discernment,
>
> how real are my rarified highs?

How real indeed? The impulse he describes elsewhere, the irresistible "whiff of carnal joy" with which "a man will come unhinged, / or try to cram the body of his longing / thru somebody else's flesh into heaven, / to never be lonesome again" is undeniably real, and so truthfully expressed as to leave one in awe. But absolution and redemption, words that Lee invokes more than once in his work, are not finally to be found in the body of the woman, and sometimes the record of that search there leaves him inarticulate: "Even the speechlessest rockface deigns to utter its pendant climbers," ends one of the *Riffs*, in as ugly a line of poetry as ever a talented poet came up with and allowed to stand.

Although they have been lauded by some critics, Lee's most recently published poetry collections, *Un* and *Yesno*, strike me frankly as unreadable. Having essayed a substitute eternity in sex and jazz, Lee turned to a kind of L-A-N-G-U-A-G-E poetry that achieves little beyond wordplay, as though he hopes, in the very cauldron of a kind of drunken vocabularianism, to find evidence of God at work. To my ear, the result is little better than babble:

> *Blah-blah was easy, we*
> *diddled the scrutable chunks;*
> *whole hog was beyond us.*
>
> *Bugspace &*
> *chugspace ahead,*
> *welcome wormlandia.*
>
> *The birds con-*
> *trive a nest. The wolves a lair.*
> *Sheer matricide is rare.*
>
> *Undernot rising. Bad*
> *OM, the*
> *holes in the wholly.*

Two whole collections of this sort of irritable reaching after fact and reason (if that is what it is) are both too little and too much. With this style we are wrestled into a universe far, far removed from the Pindaric nobility and the reasoned diction of the *Civil Elegies*, into the "here and now" which Lee regrets denying as a twenty-something in the wonderful poem "Not Abstract Harmonies But." In these poems the puritanism that plagues Lee's consciousness from the very beginning, and the harsh self-criticism that it engenders ("I came by / generations of flesh and methodists to lucid dead-end"), leaves him *in extremis* indeed: there is nothing left but syllables. If at the very darkest moment of his dark night of the soul he can survive only by proposing that "You're born; you jack off; you die," then what's left for a poet but gibberish?

By the end of *Heart Residence*, Lee admits that, having "trashed our sacramental / birthright," what remains is an unappeasable hunger, a hunger for something that he cannot name. The troubling title poem compiles the things of the world that have meaning for him—fellow creatures ("the bone fraternity / of things that are born and die," he says memorably), place, and his "dear ones" (friends, family, woman, children)—and then releases all of them in the unconsecrated certainty of "No / home but hunger." No poet has been as articulate at times about emptiness, about the loss of what he calls "passionate awe in our lives," as Dennis Lee. But what is a religious poet to do when "the breadcrumbs are gone," as he writes in the final poem in his book? There is no saving grace in language itself, that is obvious.

—

Dennis Lee, *Heart Residence: Collected Poems 1967–2017* (Toronto: Anansi, 2017).

FLOATING UP TO ZERO

K en Norris is a New York–born Canadian poet who lives, when he has to, in Orono, Maine, and teaches at the university there. For many years now he has passed his days and written his poetry as much as possible on the road, or during short lengths of stationary time in many different places, especially Thailand and China, but also Macao, Malaysia, Singapore, Cambodia, and Burma. Before that it was Europe, with sojourns in the Dominican Republic for psychic recovery. He is not so much a cosmopolitan as a Canadian traveller who is rarely in Canada, although most of his books are published there. He is as restless as a poet can be, "a traveler / in an antique land," as he says in a poem, echoing Shelley, accumulating memories but suspicious of memory as such ("Why remember? / It's only a way / to fill in the present emptiness"), living mostly in the big cities where "everything... is traffic and color," not avoiding his demons but not waiting for them to catch up with him either. He is poetically observant without designedly hunting for exotic experiences to write about. The *ewige Weiblich* is part of the wind at his back, and some of his poems are inspired by his erotic successes and failures. (One poem in *Floating Up to Zero*, called simply "Song," is that hoary old generic thing, a "come live with me and be my love" seduction poem.) But away from America he goes with the flow, as they say, and it is the "unfamiliar" that, paradoxically, "welcomes [him] home." Many of his poems are paratactic out of a desire to record his sensual experience as it plays out. "Meanwhile," a poem in *Floating Up to Zero*, is typical of this poetic mode, as it brings all the senses to bear in focusing on a normal day in Phnom Penh, a day as always when washing is done and cars honk incessantly and restaurants prepare for the lunch crowd. The catalogue of sense impressions is interrupted once or twice, as when "a green heart is being born" or when Norris speaks of "lost nights and broken promises." (The opening poem in *Zero* speaks of a green heart also.) But his attention is on the things around him rather than on any human negotiation or pattern-seeking, and the poem as a result has an intoxicating narrative essentially without beginning or ending. That is why Norris can speak of "an infinite repertoire" in the closing stanza of the final poem in *Zero*, a poem entitled "Work":

> *In solitude, in a room somewhere,*
> *in a country you have never known,*
> *within the walls of an infinite repertoire,*
> *at this table,*
> *the work goes on.*

Cosmological theory insists that the universe is finite but unbounded, which explains perhaps why an infinite repertoire can have walls around it. That is to say, there is no end of subjects for a poet who wishes not just to talk about his heart, but about the great world in which that heart beats and has its life of joy and grief.

In a poem in *Vegetables*, his first book, published over thirty-five years ago, Ken Norris tells the story of Stymie Beard, one of the child actors who made up the movies' Our Gang, and how he kept discarding the leaves of an artichoke he was served in the mistaken view that there was an edible centre to be found. When he found nothing at the centre, he threw the lot away, the "inner nothingness of the artichoke" being such a disappointment. There is an obvious metaphor in this anecdote, and while it has not in any palpable sense governed Norris's life or work in the decades that followed his first collection (and many subsequent books), it has remained a theme, along with other persistent themes: love and solitude, the seasons, travel, memory, and the realization that there is a centre to experience, but that it is always changing, evanescent, and of the moment. The poet is "the reluctant witness" to this central truth.

That at least seems to be the heart of the poetics in which *Floating Up to Zero*, Norris's most recent book, eventuates. "The Poetics" is in fact the title of the final section of the book, and the ten poems gathered under that rubric all constitute—sometimes overtly and sometimes indirectly—an *ars poetica* not so much of technique or language as of sensual and intellectual address. The poem "Mid-Day" with which the section begins combines memory (it is a poem that remembers Tonga in a book largely set in Thailand and Cambodia) with an unwavering focus on the sensual details of a moment in time, and the poet, as he often is, is "intoxicated" by what Melville once called (in *Mardi*, that strangest of his novels) the *polysensuum*. The sensual field is briefly interrupted by the prospect of a bus's arrival and the prediction that it will run over a dog on its way to where the poet is waiting, i.e., a shift of attention to the future or the prospective. But quickly the focus reverts to the present ("for now it's the white road and the flying foxes overhead"). "Sex," the poem that follows, is all about the lovely mindlessness of erotic desire and physical contact, and how in bed "time breaks apart / and a new unspoken world emerges." There are no second-hand vectors here toward a philosophy, just the witnessing of a voice speaking to passionate moments and sensual abandon, what Norris beautifully denominates in a later poem "the sweetness / of an attendance now so fully realized." Other poems in this concluding section augment Norris's "attendance" to the present. In many of his poems, and not just here, rain seems to represent temporal suspension; when the rain falls, everything else is blotted out:

> Last night I listened to the rain
> falling on the roof, falling in the street,
> falling everywhere. I was trying
> to get to sleep, and I could not
> get to sleep. Still, the rain
> comforted me. When it comes
> it comforts everyone, especially
> the green earth. ("Rainy Season")

Rain for Norris is the release into fate, then, the pleasurable abandonment of strife and need: not a permanent condition, certainly, but one where poetry often takes root.

But the poetics of Norris's *Floating Up to Zero* is not simply about paying attention to the moment which, after all, can be tiresome and hurtful as well as liberating:

> Perhaps the boredom of a moment
> and the slow passage of an age
> are indeterminably fused.

Along with a degree of Zen impassivity there is also an irrepressible sense of longing:

> I have this hunger and thirst, a longing for the clouds and dragonflies,
> a ready ear, an indirect joy. Between green swaying trees and beggars,
> between directions and complaints, I see the world
> in the new mirror and know it
> for the displaced thing it often is,

taking refuge in the green rice fields, refuge in the arms of women,
as the acetylene sun rises in the sky.

(The dragonflies appear in another poem in the book, where Norris writes that "I used to have a mission / that made me feel at one with the dragonflies," and the front cover of *Floating Up to Zero* uses a photograph of a red dragonfly perched on a lotus flower.) The longing is for work, for the work of writing poetry; having a "ready ear" is what makes a poet, finally, and, as Norris adds, the joy comes not directly from the details that fill daily life, but from the "indirect" act of transmuting them into poems. "Understand I am creating it all as I go," he contends in an earlier poem in *Zero*, and in the final poem in the book, we find him alone in a room in a foreign country, conspiring with Time to get the work of writing done.

"The Poetics" is the ninth and final section in *Zero*. Of the other eight sections, four constellate around the seasons, while the second and eighth sections focus on the United States and Asia respectively. "Winter Carousel," the section which falls exactly in the middle of the book, stands out by being comprised of off-beat prose poems (Norris has called them "wacky"), inserted despite their not belonging there for any obvious reason (he says so himself in one of them, called "The Poet's Lariat") apart from the fact that Norris had promised "George"—the poet George Bowering presumably—that he would do so. The themes of these attractive prose poems are not very different from the central concerns of the rest of the book: winter kills the spirit, old age is impending, modern life is empty (by his own admission, Norris's central concern), and so on; but he does allow himself a greater flexibility of tone, from the flippant to the epigrammatic to the very offhand to the list poem ("No to the surgical strike. Yes to fantasy. Yes to precision orgasm. No to reality TV. No to the general malaise"). Poetry normally shrinks with good reason from mere opinions, but the prose poem, with its less definite content frontier, gives room for statements such as that Herman Melville is "the Warren Oates of literature" or that "Amiri Baraka knows how to debate. Barrett Watten knows how to pontificate. No contest."

Almost in the middle of the prose poem sequence is one called "Zero." Here zero is a simple measure of temperature (Celsius, of course), the point at which winter's back is broken and "something is about to melt." Elsewhere in the book "zero" is more allusive, more metaphorical in intent. In the title poem, which comes first in the section of poems written in the United States, "zero" is the end point or the point of equilibrium achieved, blissfully, after a period of depression and despair. But in a later poem, "Zero Itself," zero is more allied to negation (it and the word "cipher" both come etymologically from an Arabic word meaning "emptiness"). Norris counsels returning to the state represented by zero, as though the search for identity were a fraud:

> The individual, negated,
> brings the sum back to zero.
> Zeros and ones.
> We live in a world of zeros and ones.
> You've tried so hard to be one.
> Now be zero.

The allusion to the binary numeral system (the zeros and ones used by computers) doesn't seem particularly crucial here. I think rather that Norris is trying to get at a state where poetry becomes possible. He says it differently in a poem entitled "The Poet":

> So close to the quiet
> and yet a voice
> still whispers.

I've cleared away
everything, in order
to hear it.

I take him to mean that it is the eccentric noise of personality that needs to be cleared away in order for the poet to be able to overhear the world, and that that is how poems are made. In the title poem, it is a "halo of anonymity" that he seeks. "Zero" is not a point of dissolution or disappearance, but a kind of balance point and much to be desired. It is where "Unity," a key poem, in my view, proposes that we must live.

"Unity" is the fifth poem in the first section, entitled "Resident," unquestionably with reference to Neruda's *Residence on Earth*, several poems from which Norris takes as a kind of skeleton over which he writes his own poems instead of translating directly, rather like Jack Spicer in his book *After Lorca*. The unity addressed in the poem of that name is something akin to a nodal congruence of the human and the natural worlds. With its imagery of greenness, water, and blood, it is hard not to be reminded of Dylan Thomas's poem "The Force That Through the Green Fuse Drives the Flower," especially as Norris's poem begins with the words "A green fuse." It doesn't matter greatly whether the allusion is deliberate or not—Thomas seems an unlikely Norris companion in poetry, and furthermore there is a Neruda poem with the same title of "Unity" that is equally germane—and Norris's poem goes in a very different direction. The centre of "Unity" is the present moment, the place where rivers merge and we are "enmeshed." The moment does not provoke clarity all the time, since it can be characterized by "an ardent confusion," but its "consonance" is uppermost and its colour is green, the colour of the natural world. Even the birds sing "their green song." The poem ends, rather unexpectedly, with a shift of imagery as Norris likens the sunlight striking the earth to "a hard slap across the mouth / drawing blood." The clarity of the moment having been described earlier in the poem as "improbable" suggests that we fall into and out of "unity" with the world all the time, and sometimes that falling out can hurt, like an unforeseen slap in the face, leaving us, as Norris says in another poem ("August in America") "in this state / of evaporating grace, watch[ing] everything / on green stems waver."

The seasons give Norris analogies for his feelings. Much of what fills the four sections with seasonal titles ("Autumn," "When the Snow Falls," "The Road to Spring," and "Summer as a Topic") presents the poet in passionate moments of ardour, longing, elegy, and fear of age and death, and in general those passions are aligned with the appropriate weather. The relationship is neither constant nor predictable. Neither is it in Vivaldi's *Four Seasons*, where surprisingly "Summer" is in a minor key, like "Winter," and, to pick another example at random, like Gershwin's song "Summertime." "Autumn" contains poems about the end of relationships, about memory, about our limitations as sentient beings ("the awful timidity / of our lives and works"), while "When the Snow Falls" contains poems addressing loss, aging, the invisibility of the sixty-year-old lover ("How the wallpaper longs / for what's in the room"), and alienation from life's fray. Spring is demonstrably Norris's favourite season, and "The Road to Spring" is full of the imagery of rebirth: crocuses poking up, reawakened desire, the shape of women as proof of intelligent design, daffodils and sunshine. "Summer as a Topic" by contrast is not especially celebratory despite the sun and the heat. The poem of the same title alludes to *Suddenly Last Summer*, the Tennessee Williams play that was made into a film with Elizabeth Taylor, in which a gay man is murdered and possibly eaten in a bacchantic fury by the Spanish boys he was trying to seduce. The "summer" of this section is not as uniformly ghastly as that allusion might portend, but on the whole Norris experiences it both as a farewell to spring and as a harbinger of worse to come, rather than as a time of ecstasy. "See you again, somehow" is the concluding line of the last poem in the section. The elegiac quality of many of the poems gathered in "Summer as a Topic" makes one realize that the polysemy of the book's title must include surcease—that the phrase "floating up to zero" encompasses, among other significations, the course of a life and its end in nothingness.

The title poem of Ken Norris's book ends with a direct allusion to A. M. Klein's wonderful "Portrait of the Poet as Landscape," Klein's most accomplished work and one of the great Canadian poems of the mid-century. Klein originally entitled his draft "Portrait of the Poet as a Nobody," and his surviving notes for this poem include the rather depressing sentence: "Cursed be the day I penned my first pentameter." "Portrait" is essentially about the poet's invisibility in society ("incognito, lost, lacunal"), but toward its conclusion Klein begins to rescue the poet from his state of *desaparecido*, or at any rate to valorize it. The poet, in the concluding lines of the poem,

> *Makes of his status as zero a rich garland,*
> *a halo of his anonymity,*
> *and lives alone, and in his secret shines*
> *like phosphorus. At the bottom of the sea.*

It is the "halo of anonymity" that Norris borrows, and it is a rich phrase, one that might generally characterize not just the poet today as in Klein's time, but that might also hint more personally at one of the motivating factors in Norris's long period of world travel. The halo is a crown of laurels, for certain, but the poet wears it wherever he goes and still remains a zero, a Baudelairean *anonyme*. If that sounds grim, in fact it is not at all. For Norris, it constitutes (to complete his line) "the silent hallelujah," a paradox to be sure, but a joyful one.

—

Ken Norris. *Floating Up to Zero.* (Vancouver: Talonbooks, 2011).

INFINITE VISTA
AND THE MIND AT PLAY

D. G. (Doug) Jones died in early March this year, just a few short months before this selection of his poems was scheduled for publication. He was eighty-seven and was, according to Jim Johnstone, the book's selector, quite ill at the end, but devoted, as he had always been, to the idea of the book. Jones had a long career. Next year, 2017, will mark the sixtieth anniversary of the publication of his first book, *Frost on the Sun*, which Louis Dudek (who taught Jones as an undergraduate student at McGill) and Raymond Souster published through Contact Press. He was one among several young poets who were interested in myth and who were associated with Northrop Frye (rightly or wrongly), including Gwendolyn MacEwen (whose *The Rising Fire* was published by Contact Press in 1963) and Margaret Atwood (Contact Press issued *The Circle Game* in 1966). *Butterfly on Rock* (1970), Jones's only critical book, is discernibly in the Frye ambit, although it is also clearly the work of a poet and not just an observer, however smart and well read. After *Frost on the Sun*, Jones went on to publish nine other collections of poems, as well as some important translations of Québécois poetry. His *Under the Thunder the Flowers Light Up the Earth* (1977)—surely the best title of any Canadian poetry book in the almost four hundred years since Robert Hayman's *Quodlibets*—won the Governor General's Award, as did Jones's translation of Normand de Bellefeuille's *Categorics: 1, 2, and 3* (1992). Jones also co-founded *Ellipse* with his then wife, Sheila Fischman, and a colleague, Joseph Bonenfant, a semi-annual journal that, unique in bilingual Canada, focused on both French and English writing, with translations of each literary work it published. *Ellipse* eventually migrated to New Brunswick and closed up shop in 2012, but during its run it made an essential contribution to bridging the two solitudes, from the beginning of the (first) Trudeau era. Jones would also resort to French in some of his original poems, although as a technique or a spiritual address, this idea has not found many followers, even among those poets comfortable in both languages.

Jones's MA thesis at Queen's University was on Ezra Pound—its title was *The City of Dioce: The Cantos of Ezra Pound as Seen Through a Study of the Images of Building*—and he was, in some obvious ways, a poet in the mid-century modernist tradition. His training at McGill by Louis Dudek would have assured that alliance and influence. But in some essential way that is perhaps truer to his instincts, he was at heart a nature poet. He grew up in Bancroft, Ontario (David Milne territory, as "A Garland of Milne" in *Under the Thunder* makes clear), and had a lifelong deep and spiritual response to birds and flowers, to weather and landscape. The second and last poems in *The Essential D. G. Jones* are about birds, and about halfway through comes "The Pioneer as Man of Letters," a poem so replete with the names of wildflowers as to be almost overwhelming. It is an alphabet poem, and yes, there are nods to myth during its evocative recital of "hepaticas, bright hips and haws" and "soapwort, saxifrage [and] black-eyed Susans"—a wyvern creeps in there as well as a reference to "the serpent's wisdom," not to mention Ugolino, the Italian count whom Dante claimed ate his own children—but essentially this wonderfully fantastic poem is about a pioneer encountering the landscape, letter by letter, as it were. Of course other poems register Jones's captivation by myth and cultural history. "Odysseus," for example, from *The Sun is Axeman* (1961), is a monologue in the voice of Odysseus based largely in the so-called Nekuia (the voyage to the underworld) in Book 11 of the *Odyssey*. This book contains the lines which Pound translated imperishably as "Canto 1." Jones's poem is not a straight translation, but it has a Homeric solidity and even grandeur that is very impressive:

> What cities, and men, what girls
> Might have known this face, these eyes,
> What faces might my eyes have known,
> Since, discarding faces, lives,
> I fled across the waters red with suns
> In search of one face, life, and home.

Homer's Greek is definitely behind some of this. (Pound often quoted the line from the opening of the *Odyssey* that describes the hero, πολλῶν δ᾽ ἀνθρώπων ἴδεν ἄστεα καὶ νόον ἔγνω, the "cities and men" bit.) But this sort of subject matter is relatively rare in Jones's poetry. He much prefers to look for poetry in his backyard, just as did his friend and colleague Ralph Gustafson. (They lived on the same street in North Hatley, Quebec, for many years.)

Jim Johnstone's very judicious selection of poems from Jones's nine collections teaches us much about the poet apart from his lifelong grounding in nature. Johnstone makes something of Jones's transition to a postmodern poet in his excellent foreword; but while there is certainly a case to be made for that evolution, what is most striking in *The Essential D. G. Jones* is the technical consistency of his poetry, at least in part. It is true that the earlier poems are more metrically conventional. Take, for example, the opening stanza from "Beautiful Creatures Brief as These" (such a lovely title!), with its almost metronomic pattern of stresses:

Like butterflies but lately come
From long cocoons of summer
These little girls start back to school
To swarm the sidewalks, playing-fields,
And litter air with colour.

Ibycus's well-known spring poem surely lies somewhere behind this poem—Pound made a version which Jones will have known, and so have Anne Carson and Ken Norris, memorably—but Jones's version is very traditional in terms of meter. That traditional approach can be heard in other early poems too, such as "Music Comes Where No Words Are," and even in later individual lines, such as "The titans he contained in a cartouche," from the aforementioned "A Garland of Milne." But as he matured, Jones began to drop regular meter (though he never gave up assonance and consonance, as no poet should), and to treat the line as a different sort of unit, more architectural than metric. He also varied his tone considerably in later poems, a change that yielded lines like "Hey man, we're on the street" or "surfing the net is no relief for the child." (The release from initial capital letters on every line happened earlier.)

As he began to pay less attention to meter, Jones began to treat the poetic line more as a unit of syntax or even breath, much as Pound and later poets like Robert Creeley did. At the same time, he resorts frequently to enjambment to give his stanzas a flowing quality, as in "Winter Comes Hardly" (again from *Under the Thunder*):

                    a constant
          grinding of small cars, trucks
          made buses, the wooden benches
          roofs, packed with baskets, bundles
          produce, a pig in a poke, all

> *rattling over the pocked, serpentine*
> *mountain roads...*

He is describing winter in a hot climate in this poem, a very un-Canadian winter chaos of pungent smells, tropical fruits, children and domestic animals at large—all the very antithesis of death ("winter is Hell / for whoever has made no confession") with which winter is usually depicted in Canadian poetry. Jones's celebration of this sensual swirl finds its technical incarnation in those run-on lines that are so characteristic of this poems and others:

> *still*
> *winter comes hardly here with bikinis*
> *sprawled on the beaches, the body splayed*
> *on the plastic deck, rocking*
> *in a leeward breeze*

Later poems are more austere in their pointing, but Jones never lost his keen eye and ear. The subject matter remained characteristic too. Jones might easily have turned into an apocalyptic eco-poet, given the widespread destruction of species, the pollution, and the threats of climate change that marked the decades of his life, even in the pastoral Eastern Townships of Quebec. But while that degradation is alluded to occasionally—he wonders how the birds manage to sleep in the glare of floodlights in a poem called "Singing Up the New Century" from *Wild Asterisks in Cloud* (1997)—he can still focus on "a forlorn bit of juniper / stuck in a vase" in the face of vastation (the unusual word is his) in a late uncollected poem tellingly titled "Ideas of the End of the World." He remained somehow cheerful to the end. While he rarely wrote about love, a Creeleyesque lyric poem like "Stumblesong" (another terrific title) nimbly and convincingly encompasses the mixed blessing of an aging life, including "a dry endearment" from the loved one, and ends with the admission, not regretted it seems, that everything is "just gently / coming apart." Maybe so, but D. G. Jones accepted that state of affairs with as much sangfroid as he'd ever had, and wrote about it (as usual) beautifully.

—

D. G. Jones, *The Essential D. G. Jones*, ed. Jim Johnstone (Erin, ON: the Porcupine's Quill, 2016).

THIS HEAVY CRAFT
P. K. PAGE'S COLLECTED POEMS

P. K. Page has had a long and interesting career as a poet, and at eighty-one years of age she has now capped it with the publication of *The Hidden Room*, her collected poems in two hefty volumes. Page first made her mark as a Montreal poet in the 1940s, when she was associated with Patrick Anderson, F. R. Scott, and the other writers who banded together to issue *Preview*, a mimeographed little magazine. She already knew John Sutherland, the editor of the rival magazine *First Statement* and the author of the first serious article on Page's poetry. But after her involvement in the Montreal poetry circles of that decade, Page went to work for the National Film Board and eventually married its chairman Arthur Irwin, the former editor of *Maclean's*. Irwin went on to a diplomatic career after his stint at the NFB, and Page left Canada to accompany him on a series of foreign postings that included Australia and Brazil. Eventually they settled in Victoria, where they still live.

The English influences on the *Preview* poets were visibly and audibly present in Page's early poetry; although her work did evolve through the 1950s and '60s, it remained formally somewhat conservative. Rhyme and traditional prosody are very prevalent in the first volume of *The Hidden Room*. The social concerns of the 1930s and '40s were very much her poetic material in her first couple of books, and a kind of bias against or resistance to the expression of highly personal concerns has never left her. Poetry, in her view, provides access to a world well beyond the personal: "earth is a briar patch" and "I fear flesh which blocks imagination" among many other instances bear witness to a theory of the poet's role that is rather austere, even magisterial at times. Though her understanding of the imagination is apparently more romantic than this would suggest—the "hidden room" of the title is the imagination, and she says that, "Like the Bodleian like the Web / like Borges' Aleph / it embodies all"—the poetry itself has strong classicist elements. A stanza like the following, from an early poem entitled "Schizophrenic," is characteristic in both its rhythm and its use of end-rhyme:

> Malleable she wore her lustre nails
> daily like a debutante and smoked,
> watching the fur her breath made as they joked,
> caught like a wind in the freedom of their sails.

Certainly these conventional qualities are less in evidence in Page's more recent work, but one can still detect them in the Wallace Stevens poem from *Hologram*, for example, published in 1994:

> Make a prime number of it, pure, and know
> it indivisible and hold it so
> in the white sky behind your lapis eyes.

Like other poets of the 1940s, such as Scott and Birney, Page did attempt to adapt to more contemporary influences, and like both of those poets, the results are not always happy. When the metrics go out the window, she is capable of writing as clunky a stanza as the opening lines of "Remembering":

> *Remembering you and reviewing*
> *our structural love*
> *the past re-arises alive*
> *from its smothering dust.*

On the other hand, a poem called "Legend" from the same section of the second volume of *The Hidden Room*, though closer in feeling to her earlier poetry, shows the intense musicality of which she is capable at her best:

> *How pack a farm at midnight?*
> *Grey sheep*
> *stupid as tombstones, cows gentle with sleep.*
> *How move the whole collection up the slope*
> *to what would still be land when stuck and seep*
> *of creeping water found its level, filled*
> *this basin in the hills?*
> *How speak when all but water's tongues were sure*
> *to hear the language that the water spoke?*

The more recent poems in the book, collected together in the final section called grimly enough "Now That I Am Dead," embody both the best and the worst of her older style and her adaptation to contemporaneity. She can write as lovely a pair of lines as the conclusion of "Autumn" ("Small / sparks spin off from the whirr / of what must be my heart") and as prosy and throwaway a poem as "Complaint," which is a complaint to God about the fact that the world is going to hell in a handcart. The final poem, "This Heavy Craft," is a brief piece that sees the poet in old age as an Icarus figure, grounded but still trying to take flight, at least in dreams.

The arrangement of this book seems to me unfortunately chosen. Perhaps I'm old-fashioned, but I would have expected that a collected poems would have printed Page's work in chronological order, from her earliest books through to recent, unpublished, or uncollected poems. Instead, Page and her editor decided to group poems non-chronologically, so that work from *As Ten As Twenty* (1946) and *The Metal and the Flower* (1954), her first two books, is broken up and appears in both volumes of *The Hidden Room*, separated from its original context. This makes it extremely difficult to construct any notion of Page's development without actually consulting the other books and trying to realign poems in the order of their publication, if not their composition. The order as settled on by Page and Stan Dragland may perhaps provide a more varied reading experience if one is reading straight through from beginning to end, but that advantage seems to me to be outweighed by what is lost. On the other hand, Page seems largely to have resisted the lure of revision, and as far as I am able to determine, such few revisions to the poems as have been made are minor. Few Canadian poets of this century have been lucky enough to see their collected poems in print, and we owe the Porcupine's Quill a debt of gratitude for giving Page this ultimate and elusive accolade. It is the rare publisher these days who is willing to bring out 500 pages of poetry. Page's "great desire to write it all" here finds its monument.

—

P. K. Page, *The Hidden Room*, ed. Stan Dragland (Erin, ON: the Porcupine's Quill, 1997).

WHERE LOVE IS
LOVELY, NOT LONELY

ON A POEM OF P. K. PAGE

P . K. Page was born one hundred years ago, on November 23, 1917. With Dorothy Livesay, she is perhaps the earliest Canadian female poet whom we read today with pertinence and pleasure and emotional recognition. With her we do not have to make an adjustment or a little mental containment for history, for an inescapably different sensibility and time, as we do for Marjorie Pickthall, say, or Isabella Valancy Crawford, or Pauline Johnson. Her loyalties as a poet were complicated, but they are mostly ours still, her ear an ear that heard the things that we too hear, her heart, hidden as it sometimes was behind an arras, nevertheless one with our hearts. There is pause only in the fact that the closer she approached autobiography, the less open she became. (Her certainty about the risks of emotional confession is nicely encoded in a comment she made, according to her biographer, when an aspiring boyfriend chided her for picking peas from a plant that had spilled out onto the sidewalk: "That's the penalty you pay for planting your peas on a public path.") The title of her verse memoir, *Hand Luggage*, determinately records that she wanted to travel lightly when she set out to look back over her life; she covered the facts adroitly, but the emotions are often spared us, if that is the right verb. That reticence, whatever its source and oxygen, can make the reader unhappy. (Ralph Gustafson's verse memoir, *Configurations at Midnight*, perhaps the only other memoir in verse by a Canadian poet, is much more expressive of feeling.) Of course reticence is not so surprising in a woman who reached the age of majority before World War II, a woman whose beloved father was a military man, a woman whose earliest erotic life had to be strictly covert and poetically unattended. The reticence became habitual—she says quite frankly in Don Winkler's NFB film about her that love poems came to her with difficulty—but it is only one small demerit in a body of work that contains so many amazements and embodies such great poetic skill.

Perhaps there is no such thing as a "normal" career for a Canadian poet, apart from the certainty that a poet's life will not be elaborated on or supported by poetry alone. Like many poets of her time and place, Page worked at a variety of jobs, in offices and retail shops mostly, until in the spring of 1946 she happily wound up at the then National Film Commission as a writer. She had been fortunate in finding supportive artistic communities twice before she moved to Ottawa, first in New Brunswick, where Miller Brittain painted a stunning portrait of her, looking startlingly patrician and resolutely unforthcoming, and later in Montreal, where she was part of the group of poets who brought out *Preview* magazine and where she met and fell in love with F. R. (Frank) Scott. It was the early 1940s, and Page had not yet published a book; but she and A. M. Klein were certainly the most accomplished poets in that mostly male group, at least from our perspective. (Like the older Klein before her, Page's poetry would first appear in a small anthology: Klein had appeared in *New Provinces* with five other poets in 1936, Page was included in *Unit of Five* with four other poets in 1944. Neither book sold well.) At the NFB (to use its later, final name) Page met Arthur Irwin, its commissioner at the time, and their marriage (she was thirty-three, he was fifty-two) transformed her life from usual-for-a-poet to rare-for-a-poet: she became the wife of the soon-to-be Canadian ambassador to Australia, Brazil, and Mexico, in that order, after Irwin left the NFB. Page later settled in Victoria for the remainder of her life when Irwin was made the publisher of the Victoria *Times* newspaper after retiring from External Affairs. She had in the meantime published several books of poetry and, despite a long spell of silence during her years as a wife-ambassadress, she became recognized gradually as one of Canada's most gifted poets. She also had a second career as a visual artist under the name P. K. Irwin. (All of this and much more is ably recounted in Sandra Djwa's excellent 2012 biography, *Journey with No Maps*.)

What do we mean when we claim that a poet is gifted? Many qualities clamour as essential: emotional openness and intellectual acumen, instinct as well as knowledge of form and poetic history, sympathy for the vast range of human nature and behaviour, an innate ability at self-analysis or self-presentation, an eye for visual forms and compelling imagery, and perhaps most importantly, an ear for the music of language—what happens inside, between, and among words when they are spoken in the mind's ear or out loud. It is music that determines the line and music that directs the choice of words in a poem, irrespective of its adherence or not to conventional techniques (metre and rhyme especially). The ugliness or brutality of actual music is usually a function of its harmony and rhythm, and poems do not embody harmony in the traditional sense of simultaneity of pitches. A poem embodies ugliness or beauty in its stresses (its rhythm), its vowel-leading or lack of it, its choices of consonants, its choices of vocabulary, its emphasis (or not) on consonance, assonance, and rhyme in the broadest sense. The great poet does not necessarily choose and plan and plot where the minutiae of these technical aspects are concerned. The great poet makes them happen and function and succeed in the poem by instinct—by ear, as the cliché rightly has it. Revision, of course, may be a more self-conscious process.

P. K. Page had this gift from the start. As far as I remember she had no musical training, but then, neither did Keats or Yeats or Jack Spicer, musical poets all. (Yeats, in fact, suffered from amusia, the congenital inability to discriminate among pitches, or "tone-deafness" in the popular appellation.) She nevertheless, and from her earliest published poems, shows a sweetness and discrimination of ear that no other Canadian poet of her time demonstrated. (Gustafson, who did have musical training, had music in his poems too, but it took him a long time to *modernize* that music. Robert Finch, another musically literate Canadian poet, emphasized meter and rhyme so persistently that his music now sounds *surannée*, to borrow the slightly fusty adjective that Baudelaire used in "Receuillement.")

I want briefly to examine an early poem entitled "Personal Landscape" to explore Page's mastery of poetic music. The title suggests both a painted landscape and personal memory (this is how I recall the prairie of my childhood, she seems to intimate), as well as the possibility that the landscape is in fact the body, a metaphor that goes back to antiquity and is perhaps most famously employed in Thomas Carew's poem "A Rapture." That the poem was originally entitled "Landscape of Love" further supports this reading. This link is strengthened in the poem by overt reference to parts of the body: lips (used as a verb), a hand, a thigh. Here is the poem, as printed in Page's *As Ten, As Twenty* (Ryerson Press, 1946), her first solo collection:

PERSONAL LANDSCAPE

Where the bog ends, there, where the ground lips, lovely
is love, not lonely.

> *Land is*
love, round with it, where the hand is;
wide with love, cleared scrubland, grain
on a coin.
Oh, the wheatfield, the rock-bound rubble;
the untouched hills

>> *as a thigh smooth;*

> *the meadow.*
> *Not only the poor soil lovely, the outworn prairie,*
> *but the green upspringing,*
> *the lark-land,*
> *the promontory.*
>
> *A lung-born land, this,*
> *a breath spilling,*
> *scanned by the valvular heart's*
> *field glasses.*

The music of this poem is carefully nuanced. The majority of its vocabulary consists of words of a single syllable, with some two-syllable words and only three with more ("upspringing," "promontory," and "valvular"). There is only a single instance of end-rhyme ("land is" with "hand is"), and internal rhyme occurs just twice ("where" and "there" in the first line, and "ground" and "round" in lines 1 and 3). By contrast the poem, especially its first half, is lush with alliteration and consonance. The *l* sound is the most obvious ("lovely," "love," "lonely," "land," "lark," "lung"), but *d* is also employed ("ends," "ground," "land," "round," et cetera), with *gr* and *r* also prominent. The vowel sounds are beautiful, especially the *o* sounds early in the poem; and the vowel sequence in the line "the untouched hills as a thigh smooth" is masterly: from short *u* to short *i* to long *i* to long *u* in a single phrase. The word that follows—"meadow"—is the final word in the first half of the poem, and a stark and game-changing one. No other word in the poem begins with an *m*, and none, apart from "promontory," even contains this letter and sound. The word stands out musically like the final chord in a perfect cadence: we stop here, at least for a long moment, as our eye, presumably, stops too, on "the meadow" that we are presented with visually.

The second half of the poem is starker from the point of view of music. There is a nice sequence of *o*'s in the line "Not only the poor soil lovely, the outworn prairie" (though one may slightly regret the single use in the poem of an inversion), and some repetition involving s's and l's (again). But just as love disappears into ambiguity in the second half, along with the possibility that it is the body that is being evoked rather than an actual painting or a remembered landscape, so the music also is more diffuse. All three words of three syllables occur in this half, and all three are dactyls, which give the pace and feel of the poem a sense of fatigue as it plays out. (The brief trochaic final line brings the reader up sharply, however.) "Valvular" is the oddest of those trisyllabic words. (I am assuming that Page herself pronounced "promontory" in the English way, as a three-syllable word, rather than in the North American way, as a four-syllable one.) We know that the heart has valves, of course, but it seems almost a truism and unhelpful (poetically, I mean) to describe it as valvular. The two v sounds do help to re-invoke the earlier use of "lovely" and "love," and perhaps that is the point. Sound in a poem is always referring back and forth, and a good poet like Page keeps every sound alive in her head as she articulates them one at a time in a poem. Ear has memory. But then the valvular heart raises binoculars to its … to its what, its eyes? Hearts don't have eyes! Yet to me, those binoculars are looking back at the beginning of the poem, where the land is wide and round and lovely, where the welcome confusion of flesh and land was proposed, and where loneliness was absent. The intake and exhalation of breath ("lung-born," "a breath spilling") denote pleasure, or surprise, or the apprehension of beauty. The poem is about the sight of beauty, its ordinariness and its necessity, whatever particular landscape this one may be. Its seeming confusions (a bog on the prairie? new growth amidst rock-rubble?) don't really matter, and the occasional puzzles (that "grain / on a coin" and the lark) do not do the poem any harm. (Although the lark is primarily an Old World bird, there is, in fact, a single species of lark that lives in North America and does inhabit the Canadian prairie.)

Sandra Djwa quotes P. K. Page as saying something essential about the composition of a poem. "Very often it's a rhythm I hear," she said, "that doesn't have words at all, and I have to fit words to the rhythm. Sometimes it's an image that doesn't have words at all, and sometimes it will be a few words...out of which can grow...the poem." That is exactly right. Despite Yeats's "I sought a theme and sought for it in vain," poets rarely sit down to their desk with the determination, today, to write a poem about mother, or God, or the snake that suddenly appeared in the garden. Poets are moved by their eyes and ears, but especially their ears. An *insistence* drives them to find the words for whatever turns out to be the subject of that niggling rhythm or word or image that has caught them in its hold. "Personal Landscape" seems to me to be just such a poem: wrought and elaborated as much by sound and rhythm as by subject, and all the more beautiful for it. It came at the outset of P. K. Page's long career—it is the opening poem in *As Ten, As Twenty*—and marked her as an extremely talented poet, one of Canada's finest.

THE ONLY NEWS
THAT ISN'T BORING
IS THE TRUTH*

LEONARD COHEN'S POETRY THEN AND NOW

I s it a coincidence that the first poem in Leonard Cohen's debut collection, *Let Us Compare Mythologies* (1956), is an elegy for Orpheus? Poet, singer, musician, songwriter, not to mention tragic lover who lost the love of his life due to distracted attention and was ultimately torn apart by women, while all his life nurturing a reputation as a "ladies' man." Few modern poets better deserve to be thought of as cast in the mold of Orpheus than Cohen who, after a promising start as a poet and novelist, transitioned to the world of popular music and became internationally famous as a songwriter and singer, while not entirely giving up on poetry. There he is, at the outset of his career, twenty-two years old and a recent McGill University graduate, protégé of poets Louis Dudek and Frank Scott, mourning the "snow-bruised body" of Orpheus, the fleshly rags of whose corpse and whose head drift "in the warm salt ocean," that very Aegean Sea, in fact, to which

---

* The title borrows a line from Cohen's notebooks, in *The Flame* (New York: Farrar, Straus and Giroux, 2018), p. 175.

272 WORK TO BE DONE

Cohen will soon betake himself and where *Flowers for Hitler* and *Beautiful Losers* will be written. The uterine warmth and "hovering coloured fish" of "Elegy" suggest rebirth, although how exactly fish "build secret nests" in the dead hero's "fluttering winding-sheet" is a bit of a mystery. Right off the mark, then, Cohen seems to be celebrating the death of the very model that he will come to aspire to himself.

Fifty years ago, when *Canadian Notes & Queries* was debuting, Cohen's *Selected Poems* won the Governor General's Award for poetry. *Selected Poems* brought together poems from four previous books, with some hitherto unpublished verse. It was a reasonably strong year for Canadian poetry: Layton, Souster, Livesay, Joe Rosenblatt, Purdy, Dennis Lee, Pat Lowther, and Jay Macpherson among others published poetry collections. Rosenblatt, Cohen, Lowther, and Lee were the youngsters in this group, all with dates of birth in the 1930s. Cohen, with those four poetry collections and two novels in print, seemed more than the rest to be at mid-career already, though he was only thirty-four years old. But of all the many awards Cohen would accrue over his long life, some for writing, more for music, and a few for the sum total of his work, the GG was the only one he declined. Mordecai Richler reportedly wanted to punch Cohen in the nose for his refusal of the prize. In his telegram to the awards committee, the poet wrote: "Much in me strives for this honour, but the poems themselves forbid it absolutely." In retrospect the decision seems more than a little highhanded and self-important. But this was a period of great change for Cohen, and his interests were shifting. His first two albums came out in the late 1960s, other artists started to cover some of his songs, and he began living in the United States where the music industry was and is centred. A musical intelligence had always underlain his poetry, sometimes elevating his language and sometimes marring it; but following the 1968 *Selected*, in the books *Book of Mercy* (1984), *Book of Longing* (1996), and his final poetry book, *The Flame* (2018), as well as a substantial second version of his selected poetry and songs called

Stranger Music (1993), the distinction between poetry (in the more high-culture sense) and song lyrics became blurrier and blurrier. *The Energy of Slaves* (1972) and *Death of a Lady's Man* (1978) fall between the two modes—still pure poetry but written from a very conflicted consciousness, if sometimes a very determined self-consciousness— and they were on the whole the least well-reviewed books of Cohen's career. Although they contain Cohen's most inventive, avant-garde writing, many readers hated them, and found themselves perhaps inclined to agree with Cohen when he spoke of "that shabby little laboratory / called my talent," in one of the more self-abnegating poems in *Slaves*. No person who had encountered "Go by Brooks" or "For Anne" (both from *The Spice-Box of Earth*, 1961) as a high-school student and had fallen in love with Cohen's early lyric voice was likely to think much of a poem like this, also from *The Energy of Slaves*:

> *I did not know*
> > *until you walked away*
> *you had the perfect ass*
> *Forgive me*
> > *for not falling in love*
> *with your face or your conversation*

Let Us Compare Mythologies and The Spice-Box of Earth both represent a young poet's work, a mix of, among other things, poems clearly meant to win girls ("Sweet merchants trading: her love / For a history-full of poems"), poems exploring Cohen's religious roots and interests (*Mythologies* is perhaps unexpectedly dominated by the figure of Christ), poems invoking a range of forms and traditional techniques (sonnet, free verse, ballad, quatrains, tercets, end-rhyme, internal rhyme, et cetera), and lyric poems that ecstatically bask in emotion and sometimes excessive language. Like many young poets, Cohen strikes dramatic poses that are occasionally effective but often unconvincing. He clearly wants to be that man who "says words so beautifully / that if he only speaks their name / women give themselves to him." He apotheosizes his mentor and friend Irving Layton ("a chorus of invalid angels / rattled their fists / and chanted odes to you"). He wants us to believe that he contemplates murder, that his lover has murdered her family, and that another lover has been brutally murdered in a Mountain Street rooming house in Montreal, none of which events presumably ever occurred. There are also many poems that foreshadow Cohen's later apostasy, if that is not too harsh a word, by which he gave over his work in serious poetry to the sort of language easily set to music. "Ballad" ("He pulled a flower / out of the moss") or "Twelve O'Clock Chant" ("Hold me hard light, soft light hold me") could readily have formed the text of a song meant for an early Cohen album like *Songs of Leonard Cohen* or *Songs from a Room*. Of course, in principle, there is nothing regrettable about this. Keats could write a musical poem like "La Belle Dame Sans Merci," and during the 1920s even Eliot and Pound indulged in quatrain poems closely organized by rhyme and regular meter. So we have Cohen's tribute to A. M. Klein, which begins like this:

> The weary psalmist paused
> His instrument beside.
> Departed was the Sabbath
> And the Sabbath Bride.
>
> The table was decayed,
> The candles black and cold.
> The bread he sang so beautifully,
> That bread was mould.

It is not a long way from this sort of writing to the poetry that dominates Cohen's last book, *The Flame*. "Winter on Mount Baldy" begins this way:

It's winter on Mount Baldy
The monks are shoveling snow
It's swinging free, the Gateless Gate
But no one seems to go

It's cold and dark and dangerous
And slippery as a lie
No one wants to be here
And me, I'd rather die

In retrospect, then, no one should have been surprised by the turn that Cohen's poetry took at the end of the 1960s. The impulse toward doggerel had always been strong in him. Even in the astoundingly anti-poetic book of poems that is *The Energy of Slaves*, a poem like "Song for My Assassin," in which the aspiration to love and the confusion of it with murder are *echt* Cohen, falls into the ballad meters and predictable rhymes of a lyric meant for music:

We were chosen, we were chosen
miles and miles apart:
I to love your kingdom
you to love my heart.

The love is intermittent
the discipline continues:
I work on your spirit
you work on my sinews.

The Flame is Leonard Cohen's final book, finished not long before his death in November 2016, and concomitant, as a work of art, with his final album, *You Want It Darker*, which was released less than three weeks before the singer died. The album received generally good reviews. Cohen knew it was his farewell album, and it is relentlessly dark. He does not make even a pretense of singing. The flame is guttering, and so is his life. "You Want It Darker" and "Leaving the Table" give the book its title. In the first song, he kills the flame at the request of "G-d." In the second, after admitting that his life as a ladies' man is over ("the wretched beast is tame"), he asks for the flame to be blown out. He's "leaving the table" and "out of the game." He feels that his heart deserves a "medal / For letting go of you." "You" is presumably the last in a long, long line of women, some with famous names and many others nameless. That long line is an essential part of the Cohen mystique.

The Flame is subtitled Poems, Notebooks, Lyrics, Drawings. The drawings consist of seventy-five black-and-white self-portraits as well as other miscellaneous pieces, a few of which are used more than once. The poems and lyrics are largely indistinguishable except when the latter are familiar (such as all but one of the texts from You Want It Darker) and some short or unrhymed poems that are, by contrast, detectably not intended for musical setting. All but a few pages of the "Notebooks" section, which comprises 40 percent of the book, are in poetic form, and can often be heard as apparent trial versions of song lyrics. The Flame is a poetry collection, then, and as such it is for the most part depressingly bad. I do not wish to be counted among those "experienced persons" whom Cohen characterizes here as dismissing his work as "cheap, superficial, pretentious, [and] insignificant," yet about whom he then goes on to say: "you do not know / how Right you are." (These off-handedly self-disparaging remarks—"I'm a regular cliché"—are typical of Cohen, and have indeed always been so at least since The Energy of Slaves. His biographer, Sylvie Simmons, cites a remark that Cohen made in 2006 in the fiftieth-anniversary reprint edition of Let Us Compare Mythologies, that, after his debut book, "it's been downhill ever since.") Yet The Flame is so replete with bad rhyming, mercilessly singsong rhythms, superficial moralizing, and adolescent self-aggrandizement ("my balls are so big / I can't buckle my belt") that one is tempted again and again to give up reading in despair in the face of so much that seems the work of a poetaster. Examples of mere rhyming abound. Here are the opening two stanzas of a poem called "Mary Full of Grace":

> *You step out of the shower*
> *Oh so cool and clean*
> *Smelling like a flower*
> *From a field of green*
> *The world is burning Mary*
> *It's hollow dark and mean*
>
> *I love to hear you laugh*
> *It takes the world away*
> *I live to hear you laugh*
> *I don't even have to pray*
> *But now the world is coming back*
> *It's coming back to stay*

Where even to begin to calculate the poverty of this sort of poetry: the unearned references to the Virgin Mary (*gratiae plena*), the predictable rhymes and metre, the overstatement ("my heart has turned to weaponry"), the lines wasted in repetition, the broad strokes in which the woman versus the mean world are delineated, and so on. And really, "oh so cool and clean"? "The water's not like water now"? It is hard to believe that any poet could get away with this sort of deficient writing in a book published by a major company (McClelland & Stewart, and Farrar, Straus and Giroux in the United States) were it not for his reputation in another sphere of influence. And the notebook selections are, if anything, even less accomplished. Cohen's guard is down in these poetic jottings. He is "hunting for pussy" and "sucking up to / the lord," and he admits to a case of pubic lice ("There are bugs / in my crotch hair") as well as to being "an evil son of a bitch." (We believe the first things, but hardly the last.) He yearns after women again and again and again, and he indulges in a sad memory of his first serious love affair ("It's all a long time gone / when I had an honest job / and Annie called me darling"), a touching moment unlike most other moments associated with the women he has chased:

> Under a greenwood tree
> two boys are sitting, talking
> about a maid, and nothing
> else matters to them.

It is just a bit unseemly that, into old age, little else mattered so much to Leonard Cohen. At seventy-something he records a moment when he is watching a woman strip on Skype. Maybe he still thinks of her as a maid. Maybe, like all the others, he thinks of her as "the only One," with a capital O.

There are better moments in the book, of course. Once in a while Cohen reveals his sense of humour, a talent that was so well developed in his youth that Irving Layton thought of him as a natural comedian. And there are moments, few but essential, of real poetry, real emotion, and real insight. A poem for his old friend Mort Rosengarten is compelling, even if it does contain the line "It is as it is," a banal colloquialism so often spoken these days as to constitute an annoying verbal tic. A poem entitled "You Want to Strike Back and You Can't" has a power too rare in *The Flame*: no rhyme, no obvious musical repetitions, no typical Cohenesque erotic picaresque:

> You want to strike back and you can't
> And you want to help but you can't
> And the gun won't shoot
> And the dynamite won't explode

And the wind is blowing the other way
And no one can hear you

This is not great poetry, but at least it possesses an austere strength of statement that Cohen largely exchanged over the course of his career for language that can be flabby and obvious: "I'm trying to finish / My shabby career / With a white cigarette / And a curtain of beer" or "I used up all my chances / And you'll never take me back / But there ain't no harm in asking / Could you cut me one more slack?" The Cohen of the earlier poetry, the poetry that aspired to something grand, would never have allowed "one more slack" to be a phrase in a poem.

In the "Notebooks," Cohen writes at one point that we his readers can "depend on [him] / ... to come down / on the side of mercy // ... to come down / on the side of love." That is the Leonard Cohen who is largely missing in action in *The Flame*, a book in which, crucially, a seventy-year-old poet gets "lucky"—gets laid—and entitles a poem about the event "The Lucky Night!!!!! Sunday March 7, 2004." Those five exclamation marks say as much about this book as anything does. He even pretends to having reserved for her something that's "been kept / for Her and Her alone." I'm afraid he didn't. A poet with Orpheus's depth of devotion certainly would have.

FIVE

THE WORLD OF BOOKS

CUI BONO? PRINTING
THE GREEK AND
LATIN CLASSICS IN
A SEMI-LITERATE AGE

"The thought of what America would be like
If the Classics had a wide circulation
Troubles my sleep."
EZRA POUND, "CANTICO DEL SOLE"

P ound's amusing squib was written at about the same time that
he composed a short essay on Hugues Salel, a French poet who
published a translation of the first ten books of the *Iliad* in 1545, and
in that essay Pound complained that "the classics have more and more
become a baton exclusively for the cudgeling of schoolboys, and less
and less a diversion for the mature." The situation has not improved at
all since then, and as far as the influence of the classical languages is
concerned, it has declined precipitously. Where the great nineteenth-
century German classicist August Boeckh could suggest without a
trace of doubt that the science of classical studies or *Altertumswissenschaft* should be a model praxis for getting at truth in any sphere of

human endeavour, a recent scholar of the humanities notes that "the contention that classical studies is not one way among many, but the best way, even the only way, to [truth] seems little short of lunacy." Those words belong to a classicist writing in the twentieth century, but let us not forget that a strain of American pedagogical thinking based in transcendentalism has long been dismissive of a classics-based education. Who can forget Emerson's characterization of "the American scholar" as the man who studies nature in order to know himself, and his concomitant rejection of the very basics of an unnamed but clearly intended *Altertumswissenschaft*:

> Hence, instead of Man Thinking, we have the bookworm. Hence the book-learned class, who value books, as such; not as related to nature and the human constitution, but as making a sort of Third Estate with the world and the soul. Hence the restorers of readings, the emendators, the bibliomaniacs of all degrees.

Jeremiads on the regrettable death of the study of the classics unfortunately tend to lead to neo-conservative ideals-bashing and unreflective *ubi sunts*. *Who Killed Homer?*, a book published in 1998 by Victor Davis Hanson and John Heath, two highly opinionated California classicists, tended among other things to explain the dreariness of contemporary American life, culture, and moral values through the educational disappearance of the example of the Greeks. *Who Killed Homer?* constituted as much a symptom as it did a course of treatment for the classics, coming as it did from what one reviewer called "the kind of beleaguered outpost that characterizes most classics departments in this country." They are beleaguered for a number of reasons, but the essential fact is that the enrollments in college and university courses that require Greek or Latin language skills "seem hardly visible," as Lee Pearcy has written, "against the background of American education." He thinks it distinctly possible that if his great-great-great-grandchildren decide to learn Latin, they will have to seek out some informal way to accomplish it, much as one does now to learn "heraldry, or how to use an astrolabe."

It has long been the case, then, that to be on the side of the classics in contemporary America and England is to be fighting a losing, rearguard battle. Printers, for their part, have been happy to be on the losing side, especially in the last few decades. It is obvious, of course, that letterpress printing is itself the technological equivalent of an area of study—the classics—that had a tremendous influence from the Renaissance to World War I, but whose relevance has been in steady and inevitable decline ever since, and I will return to that almost irresistible analogy below. But first let us look at the relationship between fine printers and the classics historically. Ultimately I want to concentrate on the recent past, for in its beginnings the private press turned only occasionally to classical texts. Horace Walpole, for example, whose Strawberry Hill Press is considered by many to be the first truly private press in the English-speaking West, printed English-language texts almost exclusively, and no translations among them; but in 1760 he did an edition of Lucan's *Pharsalia* in five hundred copies. Printers often take on projects because a friend knows someone who knows someone who has a manuscript, and in the case of the Lucan, it came about largely because Walpole knew the son of Richard Bentley, the great English classicist who had died in 1742. The son had Bentley's notes on the *Pharsalia*, and they were incorporated into the Strawberry Hill Press edition. (Walpole commented in a letter, alluding to Bentley's notorious self-assurance as an editor, that "Lucan was muscular enough to bear his rough hand.") But printers also take on projects because of personal obsession, or devotion, or contemporary politics, among other reasons, and Walpole's decision to publish Lucan's epic of war doubtless had something to do with the fact that Britain in 1760 was in the midst of the Seven Years' War. He later wrote in French that "for we ... near-republicans, Lucan should be a valued writer."

The great English private printers of the *fin de siècle* and the early twentieth century printed relatively few classical texts. The Daniel Press did none, William Morris did none, and the Doves Press did just one: an edition of Tacitus's *Agricola* that Cobden-Sanderson published in 1900 in Latin. One could add the Doves Press *Pervigilium Veneris*, but the former, though in Latin, is hardly classical—Pound said that its trochaic metric "indicated as great a change of sensibility in its day as the change from Viennese waltzes to jazz may indicate in our own." St John Hornby at the Ashendene Press took a little more interest in classical texts, issuing an edition of Lucretius's *De rerum natura* in 1912 and a very limited edition of Horace's *Carmina sapphica* in Latin, as well as Apuleius and Thucydides in English, *Daphnis and Chloe* in French, and small bits of Plutarch and Marcus Aurelius, again in English. The Eragny Press printed nothing classical, and Charles Shannon and Charles Ricketts at the Vale Press did only an excerpt from Apuleius (the Eros and Psyche story) in English in 1897 and in Latin in 1901, and, again, a *Daphnis and Chloe*, in George Thornley's seventeenth-century English translation this time. In other words, during the silver age of classical education in England, when most educated readers could handily read Latin and many had also mastered Greek, the private presses largely ignored the corpus of ancient Greek and Latin literary and other texts. The relative popularity of Apuleius and Longus in this decadent period is not hard to explain: in classical terms their language is decadent too, since both authors were writing at the very end of classical antiquity.

—

A few European fine press editions from the following generation need to be mentioned before I move on to some books from the last twenty-five or so years. The first is the Bremer Presse Homer's *Odyssey* of 1924, as magisterial and austere a book as imaginable, printed in folio without a trace of anything but the Greek, save for some textual notes in

Latin. The second is the Cranach-Presse's Virgil's *Eclogues* of 1927, with lovely illustrations by that most classical of all twentieth-century French artists, Aristide Maillol. François-Louis Schmied, an artist whose sensibility was equal parts Parisian and Mediterranean, also provides several stunning examples. His Homer's *Odyssey* of 1930 was designed but not executed by him, and it has been criticized on account of Maurice Darantière's conservative printing. (It was Darantière's unilingual francophone typesetters who set the first edition of Joyce's *Ulysses*, published in Paris in 1922.) Ward Ritchie has remarked on the fact that although the two printers collaborated on this complex book, each hated the other's work. Finally, another Schmied centaur, the Aeschylus *Prometheus Bound* of 1941, was designed and illustrated by the master but the blocks were cut and the printing executed by his son, Théo. The two German books represent private press projects of the purer sort: books without commissions created for the sheer pleasure of making a beautiful object. Harry Kessler's Cranach Presse operated, as Roderick Cave has written, "in the grand tradition in which neither time nor cost was important," and the existence of an audience for Greek and Latin books was not a consideration. The French books responded to outside commissions, but nevertheless were mostly free of any motivation save, again, the ideal of the book beautiful. Well, perhaps not quite. One cannot but wonder whether the Aeschylus, published a year after the fall of Paris in June of 1940, does not have a strong political subtext, Prometheus standing in for *le peuple français* itself under the German yoke.

The provocative adjective in my subtitle, "semi-literate," can be taken with a grain of salt, of course. After all, although fewer and fewer people read Greek and Latin anymore, one can by contrast point to the fact that fresh translations of classical literary texts (and Herodotus, thanks to *The English Patient*) continue to interest commercial publishers and to find an audience. Much of Horace, Virgil, Ovid, and Homer has been published in new English versions in the last half decade, and

Christopher Logue's *All Day Permanent Red* and *War Music*—"accounts," as he calls them, of parts of the *Iliad*—demonstrate that the contemporaneity of the Homeric texts can be reified in forms much more cutting-edge than straight translation. The motivation of many recent private press / fine press editions of various classical texts is perhaps not so very different from that of Logue's Homeric transmutations.

Jack Stauffacher's Horace's *Odes* of 1992, for example, as austere a book in its way as the Bremer Presse Homer, represents the end point of a complex of motivations that includes a typographic homage and a deep admiration for Horace's ability—as the translator of Stauffacher's edition, Michael Taylor, put it—to "[observe] his fellow men in an age of upheaval and change," a sentiment with rather obvious contemporary relevance. Stauffacher's brief annotations to the illustrations of Horatian manuscripts and printed editions in the booklet that accompanies his *Odes* exhibit an excitement arising from the fact that his own version comes at the end of a line of Horaces that begins in the early tenth century, over a thousand years before the Greenwood Press version. As he wrote in 1992, "my typographic exploration began with the question: how were these texts [Horace and Plato] transmitted from the earliest times to the present?"

Not all printers are as deeply interested in the typographic and transmission histories of their texts, but Peter Koch's editions of pre-Socratic Greek philosophical texts demonstrate a similar multivalent genealogical obsession. Two of these, his Herakleitos and his Parmenides, try in very different ways to pay attention both to the ageless quality of the texts and to the unique ability of the letterpress printer to match medium and message. Compared to the later Parmenides, Koch's Herakleitos of 1990, in Guy Davenport's translation, is extraordinarily austere. The Greek is there with the English *en face*, in Eric Gill's Gill Sans Greek, but in upper case only, for its inscriptional effect; and the binding attempts to reproduce Coptic-style wooden boards with paste papers—an unexpected choice perhaps for a text with no Coptic affiliations, but it makes a handsome object all the same. The Bembo Roman was chosen as a direct homage to Aldus Manutius, Koch later declared. *The Fragments of Parmenides* of 2003 is a project on a wholly different scale. Set in a proprietary Greek inscriptional font cut and cast for Koch by Dan Carr, the Greek setting, though not unwaveringly imitative of the written texts of its own time (which were probably boustrophedonic and certainly did not employ word spacing), looks extraordinarily convincing. The English translation, by Robert Bringhurst, is a new one, and it is accompanied (unlike the earlier Herakleitos) by an essay that traces the survival and publication of "On Nature," Parmenides's poem, and briefly makes a case for the work's attractiveness to an audience 2,500 years *post mortem poetae.* The book is also illustrated, which is unusual for an edition of a philosophical text, even in poetic form. Richard Wagener's wood engravings feel both antique and postmodern, and while they illustrate nothing in particular, they add both edge and depth to the book as a book.

—

I want to comment on one further book, and that is the massive, magisterial, and fascinating *Oresteia* from the Gehenna Press. This was one of Leonard Baskin's last projects, and indeed the colophon is signed not by him and the poet-translator, Ted Hughes, because they had both died before the book was completed, but by their surviving spouses, Lisa Baskin and Carol Hughes. The three plays were produced as separate volumes, tall folios with lovely large Centaur and Arrighi types, and with many compelling illustrations by Leonard Baskin. Flawlessly executed, this is nevertheless a classical text brought into the contemporary world with a motivation that surely has to be called psychiatric. Ted Hughes has taken Aeschylus's trilogy and made it even more chthonic, blood-mad, and revenge-bent than it was in the sixth century BC. It is hard not to hear Hughes's own autobiographical conundrums in such lines as these, from the close of the second play, the *Choephori*:

> *Can the poor scorched brains of Orestes*
> *Figure out all the factors?—Can he solve*
> *The arithmetic of the unfinished*
> *That shunts this curse from one generation*
> *to the next?*
> *Who can bring it to an end?*
> *When can it be brought to an end?*
> *How can it be brought to an end?*

Baskin's forty-seven woodcuts manage very deftly to parallel the violent armature of Hughes's poetry, but they gothicize the Greek spirit and definitely would have frightened Winckelmann to death. No "sweetness, truth, and force of the Antique" here, as Thomas Frognall Dibdin said of the beautiful 1795 Foulis Press edition of Aeschylus in Greek.

In conclusion, I want to begin with a quote from Burton's *Book-Hunter*. "The possession of a private printing press," he says, "is, no doubt, a very appalling type of bibliomania." He then goes on to say that the "owner of such an establishment...dictates his own terms; he is master of the situation, as the French say, and is the true autocrat of literature." The private or fine printer, in other less provocative words, prints what text she or he likes in the manner he or she desires. In our era, choosing a classical text in itself is provocative, particularly if one prints it in the original language, with or without a translation. There is a typographic challenge in printing Greek, obviously, that printers sometimes want to take on. The printer of the Libanus Press edition of Plato's *Symposium* of 1986 has related how he found it necessary to use Peter Forster's illustrations mainly on the Greek sides of his two-page spreads that had Greek on the versos and English on the rectos, because the Greek took up much less space. Printers believe in their texts, however obscure or little read they may be; and while most are not printing merely for the challenge or the fun, and do need readers to buy their work, they can trust their audience to believe in the work as well, both as text and as object. And so I return to my earlier observation, the one that finds a connection between letterpress printing as a means of communication and the increasing absence of the works of classical antiquity in our culture. Stephen Leacock humorously rejected any loving attention to the classics in this way:

> I have seen thus a deceived dog value a pup with a broken leg, and a pauper child nurse a dead doll with the sawdust out of it. So I nursed my dead Homer and my broken Demosthenes.

Printers and the diminishing band of readers for Greek and Latin literature know better.

ONLY COPY KNOWN
RANDOM REFLECTIONS ON RARITY

J ust what exactly constitutes a rare book is a question that casual visitors to book fairs or to rare book libraries often pose to booksellers and librarians. The waggish answer—a rare book is a book I want to buy for stock or for my collection but cannot find—is tempting but not really satisfactory. A bookseller friend of mind likes to say, in a gastronomic pun, that he specializes in medium-rare books, although in fact the English word "rare," as applied to books and to filet mignon, actually represents two homophonous words with distinct etymologies. "Rare" as applied to cooking comes from an Anglo-Saxon word meaning uncooked or partially cooked, and was originally used only of eggs, not meat. Through its Indo-European root it is related to the word "idiosyncrasy," a trait exhibited by many book collectors. "Rare" as applied to books has a different Indo-European root, and in a variant form is allied to the word "hermit," which some bibliophiles certainly are. "Hermit" in turn comes from a Greek word meaning desolate or empty, a feeling shared by many collectors when the book they coveted is discovered already to have been sold before their email was sent or their phone call placed. "Rarus" in Latin has the basic sense of thin, far apart, or infrequent. The *Oxford English Dictionary*, by the way, can only rather lamely cite an 1862 use of "rare book" (in Burton's *Book-*

Hunter) as the earliest recorded, although there are many at a much earlier date in more obscure sources.

In a certain quarter of the book business, rarity is not what it used to be. "Rarity," Nicholson Baker has said in a context that has nothing to do with books, "is an emotion as much as it is a statistical truth."* How often did one use to hear—as an emotional avowal rather than as a strictly statistical fact—that a bookseller had seen only two copies of X in twenty-five years, or had not handled a copy of Y since 1970, or had never seen Z in thirty-five years in the trade. This is what might be thought of as the empirical theorem: I, who am a dealer in a single city in a certain country during a particular period of time, can extrapolate my own experience to a universal truth. What has altered all of this is, of course, the internet. Many booksellers who thought that certain books, which were rare because they seldom if ever showed up over twenty or thirty or forty years, now know to their grief that the net lists multiple copies at quite various prices. It may be, of course, that a particular book, once thought rare, and now for sale by a dozen or more booksellers all across the world, will lapse into genuine scarcity after those copies are absorbed, following the same pre-internet principle, universally acknowledged by experienced bibliophiles, that genuinely rare books sometimes appear on the market in multiple copies in close temporal proximity.

On the other hand, it may be that John Carter's principle of "localized rarity" no longer obtains in a market that has no remaining local aspect.† If ever there were copies of, say, Canadian poet Irving Layton's rare first book, *Here and Now* (1945), that might have made their way to Mexico or France or South Africa, the chances of their subsequently finding their way onto the market are now increased exponentially, and the traditionally invoked rarity of that book might well have to be altered.

---

* Nicholson Baker, "Rarity," in *The Size of Thoughts: Essays and Other Lumber* (New York: Vintage Books, 1997), p. 19.

† John Carter and Nicolas Barker, ABC *for Book Collectors* (Newcastle and London: Oak Knoll Press and the British Library, 2004), p. 182.

Many collectors, I am sure, will remember a catalogue devoted to Henry Fielding issued by Ximenes Rare Books in the fall of 1991. It was the earliest bookseller's catalogue I can recall in which the availability of the *English Short-Title Catalogue* (ESTC), published the year before, made an extraordinary difference to the number of recorded copies that were cited. In the pre-ESTC days a dealer might have said of a Fielding item that the *National Union Catalog* (NUC) recorded four copies, in addition to, let us say, the British Museum copy, the Rothschild copy, and the copies known to the bookseller to be at the University of Toronto or the Beinecke Library, or in a private collection in Los Angeles.* With the ESTC, all of a sudden the total number of seven or eight recorded copies swelled to twenty or thirty or forty, as copies in rural England and the American Midwest and Göttingen and other locations turned up. What was rare before the ESTC went live was not necessarily so afterwards. That worked both ways, however, as certain books one could not imagine being rare turned out, surprisingly, to be so. Charlotte Cowley's *Ladies History of England* (1780) is a good example. This is an imposing late-eighteenth-century illustrated folio that ought, instinctually, one thinks, to be everywhere. But the ESTC proves otherwise: it records only six copies in England and two—one at Kent State and one at the University of Toronto—in North America. (A ninth, unrecorded copy, previously at the Public Library in Oakland, California, is now at UCLA's Clark Library.)

We do not like to admit it, but rarity is to some extent a relative term and it can be twisted when the point is to turn something common and unattractive into something desirable. I have never forgotten the description of a copy of Edward FitzGerald's *Euphranor* (1851), a little Platonic dialogue of eighty-four pages, which appeared in a Bernard Quaritch catalogue a dozen or so years ago. *Euphranor* is not a scarce book. When FitzGerald died in 1883, Quaritch purchased a batch of unsold copies, with the result that the book is found more often than not in perfect con-

---

* Ximenes Rare Books, Inc., *Occasional List No. 92* (New York: Ximenes Rare Books, 1991).

dition. This particular Quaritch copy, however, was "somewhat stained and faded, spine worn... [and with an] owner's inscription." In other words, it was a ratty copy. But nothing daunted, the Quaritch cataloguer described this copy in this condition as "rare," precisely because it bore "evidence of contemporary readership"! Clever bookselling and outright gall often go hand in hand, but this is an especially impressive example.

I was recently moved to think more doggedly about rarity when I came across a passage in a book I was reviewing that commented on *Pauline*, Robert Browning's first book. The author called it "very rare" and then estimated that "only about a dozen copies of the original exist." Anyone engaged daily in the business of buying or selling old books sees this statement, or versions of it, all the time, and nothing about this particular example should have been striking. But even I, as someone who has no specialized knowledge of Browning bibliography, realized that I could think of several copies of *Pauline* without even trying. My own library had one—and William Andrews Clark did not specialize in the Victorians; there was certainly one in the Ashley Library at the British Library; and there must surely be one at Texas among the Wrenn books, et cetera. So I wondered how accurate that statement about *Pauline* really was.* I was wrong, incidentally, about the Wrenn Library, although I was right about Texas. Thomas James Wise tried hard to secure a copy of *Pauline* for John Henry Wrenn, but he never managed it; when Wrenn died in 1911, his library did not include the book. But a copy he had missed at Sotheby's was bought by Maggs Bros. Ltd. for £325 in June of 1904 and resold to the Chicago collector John A. Spoor. Spoor's books were not sold until twelve years after his death, and at the sale, in the spring of 1939, Texas acquired *Pauline* for $3,900—a bargain, given the fact that the Jerome Kern copy had fetched $16,000 ten years earlier.

---

* The review was of Joseph Rosenbaum's *Practice to Deceive: The Amazing Stories of Literary Forgery's Most Notorious Practitioners* (New Castle: Oak Knoll, 2000), and it was published in the *Papers of the Bibliographical Society of Canada* 39, 1 (Spring 2000): 109–111. To prove once again how error can be added to error where copies of rare books are concerned, I there stated that McGill also owned a copy of *Pauline*. This is not so. McGill owns only a copy of the 1886 Wise facsimile reprint.

So how rare, exactly, is *Pauline*? In his Browning bibliography, issued in 1929, Wise called the book "one of the scarcest volumes in the list of modern poetical rarities."* As early as 1894, in his guide to collecting modern authors, J. H. Slater had stated that there are eight known copies.† In 1921, Seymour de Ricci detailed eighteen copies in his guide to collecting.‡ Fannie Ratchford, writing about the Texas copy in 1943, unaware perhaps of De Ricci's census, prefigured the book I began all of this with and stated that "approximately a dozen [copies] are recorded as extant."§ The most recent census, published in 1984, lists twenty-three copies, of which one, stolen in 1940, has not yet resurfaced.¶ Not in the census are a copy at the University of South Carolina which belonged to F. J. Furnivall, and a copy that may or may not be at Case Western Reserve University Library. That makes possibly twenty-four or twenty-five recorded copies, all but one of which are in institutional collections. The one privately owned copy, listed in the 1984 census as belonging then to H. Bradley Martin, is now in a private collection in North Dakota. It fetched $70,000 to a bookseller at the Martin sale in 1990. It is worth mentioning that even the wonders of online bibliographic databases and the web do not necessarily make it easier to locate copies of rare books and to be precise about numbers. If one searches *Pauline* in the Online Computer Library Center (OCLC) database, for example, you will find fifteen libraries reporting copies, including several not listed in the 1984 census. However, if you take the next step and check the various institutional online catalogues, you will find that at least three of these copies

---

* Thomas James Wise, *A Browning Library: A Catalogue of Printed Books, Manuscripts, and Autograph Letters by Robert Browning and Elizabeth Barrett Browning* (London: printed for private circulation only, 1929), p. 4.

† J. H. Slater, *Early Editions: A Bibliographical Survey of the Works of Some Popular Modern Authors* (London: Kegan Paul, Trench, Trübner, 1894), p. 46.

‡ Seymour de Ricci, *The Book Collector's Guide: A Practical Handbook of British and American Bibliography* (Philadelphia and New York: the Rosenbach Company, 1921), p. 77.

§ Fannie Ratchford, "Browning's Pauline Comes to Texas," *Southwest Review* 28, 3 (Spring 1943): 282.

¶ Philip Kelley and Betty A. Coley, *The Browning Collections: A Reconstruction with Other Memorabilia* (Winfield, KS: Wedgestone Press, 1984), pp. 215–218.

are surrogates—two photocopies and one microfiche—despite their being listed as books. One copy, recorded as being at the New Haven Free Public Library, is apparently listed in error.

So *Pauline*, like many books thought to be rare, really is not. A book that exists in more than two dozen copies cannot be considered rare in the strict sense, though "rare on the market" and expensive it obviously is. Many so-called rare books fall into this category, and many, clearly much less rare than *Pauline* and even more expensive, are really rather common.

Let me take an earlier book as a further example. Newton's *Principia*, published in 1687 and universally regarded as one of the most important scientific works ever written, is a stout quarto that, in its day, would have had a small audience. All the same, something over two hundred copies have survived, over sixty of which are in North American libraries. In the 1940s, John Carter commented on how the *Principia*, which had long been considered a "fairly common" book, then seemed to have become "scarcer."* A. N. L. Munby, in his essay on the distribution of the *Principia*, said in October 1952 that it "can never be described as a *rare* book."† However valid these impressions were then, the *Principia* today seems to have become common on the market again. In the fall of 2002, there were two copies for sale by booksellers in Los Angeles alone, not to mention others available in the English trade. One can quibble about these copies—from which issue do they come (there were two, and one is decidedly less common)? What condition are they in? and so on—and some of this sort of quibbling partially accounts for the variations in price that the copies now on the market exhibit, from a low of $175,000 to a high of over $310,000. A bookseller of my acquaintance believes that the day is not far off when a *Principia* will fetch half a million

---

* John Carter, *Taste and Technique in Book Collecting: A Study of Recent Developments in Great Britain and the United States* (New York: R. R. Bowker, 1948), p. 143.

† A. N. L. Munby, "The Distribution of the First Edition of Newton's *Principia*," in *Essays and Papers*, ed. Nicolas Barker (London: the Scolar Press, 1977), p. 53.

dollars. In any case, a book that you can buy in any month of the year, if you have the money, is not an especially rare book.

Both collectors and booksellers have long played fast and loose with the word "rare," each for slightly different reasons. As early as the eighteenth century, a number of guides to books were published in Europe in which rarity was defined in greater or lesser detail, and many reasons were adduced to explain why certain books are rare.* Most of the reasons suggested then still apply, as one might guess. An essay by Johann Georg Schelhorn, for example, which fills 115 pages of his book *Amoenitates literariae* (1725, new edition 1730), lists fourteen reasons for the rarity of books, including suppression by the authorities or by the author or publisher, export abroad, small physical size, et cetera.† As the eighteenth century progressed and collecting became less a scholar's and more a connoisseur's pursuit, vade mecums came to be more prevalent and the relationship between rarity and financial value was emphasized more. With that relationship solidly established, the language of description in auction, bookseller, and library catalogues became more fixed around the notions of rarity and uniqueness. This was so much the case that the bibliographer Thomas Frognall Dibdin, whose own use of language is definitely not known for self-control or subtlety, warned the "sober and cautious collector" in his *Bibliomania* (1809) "not to be fascinated by the terms '*Matchless, and Unique;*' which...are studiously introduced into Booksellers' catalogues to lead the unwary astray."‡

A couple of examples—one a rather obscure auction sale catalogue from the early nineteenth century and the other a rather famous private library catalogue from the late-nineteenth century—bear out the ways in which words and phrases like "rare," "unique," or "only copy known"

---

* M. S. Batts, "The 18th-Century Concept of the Rare Book," *The Book Collector* 24, 3 (Autumn 1975): 381–400.
† Johann Georg Schelhorn, *Amoenitates literariae*, new and corrected ed. (Frankfurt and Leipzig: Daniel Bartholomaeus, 1730): II, 321–435.
‡ Thomas Frognall Dibdin, *The Bibliomania; or, Book-Madness* (London: Longman, Hurstd, Rees, 1809), p. 65.

came later increasingly to dominate bibliophily. The sale in 1818 of the "library of an eminent collector, removed from the north of England," was typical for the period.* It took six days to put the 790 lots under the hammer, and the contents of the collection were largely what one would expect for the time: English poetry, topography, and illustrated books. The owner seems to have been James Midgely, Jr, of Rochdale, north-east of Manchester, although the sale also included books from the *Bibliotheca Anglo-Poetica*, a quite spectacular catalogue issued by Long-man's in 1815 that had not done at all well. Midgely owned no Caxtons, indeed no fifteenth-century books at all; but he did have black-letter books (books printed in Gothic types), and the catalogue singled these out. (The "black letter dogs of the present day," as Dibdin had called them, were still very much a force in the book world then.)† Midgely had many extra-illustrated sets, and indeed the highest price realized at the sale—£262—was for one of these. Another, an extra-illustrated copy of Byron's *English Bards and Scotch Reviewers* (in 1818, a book that was less than a decade old), fetched the amazing price of £18.18.0. But the book in the sale catalogue one would most like to have a time machine at hand to pursue was Midgley's copy, apparently in an undisturbed seventeenth-century binding, of the Shakespeare First Folio, 1623, which was bought by booksellers Payne and Foss for £121.16.0. (They sold it to Thomas Grenville, and it passed from him to the British Museum in 1846—not, unfortunately, before Grenville had had it rebound.) That very substantial price, by the way, can be compared to a copy of the First Folio which had been in the sale, five years earlier in

---

* *Bibliotheca selecta: A Catalogue of the Library of an Eminent Collector, Removed from the North of England* (London: Robert Saunders, 1818). A copy of this catalogue at the Clark Library, UCLA, has the name "Midgely" added in pen on the title page. Seymour de Ricci, in his *English Collectors of Books and Manuscripts, 1530–1930, and Their Marks of Ownership* (Cambridge: Cambridge University Press, 1930), p. 92, says only that the collector in question "was said at the time by gossips to be one 'Midgely,' about whom I have no further information, but he doubtless only possessed a portion of the books in the sale." Marc Vaulbert de Chantilly has identified the collector as James Midgely, Jr.

† Dibdin, *Bibliomania*, p. 56, n. 45.

1813, of the library of Colonel Thomas Stanley, which, if less wonderful, was still respectable, and which had fetched only £37.16.0.*

But let us have a look at the auction house's annotations to the books. Here we find a variety of phrases, variations of which are repeated any number of times: "so rare that one copy only is known besides the present" (lot 33, Richard Braithwayte's *Times Curtaine Drawne*, 1621, now known in ten copies); "of the most extreme rarity" (lot 415, Samuel Madden's *Memoirs of the Twentieth Century*, 1733, recorded now in fifteen copies); "of such extreme rarity that the present copy is probably unique" (lot 433, Arthur Newman's *Pleasure's Vision*, 1619, now known in six copies); "probably unique" (lot 379, Robert Holland's *Holie History of Our Lord and Saviour Jesus Christ*, 1594, now known in three copies); and just "unique" (lot 389, *The Husband, A Poem*, 1614, even today known in only two copies). To be fair, there are at least two books in the sale which, described as "unique," remain so today: the 1530 edition of Chaucer's *Parliament of Foules* (lot 108, today at the Huntington Library) and An Collins's *Divine Songs and Meditacions*, 1653 (lot 176, today also at the Huntington). These examples do not detract from my main point, however, that despite the validity sometimes of the vocabulary of rarity, many books described as rare simply are not.

At the end of the century, the published catalogue of a famous and influential collection provides an interesting example of the continuing use of the booksellers' vocabulary of rarity being assumed by an owner and his librarians and compilers. I am referring to the catalogue of the Rowfant Library, accumulated by Frederick Locker-Lampson and described in a one-volume catalogue in 1886 put together by A. W. Pollard and R. H. Lister, both librarians.† Locker-Lampson's approach to collecting was very persuasive to his generation and those that followed. Instead of building an enormous library like most of his distinguished

---

* Thomas Hartwell Horne, *An Introduction to the Study of Bibliography* (London: Cadell & Davies, 1814), p. 674. The First Folio was lot 426 in the Stanley sale.

† A. W. Pollard and R. H. Lister, *The Rowfant Library. A Catalogue of the Printed Books, Manuscripts, Autograph Letters, Drawings, and Pictures, Collected by Frederick Locker-Lampson* (London: Bernard Quaritch, 1886).

predecessors, he wanted only a small but choice collection of great English poets from Chaucer to Swinburne. The first section of the catalogue covers the period from 1480 to 1700 and contains just 529 books, not counting duplicates. Among these are twenty-three that are described as "unique," or "the only copy known," or "almost unique," or, in one case, "of the greatest rarity." Six of these books are still, in fact, known only in the single copy that belonged to Locker-Lampson, and they are now in various institutional libraries. More typical are examples like Samuel Daniel's *Delia*, 1592, described in the Rowfant catalogue as "stated to be unique," but recorded now in ten copies,* or John Davies's *Microcosmos*, 1603, "according to Dr. Grosart...almost unique," now recorded in the ESTC in more than ten copies.†

Locker-Lampson, by the way, owned a copy of *Pauline*, indeed perhaps the most important copy of all. Browning used it to correct and revise the poem in 1868. He presented it to Locker-Lampson the following year and inscribed it warmly. The booksellers Dodd, Mead offered it for sale in a catalogue around 1905 for the amazingly high price of $2,500. The copy was bought by the poet Amy Lowell, who later gave it to Harvard. To demonstrate how comparative values change, I would point out that Dodd, Mead offered in the same catalogue Locker-Lampson's copy of Blake's *Songs of Innocence* (1789) for $750. Today, the Blake would bring many times the price of *Pauline*.

At a slightly earlier period, collectors' passion for the rarest of the rare led to the most famous bibliophilic leg-pull of the nineteenth century, the Fortsas Hoax. The Brussels bookseller René Chalons printed an auction catalogue for the sale of the imaginary Count Fortsas's library, which was to take place in the small Belgian town of Binche on August 10, 1840. The count was said to have collected only books that were unique, discarding even great rarities when he learned of a second copy

---

* Locker-Lampson's copy is now at the Huntington Library (RB 58734).
† This is Alexander Balloch Grosart, 1827–1899, whose collection was sold at Sotheby, Wilkinson, Hodge on December 11, 1899.

anywhere. No library so deserved the standard compliment of "small but choice." Chalons not only invented Fortsas, of course, but all of the books in his imaginary library as well, some of which Chalons annotated amusingly. Lot 43, for example, is an anonymous work entitled *The Wages of Love, or, The Great King Uncomfortable in the Low Countries*, 1686, a duodecimo of 152 pages, illustrated, bound in black Morocco, and so on. The annotation reads: "A libel of quite disgusting black humour concerning Louis xiv's fistula. One plate shows the royal behind in the form of a sun [The Sun King!] encircled with rays, with the famous motto: *nec pluribus impar.*"* (A free translation of this might be "Come one, come all.") Many well-known bookmen made the trip to Binche for the sale, to the utter confusion of the citizenry who had never heard of Count Fortsas or his books.

Needless to say, despite this elaborate satire on the world of booksellers and collectors, the allure of the unique was in no way driven out by laughter. It was inevitable that a bookseller would eventually produce a catalogue devoted to genuinely unique books, and in 1902, London dealer Wilfrid Michael Voynich did just that. Voynich was born in 1865 in Poland, and he moved to London in 1890. E. Millicent Sowerby, who began working for him in 1912, described him vividly in her memoirs, *Rare People and Rare Books*, where she calls him "the greatest international rare book dealer of his time."† Voynich sold the British Museum more than 3,800 books during a thirty-year period; so unusual were many of them that the museum gave them a separate "Voynich" shelfmark.‡ His *An Eighth List of Books on Exhibition* contained only "unknown and lost books," although he was admirably circumspect about his claims. "It would be too much to hope," he wrote in the preface to the catalogue,

---

* *Catalogue d'un très-riche mais peu nombreuse collection de livres provenant de feu Mr. le comte J.-N.-A de Fortsas* (Mons: Typographie d'Em Hoyois, Libraire, [1840]), lot 43. The translations are mine.
† E. Millicent Sowerby, *Rare People and Rare Books* (London: Constable, 1967), p. 8.
‡ I am grateful to Nicolas Barker for this information.

That no book in this list has ever been described by any specialist. We particularly wish to guard ourselves from asserting that no other copies exist. At the same time we must confess to believing that if the term could ever be applied to books not printed in one sole copy, most of those in the present catalog could be described as "unique."

Voynich also took pains to assure his readers that he "had, of course, not searched works of recognized unreliability, such as sales catalogues and booksellers' lists."[*]

Voynich had warmed up in his *A First List of Books*, in which he catalogued twenty-five "unknown, lost, or undescribed books after 1525" in a separate subsection.[†] In his eighth list, however, there were 158 items, and they were offered first as a collection. Naturally, many of the books are no longer known only in the copy catalogued by Voynich. A 1572 London-printed piece entitled *Progymnasmata*, by fourth-century Sophist Aphthonius, is now ESTC 700 and is known in three copies, while a Greek version of the *Catachesis tes Chritianikes Pisteos* (London, 1655) is now Wing 1463A and is bountifully recorded in five copies. The first edition of a work on meteors by Themon Judaeus (dated not after 1480), Voynich said, was "an entirely unknown book."[‡] Ten copies are now recorded, including the British Library's, where Voynich's copy not surprisingly went,[§] bearing out his own skepticism in the preface to his Catalogue 2 as to "the existence of unique books... [W]hen one copy of a book has been recorded, other copies tend to appear from time to time' and the use of the word 'unique' appears to me unjustified and misleading."[¶]

There is one other figure who needs to be mentioned in the context of emphasizing rarity and uniqueness as the heart and soul of book

---

[*] Wilfrid Michael Voynich, *An Eighth List of Books on Exhibition* (London: 1902, p. 3.

[†] Wilfrid Michael Voynich, *A First List of Books on Exhibition* (London: n.d.).

[‡] Wilfrid Michael Voynich, *A Second List of Books* (London: 1900), p. [65].

[§] *Catalogue of Books Printed in the xvth Century Now in the British Museum* (London: Trustees of the British Museum, 1908), 7, 977.

[¶] Voynich, *A Second List of Books*, p. [65].

collecting, and that is Thomas James Wise. *The Ashley Library Catalogue*, the eleven-volume catalogue of his collection that Wise had printed between 1922 and 1936, is something of a monument to the centrality of rarity in the collecting enterprise. In the introduction to each volume, penned successively by Richard Curle, Edmund Gosse, Augustine Birrell, John Drinkwater, E. V. Lucas, and other writer-collectors, rarities in the Wise collection are marvelled at. Curle, who was a writer, collector, and friend of Joseph Conrad, as well as of Wise, and who outlived Wise by over thirty years and doubtless therefore lived to regret some of his more innocently fawning compliments in his introduction to volume 1, cites a score of books from Wise's collection of which he says variously that there is "only one other copy known," "only two or three copies known," or "the only other copy is in the British Museum." Most of these numbers do not stand any longer. Lyly's 1597 *Woman in the Moone*, for example, which Curle claimed to be one of only two or three known copies, is now known in nine; Pope's 1716 *God's Revenge Against Punning*, called unique, is now recorded in fifteen copies spread among three editions; and likewise Gay's 1725 *To a Lady on Her Passion for Old China*, which Curle also claimed to be unique and is now known in two editions for a total of nine copies.* I would emphasize that this sort of numbers game, played by collectors and booksellers ever since the days of Dibdin, remains with us today, though the focus has shifted as collectors have begun to collect books, such as modern first editions, where true rarity or uniqueness is to all intents and purposes non-existent.

The Clark Library recently acquired an uncommon little pamphlet from 1762, printed in Sweden, by Andreas Wallin, called *Dissertatio academica de bibliomania* (An Academic Thesis on Bibliomania). In it, Wallin says, "*Quot caelum stellas, tot habet Europa libellos*" (Europe has

---

* Thomas James Wise, *The Ashley Library: A Catalogue of Printed Books, Manuscripts and Autograph Letters Collected by Thomas James Wise*, vol. 1 (London: printed for private circulation, 1922), pp. xi–xii.

as many books as there are stars in the sky).* Only a few of those books are unique, despite the fact that many fifteenth-century books, to cite just one group, survive in quite small numbers. Perhaps I can close with an example. The Clark Library has been collecting for some years translations into European languages of British books of the seventeenth and eighteenth centuries. This collection has reached the point where, if you need to read Locke in Swedish or Hume in German, the Clark is the place to do it. I recently acquired a number of editions of Samuel Richardson's novel *Pamela* and so-called Pamelaiana, which included a 1744 translation of the novel into Italian. I bought this book from an English bookseller who bought it at an auction in Rome, where the underbidder was the Biblioteca Nazionale. It is apparently unique. I cannot find it in any database or catalogue, and the only mid-eighteenth-century Italian translation of the book I can find is from a decade later, and that is in only one copy too, at Harvard. All the same, it is hard to believe that this is a unique survivor. The publisher is a known one, the novel was famous almost instantly in England and in Europe, and the translator says in the preface that the translation was made "with the consent of the author, who kindly passed on to me some additions and corrections."† Even if the edition was small, other copies must be "out there" that have simply escaped the usual databases and catalogues. The fact that the Catholic Church listed it on its Index of Prohibited Books makes it more, not less, likely that copies were read and kept. For the moment, the book is certainly rare. But unique? I doubt it very much.‡

---

* Andreas J. Wallin, *Dissertatio academica, de bibliomania, quam, venia incliti colegii phiolosophici, ad regium upaliense lyceuym* [etc.] (Uppsala: s.n., 1762), p. 11.

† Samzuel Richardson, *Pamela, ovvero la vurtu' premiata* (Venice: Giuseppe Bettinelli, 1744), leaf *4^V: "Altro più non mi ramane a dire, se non che questa Traduzione è fatta col consenso dell'Autore ch'ebbe la bontà di somministarmi alcune poche aggiunte e correzioni." I am grateful to Stefania Tutino for reading and translating the preface for me.

‡ Since delivering this paper, and in apparent fulfillment of my prophecy, a copy of the Italian *Pamela*, complete in four volumes, turned up at the Bayerische Staatsbibliothek in Munich. I am grateful to the bookseller Peter Young for telling me of this copy.

WAITING FOR
THE BARBARIANS

RARE BOOKS AND THE NEW
UNIVERSITY IN CANADA

M any of you, I am sure, will recognize in my rather rhetorical title the name of one of the best-known poems of Constantine Cavafy, the Greek poet born in Alexandria who haunts Lawrence Durrell's Alexandria Quartet series of related novels. In his poem, Cavafy describes the residents of Rome patiently awaiting the arrival of the barbarians, whose coming is expected and seemingly inevitable. These barbarians are dazzled by beautiful silver and gold work, and are "bored by rhetoric and public speaking," a detail in the poem which ought perhaps to have given me pause, but did not. I will return to Cavafy's poem and the irony of its conclusion later in my remarks.

Our conference this week takes place during the fiftieth-anniversary year of the Bibliographical Society of Canada, an organization which was founded by Lorne Pierce and his fellow bibliographers in 1946. That is reason enough for all of us to celebrate, and as I am on the whole a mainly optimistic sort of person, I hesitate to inject a note of gloom into what deserves to be a high-spirited occasion. But for many reasons, some of them personal and some of them professional, I have been giving a good deal of thought recently to what it is that I—and many of you—do, and how the sort of collection I curate fits into the current culture of libraries and higher education which, as we know, is changing radically these days. What I see—at McGill, more generally in Quebec, and even more generally in the rest of Canada—depresses me somewhat; and unless I have unwittingly entered on the male climacteric and am mistaking my own decline for the decline of the world of institutional rare book collections, I think that I have just cause to be depressed.

Those of us who work in long-established collections are used to taking a long-term perspective on things. We know that in the history of any institution, whether a university or a library within a university, there are good times and bad times, times of plenty and times of dearth, times of idiocy and times of remarkable intellectual and cultural flowering. At another level we also know that instances of immense change in the past have been met usually by equally immense flexibility and intelligence by that most flexible and intelligent of all creatures, *Homo sapiens*. The printing press replaced the copyist, the typewriter replaced the holograph, the linotype machine replaced the compositor, and so on; and whatever local resistance these changes produced died out and was subsumed into what we like to call "progress," a word which Mary Russell Mitford with foresight called "an expressive Americanism." Knowing these things makes it less easy to be an accurate pessimist; and no one, of course, looks sillier in retrospect than an *inaccurate* pessimist.

So just what is it, you will be thinking, that I am depressed and pessimistic about? In a nutshell, it is this: first, that I see the generalized culture of librarianship turning its face from "the book" in a spirit of aggressive anti-historicism and placing its faith, with an almost Gnostic intensity, in the computer; second, that this abandonment of librarianship's traditional focus is reaching an almost frenzied peak of devotion at a time of economic transformation and fiscal shortages that, quite by themselves, may well completely change the role and aspect of institutional libraries of all stripes; and third, that the increasing "MBA-ization" of senior library administrators everywhere is contributing to a process of cutting libraries off from their rootedness in a broad-based culture, scientific and humanistic, that has nourished them for half a millennium in the West.

Let me assure you that I am not a Luddite and do not regret the presence of the computer in the library. It is a remarkable machine for certain functions; and although, for example, I do sympathize with some of the points made by Nicholson Baker in his now infamous *New Yorker* article on library discards, published a couple of years ago, I am the first to confess to an admiration for the online catalogue at my institution and the almost surreal searching capabilities it possesses. The *English Short Title Catalogue* (ESTC) is even more impressive. As a writer, I sold my typewriter several years ago; and even if I do continue for reasons of physical pleasure to write first drafts by hand in a notebook, the advantages of word processing over the "typer" are obvious and irresistible. So you see that I am not what Arthur and Marilouise Kroker of Concordia University, the gurus of the information society, might call a "retrotechnophobe."

What I have watched with alarm is, first of all, the enormous sums of money which have been invested in library technology, almost always defended with the rhetoric of manpower saving and "increased access," as though we do not already have too much access and too many people out of work; and second, the progress of the myth that access will replace ownership, that a virtual copy of, say, the 1472 Foligno edition of the *Divine Comedy* will forever make it unnecessary for any library to buy a copy of the book, or to worry about preserving its copy if it already has one. I was once asked by one of the computer specialists in my library why, now that a certain book was available on the internet, we would want or need to have the real thing in the Rare Book Department, just as I was once asked by another colleague why we were keeping the pre-Confederation pamphlets which he had noticed coming back from being filmed by the Canadian Institute for Historical Microreproductions. These rustically Platonic views of what constitutes research material no longer constitute a minority opinion. Their purveyors will not end up as rare book curators, of course; but they have a good chance of ending up as the bosses of rare book curators, and I am fearful for the day that happens.

Terry Belanger, in the afterword to *The Book Encompassed*, a collection issued in 1992 to mark the one-hundredth anniversary of the founding of the Bibliographical Society in Great Britain, sees a revolution coming in the world of institutional rare book collections, a revolutionary dismantling of collections and a dispersal of books more far-reaching than anything since the Napoleonic era. The onward rush toward downsizing in the higher education sector in Canada which is being overseen and demanded by politicians of every stripe—the Liberals in Ottawa, the Tories in Ontario and Alberta, the Péquistes in Quebec City, and so on—is bound to affect the humanities more than the other faculties within the universities, if McGill is any measure. The lawyers, the doctors, and the scientists have a kind of respect and clout that will help them to weather the storm; these are the disciplines which are by definition largely ahistorical and whose research is far less dependent on books, for one thing, than humanities research, and infinitely more likely to produce practical applications, for another. Think how pervasive has become the vocabulary of neo-conservative business thinking—accountability, profitability, global economy, everything reduced to its financial implications and little else—and now think of the traditional strengths of humanistic research, and you begin to understand that old books may become as endangered as the tropical rainforest. The University of Québec at Montréal is slowly selling off its rare book collection; the Toronto Public Library is rumoured to be looking to sell its Audubon *Birds of America*, a copy brought to Toronto by Audubon himself and sold to William Allan, from whose estate it was bought by the Toronto Public Library in 1902 for $1,900; the University of British Columbia went for several years without a special collections librarian. And these facts represent, I am sure of it, only the preliminary skirmishes in an approaching battle that will see other, equally discouraging casualties.

As far as one can guess, the new university in Canada is likely to be very different from the sort of university I grew up with and have been associated with for the past twenty-five years as either a student or an employee. It will be smaller, it will cost students a great deal more to attend, and its research focus will be angled much more flagrantly toward profitable enterprises than toward the traditional disinterested search for truth. Its senior administrators will increasingly be drawn from the business sector rather than from the professoriate, and faculties and departments will have to attract much of their own money or face extinction. With fewer faculty to teach, pedagogy will become more and more dependent on the computer in various ways; and as more money is put into automation (as endless a sinkhole for money as libraries ever were), library budgets will continue to shrink, even as the number of books published goes on rising along with their cost. This will make the attraction of selling off parts of the retrospective collection ever more irresistible, a course of action which will be defended by recourse to what I now call the reasoning of the "internitwits": it's all there in cyberspace, so why keep the real thing?

I was struck recently in reading a report from McGill University's Planning and Priorities Sub-Committee of the Academic Policy and Planning Committee, a very powerful committee of the University Senate, by the prevalence of the business vocabulary used in describing McGill's current and future academic and financial situation. Words and phrases like "economically sustainable," "short-term academic benefit," "a diverse portfolio of individual research projects," "competitive," "optimize our investments," "commercially applicable research," even "the academic enterprise," among others, bespeak a mindset far, far from that which predominated during my institution's first 175 years, and it says something that the term "higher learning" now has a curious and vaguely deplorable antiquarian ring to it.

Let me pause here to indulge myself in a brief description of three of the books in the collection at McGill which best represent, to my way of thinking, the characteristics of a rare book collection that surrogates simply cannot equal or replace. I know that all of you who work with antiquarian books and manuscripts could easily furnish a similar list from your own collections. I begin with a copy—beautifully fresh and in the original medium blue paper boards and labels—of a three-volume novel entitled *Glenarvon*, issued anonymously in 1816 by the London publisher Henry Colburn. It is a scarce work—Sadleir did not own a copy and Robert Lee Wolff's copy was rebound and lacked the half-titles, the blanks, and the advertisement leaf in volume 3—and as you may know, its author is Lady Caroline Lamb. It is a *roman à clef* about Byron, Lady Caroline, her family, and some members of Elizabeth Lamb, Lady Melbourne's circle, and it was written mainly in revenge after Byron married Annabella Milbanke on the second of January, 1815. "Is a woman in low spirits?," Hannah More once wrote. "Let her console herself by writing a novel." And so Lady Caroline Lamb did, to the distress of many members of the Regency's highest circles. I cite this example not because of its condition or rarity, however, but because the McGill copy bears the bookplate of William Wilberforce, the evangelical politician through whose efforts the slave trade was abolished in Britain in 1807. *Glenarvon* is not perhaps a book that we would associate with the saintly Wilberforce, and it is exactly for that reason that this copy is instructive and evocative. To handle it is to establish briefly a direct line to a particular place and time in all their complexities: Byron and Wilberforce, we understand in looking at this novel, inhabited the same world, if not exactly the same sensibility, and the books they bought often looked just like this copy of this novel.

My second example, drawn to my attention by Martin Davies, is a copy of an incunable edition of Pseudo-Augustine, *Sermones ad heremitas*, published without date in Strasbourg by Johann Prüss. Most authorities date the book as "not after 1488." Our copy is in a monastic binding of quarter pigskin over wooden boards, and it came to McGill in the 1920s as the gift of Cleveland Morgan, who bought it from Leighton in London, who had it from the well-known collection of George Dunn of Woolley Hall. The most interesting feature of this copy, however, is the contemporary buyer's note on the rear pastedown, which reads as follows: "*Paulus murator[us] [e]mit [hunc?] libru[m] [?] gross[chen] anno lxxxvii,*" which translates as "Paul Muratorus bought this book for [?] groschen in the year 87," i.e., 1487. This note does not allow us to date the edition exactly, but it does at least push the "not after" date by one year, and 1487 may well be the correct year of issue. Furthermore, Paulus wrote his Christian name in red ink on the verso of the title-leaf, and there is little question that the modest rubrication throughout this copy is in the same hand and was done by him, a demonstration of the fact that individual owners of early printed books sometimes executed their own decorations rather than commissioning a professional flourisher to do the job. Paulus's work consists merely in touching with a little red ink virtually every upper-case letter in the text, as well as adding the initial capitals needed at the beginning of each sermon following the guide letters.

Lastly, and perhaps closest to home for this society, is a copy of A. M. Klein's first book, *Poems*, which Klein inscribed for F. R. Scott with the words "For Frank Scott | With hosannas for his politics | and hallelujahs for his art" and dated 8 February 1945. This is not just an association copy of a book by an important writer who did not often inscribe his books; it is a book which connects two of Montreal's most talented modernist poets who also shared strong political instincts and who were, moreover, students together at McGill and associated in the 1920s around the founding of the important little magazine the *McGill Fortnightly Review*.

Books like these do not represent merely bibliophilic icing on the bibliographic cake. They demonstrate some of the unique characteristics books in individual copies frequently embody, characteristics which facsimiles of any kind naturally eliminate. As such they are rich potential research material, and it would be folly and mania to ignore or to get rid of them simply because the Klein corpus is available in a scholarly edition from the University of Toronto Press, or because Sir Charles Chadwyck-Healey has issued the *Patrologia Latina* as a searchable database.

Who, then, you will be asking, are the barbarians? I will answer this question, as you expect me to; but let me return for a moment to the Cavafy poem from which I borrowed my title. Cavafy brings his poem to a conclusion with a surprising irony, for the barbarians do not actually show up, and the reaction of those who were waiting for them is not relief, as we might expect, but rather disappointment. Why? Because, as the poet says, the barbarians were a solution, rather than a problem—a solution, I suppose, to history in a sense, or at least to the specific historical problem of what a society is to do when it appears to have come to the end of a cycle in its natural life, even to the end of its natural life altogether. Change by force is perhaps easier in some ways to accept than the responsibility of deciding one's own future. Cavafy's group of civilized men and women, left to themselves at the end of the poem, must solve their own problems.

For me, then, the barbarians are, first, the "internitwits" who do not possess a developed and complex understanding of how good research works, and, second, the new corps of academic and library administrators who, having lost touch with the traditional strengths and raison d'être of research libraries, have become mesmerized by the bright light of technology. These two groups together represent the apparent leaders of the academic library world and the formulators of our collective future. They are unlikely to be kind to us and to the collections of old books and manuscripts that we look after. We always need more money, more space, and more staff, and it is these three things—already in short supply—which are certain to become rarer than a copy of the Jacques Cartier *Bref récit* of 1545.

But I have to add a third class of barbarians to the other two, in a reversal that parallels both the Cavafy poem and the novel by J. M. Coetzee which shares its and my title. This third class, I am afraid, is ourselves—not because we share the blinkered world view of our less bookish colleagues, but because we have failed, miserably at times, to explain and to justify our role in the process of education and research. We have too often turned our collections into museums, where objects may be seen but not touched. We look down on, when we do not refuse to admit, high school students and undergraduates. We compete fiercely with each other instead of building collections cooperatively. We are wont to babble incomprehensibly with colleagues who do not share our passion for bibliophily, the book trade, the intricacies of analytical bibliography, and so on. We are given to boasting of the rarities and high spots in our care, as though the more *Printing and the Mind of Man* books we have, the better the collection. We do not lament the fact that what we do often has too little administrative relation to what is done in the rest of the library or library system of which we are a part.

For rare book collections to survive in the evolving higher education ecology—and for people who use them, like bibliographers, also to survive—we must do a far better job of demonstrating, tangibly and visibly, the importance of books in research and teaching, to say nothing of their importance in cultural history construed in its broadest sense. The rapidly growing interest in the history of the book is a good sign and potentially a blessing to bibliographers and rare book curators everywhere. We must ensure that our managers are kept aware of such developments, even as we must encourage our academic colleagues to take up the cudgels for *l'histoire du livre*.

R. Howard Bloch, in a recent book called *God's Plagiarist* (1994) about Jacques-Paul Migne, the publisher of the *Patrologia Latina* and the *Patrologia Graeca* among other sets of books, quotes a remark of Migne's which he borrowed from Tertullian and used in many of his sales prospectuses: "In this world anxious for Progress, we offer the tradition of the past in order to march forward." Perhaps it is in a seemingly paradoxical formulation of this kind that the continuing importance of rare book collections can be expressed. We as curators and bibliographers—the developers and users of such collections— often take the value of our books to be self-evident. That complacency must evolve, however, if we and the books are to survive. The old technology of the book and the new technology of the computer clearly can coexist, just as manuscripts continued and continue even now to coexist with printed books. If at times we seem, like Tertullian himself, to be on the brink of a dark age for learning, then we must renew and expand our efforts to remind our administrators and our users of the centrality and irreplaceability of the book. By those efforts we shall live or not live. Let us hope that in CE 2046 my counterpart at the Bibliographical Society of Canada's one-hundredth anniversary dinner will be able to reflect on my talk this evening and wonder why on earth I could have been so gloomy about the future of books.

ACKNOWLEDGEMENTS

I am deeply grateful to the journal and newspaper editors who, over a period of more than four decades, have commissioned or accepted for publication the essays and reviews collected in this book, as well as many others not included here. I offer special thanks to Jack David and Robert Lecker, who published my earliest reviews in *Essays on Canadian Writing*; to Paula Dietz and Ron Koury at *The Hudson Review* for, beginning in 2011, offering me a steady stream of books for review on several subjects; and to Emily Donaldson of *Canadian Notes & Queries* for her support and friendship and regular assignments. No book reviewer in Canada makes a living from such work, but these editors made my literary life deeper and more rewarding on another level.

I owe a special debt of gratitude to my editor, John Metcalf, for seeing in my disparate review-and-essay work a viable book about which he has been unremittingly complimentary.

The following essays and reviews were first published in *The Hudson Review* and are reprinted by permission. The copyright for them remains with The Hudson Review, Inc. "Sappho; Or, On Loss" (vol. LXVI, no. 4, Winter 2014); "The Muses Taught Me Song Beyond Divine" (vol. LXXI, no. 2, Summer 2018); "I Suppose You to Be No Mean Reader, Since You Intend to Read Homer" (vol. LXVII, no. 2, Summer 2014); "The Place to Rest from All You Have Undergone" (vol. LXXI, no. 1, Spring 2018);

"Vivet" (vol. LXXII, no. 4, Winter 2020); "I Who Was Once the Favorite of the Gods" (vol. LXX, no. 4, Winter 2018); "A Viking on the Loose from His Longboat" (vol. LXX, no. 1, Spring 2017); "Have Faith and Have No Fear" (vol. LXXIV, no. 1, Spring 2021); "I Bite Rooks" (vol. LXVIII, no. 2, Summer 2015); "The Universe Is So Very Marvellous; or, What You Have Done, Odysseus" (vol. LXIX, no. 1, Spring 2016); "Dream of Fair to Middling Poetry" (vol. LXVIII, no. 1, Spring 2015); "Fulfillment's Desolate Attic: Philip Larkin's *Complete Poems*" (vol. LXV, no. 2, Summer 2012). "Epics Manqués" was also first printed in *The Hudson Review* (vol. LXIV, no. 3, Autumn 2011).

The following first appeared in *Canadian Notes & Queries*, and are reprinted by permission: "Embracing Everybody and Wrestling Trees: Walt Whitman Turns Two Hundred" (no. 104, Spring 2019); "Set Apart for a Real Ministry" (no. 88, Summer–Fall 2013); "The Impossibly/Beautiful": Phyllis Webb (no. 94, Winter 2016); "'A Slam-Bang Case of *Extremis*'" (no. 100, Fall 2017); "Infinite Vista and the Mind at Play" (no. 98, Winter 2017); "Where Love Is Lovely, Not Lonely: On a Poem of P. K. Page" (no. 97, Fall 2016); "'The Only News That Isn't Boring Is the Truth': Leonard Cohen's Poetry Then and Now" (no. 103, Fall 2018).

The remaining essays and reviews were published in the following journals, both print and online: "What's Poetry?" first appeared in *Rattle* (Spring 2012). The pieces on John Sutherland, Anne Wilkinson, the avant-garde in Canadian poetry, and Raymond Souster and the 1950s were originally part of a series entitled "The Tradition" that appeared in *Poetry Canada Review* (Summer 1987, Fall 1987, Summer 1988, and Summer 1989 respectively). The Souster/Dudek review was published in *The Fiddlehead* (no. 133, July 1982). The review of Brian Busby's biography of John Glassco first appeared in *TriQuarterly* (online) in June 2011. "This Heavy Craft: P. K. Page's Collected Poems" was published in *The Canadian Forum* (January–February 1998). The review of Ken Norris's *Floating Up to Zero* first appeared on the website of Talonbooks (Meta-Talon) in January 2012. "*Cui Bono?*" first appeared in

Parenthesis 15 (Autumn 2008). "Only Copy Known" was given as the John Seltzer and Mark Seltzer Memorial Lecture at the Thomas Fisher Rare Book Library, University of Toronto, and was printed in *Book Talk: Essays on Books, Booksellers, Collecting, and Special Collections*, edited by Robert H. Jackson and Carol Z. Rothkopf (Newcastle: Oak Knoll Press, 2006). "Waiting for the Barbarians: Rare Books and the New University in Canada" was given as a lecture at the fiftieth annual general meeting of the Bibliographical Society of Canada on June 10, 1996, and was first printed in the *Papers of the Bibliographical Society of Canada* (vol. 34, no. 2, Fall 1996).

BRUCE WHITEMAN was a rare book specialist for over thirty years. He worked at McMaster and McGill Universities in Canada, and later ran the William Andrews Clark Memorial Library at UCLA. He is now a poet, translator, and reviewer. He teaches courses in the School of Continuing Studies at the University of Toronto, and for several years was the Poet in Residence at Scattergood Friends School, a Quaker boarding school in Iowa. The final book of his long poem, *The Invisible World Is in Decline*, was published in 2022.